Visions And Tasks, And Other Sermons

Phillips Brooks's Sermons

In Ten Volumes

1st Series — **The Purpose and Use of Comfort**
And Other Sermons

2d Series — **The Candle of the Lord**
And Other Sermons

3d Series — **Sermons Preached in English Churches**
And Other Sermons

4th Series — **Visions and Tasks**   And Other Sermons

5th Series — **The Light of the World**
And Other Sermons

6th Series — **The Battle of Life**   And Other Sermons

7th Series — **Sermons for the Principal Festivals and Fasts of the Church Year**
Edited by the Rev. John Cotton Brooks

8th Series — **New Starts in Life**   And Other Sermons

9th Series — **The Law of Growth**
And Other Sermons

10th Series — **Seeking Life**   And Other Sermons

E. P. Dutton and Company
681 Fifth Avenue   New York

Visions and Tasks

And Other Sermons

By the
Rt. Rev. Phillips Brooks, D.D.

Fourth Series

NEW YORK
E. P. DUTTON & COMPANY
681 Fifth Ave.

COPYRIGHT, 1886
(Twenty Sermons)
BY
E. P. DUTTON & COMPANY

PUBLISHERS' NOTE

This volume was originally published as " Twenty Sermons"

TO THE MEMORY OF
𝔉𝔯𝔢𝔡𝔢𝔯𝔦𝔠𝔨 𝔅𝔯𝔬𝔬𝔨𝔰
I INSCRIBE THESE SERMONS.

CONTENTS.

SERMON I.
Visions and Tasks.

"*While Peter thought on the vision, the Spirit said unto him, Behold, three men seek thee.*"—ACTS x. 19 1

SERMON II.
The Mother's Wonder.

"*Son, why hast thou thus dealt with us?*"—LUKE ii. 48 . . 20

SERMON III.
The Church of the Living God.

"*The Church of the living God.*"—1 TIM. iii. 15 . . . 42

SERMON IV.
Standing Before God.

"*And I saw the dead, small and great, stand before God.*"—REVELATION xx. 12 60

SERMON V.
Brotherhood in Christ.

"*Simon, called Peter, and Andrew, his brother; James the son of Zebedee, and John his brother.*"—MATTHEW x. 2 . . 76

SERMON VI.

The Giant with the Wounded Heel.

"*And I will put enmity between thee and the woman, and between thy seed and her seed. It shall bruise thy head, and thou shalt bruise his heel.*"—GENESIS iii. 15.   . . . 93

SERMON VII.

The Sea of Glass Mingled with Fire.

"*And I saw as it were a sea of glass mingled with fire, and them that had gotten the victory over the beast*" . . . *stand on the sea of glass, having the* "*harps of God.*"—REVELATION xv. 2. 110

SERMON VIII.

The Beautiful Gate of the Temple.

"*The Beautiful gate of the temple.*"—ACTS iii. 10. . . . 127

SERMON IX.

Disciples and Apostles.

"*And when it was day he called unto him his disciples, and of them he chose twelve, whom also he named Apostles.*"—LUKE vi. 13. 152

SERMON X.

The Earth of the Redemption.

"*The heavens, even the heavens are the Lord's: but the earth hath he given to the children of men.*"—PSALM cxv. 16.   . 173

SERMON XI.

The Man with Two Talents.

"*To another he gave two talents.*"—MATTHEW xxv. 15   . 192

SERMON XII.
Destruction and Fulfilment.
"*I am not come to destroy, but to fulfil.*"—Matthew v. 17. . 219

SERMON XIII.
Make the Men Sit Down.
"*And Jesus said, Make the men sit down.*"—John vi. 10. . 236

SERMON XIV.
Timeliness.
"*He hath made everything beautiful in his time.*"—Ecclesiastes iii. 11. 244

SERMON XV.
The Sword Bathed in Heaven.
"*For my sword shall be bathed in heaven.*"—Isaiah xxxiv. 5. . 262

SERMON XVI.
The Knowledge of God.
"*As the Father knoweth me, even so know I the Father.*"—St. John x. 15
"*Then shall I know even as also I am known.*"—1 Corinthians xiii. 12. 280

SERMON XVII.
An Evil Spirit from the Lord.
"*The spirit of the Lord departed from Saul, and an evil spirit from the Lord troubled him.*"—1 Samuel xvi. 14. . . 297

SERMON XVIII.

Going up to Jerusalem.

"*Then Jesus took unto him the twelve, and said unto them, Behold, we go up to Jerusalem, and all things that are written concerning the Son of man shall be accomplished.*"—LUKE xviii. 30. . . . 316

SERMON XIX.

The Safety and Helpfulness of Faith.

"*They shall take up serpents, and if they drink any deadly thing it shall not harm them. They shall lay hands on the sick and they shall recover.*"—MARK xvi. 18. 333

SERMON XX.

The Great Expectation.

"*Let your moderation be known unto all men. The Lord is at hand.*"—PHILLIPPIANS iv. 4. 358

SERMON I.

Visions and Tasks.

"While Peter thought on the vision, the Spirit said unto him, Behold, three men seek thee."—ACTS x. 19.

THESE words recall to many of you a most familiar picture, for the story of St. Peter's vision is one of those passages of the New Testament which have almost become the proverbs of mankind. Peter had been sitting on the top of Simon's house at Jaffa, and there had been shown to him the sight of the great sheet full of all living beasts, of which he had been bidden to take and eat. And when he hesitated, you remember how a voice had spoken to him, and rebuked the narrow punctiliousness with which he drew distinctions, and thought some of God's creatures clean and others unclean. He was sitting there, pondering this vision, "doubting in himself what the vision which he had seen should mean." A new idea had come to him. He saw it very vaguely; and its developments, what it would lead to if he followed it out, he could not see at all. It was all abstract and impalpable. It just bewildered and eluded him. But as he sat there, steps were heard below, and to his mind the Spirit spoke, saying,

"Three men are asking for thee." They were the servants of Cornelius, the Gentile, coming to ask him to visit their master. Their visit gave him immediately the chance to put in action the idea which had possessed him. Our verse shows him then standing between the vision and its application. On the one side of him was the mysterious sheet full of the multitude of beasts; on the other side were the three men who needed just the principle which the sheet-full of beasts involved. It was a critical moment. The question was whether the vision could pass through Peter to the three men and Cornelius. When on the morrow he "went away with them," the question was decided, and the idea and its appropriate duty had joined hands.

Man standing between his visions and his tasks—that is the subject of our verse then. That is our subject for this morning. It is the place where certain men are often called upon peculiarly to stand; and in some degree it is the place in which all men are standing always. For every man has visions, glimpses clearer or duller, now bright and beautiful, now clouded and obscure, of what is absolutely and abstractly true; and every man also has pressing on him the warm, clear lives of fellow-men. There is the world of truths on one side, and there is the world of men upon the other. Between the two stands man; and these two worlds, if man is what he ought to be, meet through his nature.

Think of an instance, and you will see what I mean. Here are you, a thoughtful, meditative man.

You have been pondering and studying. Somehow it has become clear to you, let us say, that there is a God. The supernatural behind the natural, the will behind all forces, has revealed itself to you. For the moment, it is enough for you just to know that mighty truth. Turning it this way and that, you think in one view and another how mighty it is. But very soon, if you are a true man, your nature begins to hear and feel a stir upon the other side of it. Under the windows which look towards the world, the tumult of the needy life of your fellow-men comes rising up to you. Perhaps it is more definite than that, and certain special fellow-men come, with footsteps which you can hear, up to your hearts' doors and knock. At first their coming seems to be only an intrusion. Why can they not leave you alone with your great idea? What right have they to claim a share of the sunshine in which you are sitting? But by-and-by you see more wisely. You begin to wonder whether their coming on this side of you is not the true correlative and correspondent of the coming of the vision on the other side of you. You begin to feel that the practical life may be needed to complete the meditative life. If you open the door to your intrusive fellow-men you find that it indeed is so. Your idea of God falling upon the many mirrors of their various needs and natures, gains new interpretations and illuminations. Their human hearts get hold of the reality of God, which they never could have found out for themselves, through your belief in it. And your own life, open on both sides, on this side to the vision, and on that side to the men, grows rich and sacred as being the room in which that most deep and interesting transaction which the world can witness, the meeting of truth with the human mind, takes place.

Truth is vague and helpless until men believe it. Men are weak and frivolous till they believe in truth. To furnish truth to the believing heart, and to furnish believing hearts to truth, certainly there is no nobler office for a human life than that; and the doctrine which I want to preach to you to-day is that the human life or human nature is so made as to fulfil just that office. How can we better tell the story of you who first believe in God yourself and then are drawn out to make your fellow-men believe in Him, and in making them believe in Him find your own belief grow steadier and clearer—how shall we better depict this human life which never learns anything without hearing other human lives clamoring to share the blessings of its knowledge than by recurring to the story of Peter, to whom, "as he thought on the vision, the Spirit said, Behold three men seek thee."

It is illustrated, this central and critical position in which a man may stand, by the way in which the artist stands between the whole world of beautiful ideas and the hard world of matter, in which these ideas at last find their expression through him. The artist dreams his dream, and as he thinks upon the vision, the Spirit says, Behold the marble seeks thee;" and instantly the chisel is in his hand and the work of carving has begun. Ideas would hover like a great vague cloud over a world all hard and gross and meaningless, if it were not for man who brings the fire down and makes the whole of nature significant and vocal. If civilization has changed the face of nature, and out of rocks and trees built monuments and cities, the whole long history is but the record of the meeting within the transmitting intelligence of man of the abstract idea with the adaptable material.

But to return from our illustration to our truth. There are some moments in life when this position of man, as standing between the visions which he has seen and his fellow-men on whom he is to bring them into power, is peculiarly manifest. There are perhaps some young men here to-day who stands just at one of those moments now. When any process of education has been finished, when the college doors have just dismissed their graduate, when the professional student stands upon the brink of the troubled waters of his profession with the calm scholar-days behind him, when the young minister is just feeling the hands of ordination on his bowed head, in all these days how real this sense of the two worlds between which he stands is to any truly thoughtful man. Between the silence and the stir, between the calm accumulation and the active employment of his truth, the young man stands with a strange consciousness which is never so vividly repeated at any other moment of his life. The two worlds, one on each side of him, receive illumination from each other, and this illumination is sent back and forth through him. Truth never seemed so sacred as when he comes in sight of its true uses; and the world never seemed so well worth living for as when he sees how much it needs his truth. Sad is the lot, sad is the nature of any man who can pass through such a moment and not be solemnized and exalted by it. Sad is the man who can graduate from college and go out into the world, and think of his education only as a drudgery from which he has at last escaped, or as an equipment with which he is to earn his daily bread.

Sad is the lot and nature of any man who sees his youth fading back behind him, finds himself growing out of the specially vision-seeing period of life, and counts his visions as they fade, mere pleasant recollections, or, it may be, things to laugh at and to be ashamed of. Sometimes you see a happy man, of whom, as he grows older, nothing of that kind is true. A man we see sometimes who, as he comes to middle-life, finds his immediate enthusiastic sight of ideal things grown dull; that is the almost necessary condition of his ripening life. He does not spring as quickly as he once did to seize each newly offered hope for man. A thousand disenchantments have made him serious and sober. He looks back, and the glow and sparkle which he once saw in life he sees no longer. He wonders at his recollection of himself, and asks how it is possible that life ever should have seemed to him as he remembers that it did seem. But the fact that it really did

once seem so to him is his most valued certainty.
He would not part with that assurance for anything.
All the hard work that he does now is done in the
strength and light of that remembered enthusiasm.
To have been born into the world as he is now; never
to have had any years in which the sky seemed
brighter and the fields greener, and man more noble,
and the world more hopeful than they seem to-day,
would make all life for him another and a drearier
thing. Every day the dreams of his boyhood, which
seem dead, are really the live inspirations of his life.
To such a man there surely came, some day or other
in the past, a Peter-hour, a time at which the visions
of his youth and the hard work of his manhood met
and knew each other. From that time on the
power of his vision passed into his work; and now,
as, with his calm, dry face, seeming so unemotional,
so unmoved, he goes about his labor, doing his duty
and serving his generation, it is really the fire of his
youth which no longer blazes, but still burns within
him that makes the active power of that dry, prudent,
conscientious, useful man. Peter plodding over the
dusty hills to reach Cornelius, may seem to have lost
the glory which was on his face while he sat and
thought upon the vision, and caught glimpses of the
essential nobleness of man—but the vision was at
the soul of his journey all the time, and was what
made his journey different from that of any peddler
whom he met upon the road.

One longs to speak to men whom the hard work
and dry details of life are just claiming, as they are

leaving their youth behind and passing into middle life. You may expect to grow less enthusiastic and excited. Do not be surprised at that. But in the meeting of the facts of life with those accumulated convictions which must be the real heart of any true enthusiast, you ought to be growing more and more earnest the longer that you live. There are trees whose fruit does not ripen till their leaves have fallen; but we are sure that the ripe fruit does not laugh at the fallen leaves whose strength it has drawn out into its own perfected shape and color. If you do not see the visions which you saw when you were a boy, that does not prove that the vision was not true. That boy's belief that man is essentially noble, and the world is full of hope, is as genuinely a part of your total life as this man's experience that men will cheat, and that the world's great wheels move very slowly. The emotions grow less eager and excited, but the convictions ought to be growing always stronger— as the kernel ripens in the withering shell. Believe in man with all your childhood's confidence, while you work for man with all a man's prudence and circumspection. Such union of energy and wisdom makes the completest character, and the most powerful life.

I have been wandering a little from my subject. The power of man to stand between abstract truth upon the one side and the concrete facts of life upon the other, comes from the co-existence in his human nature of two different powers, without the possession of both of which no man possesses a complete humanity. One of these powers is the power of knowing, and the other is the power of loving. I ask you to give to both of the words their fullest meaning, and then how rich the nature grows which has them both—this human nature, which is not truly human if either of them be left out. The power of knowing, however the knowledge may be sought or won, whether by patient study or quick-leaping intuition, including imagination and all the poetic power, faith, trust in authority, the faculty of getting wisdom by experience, everything by which the human nature comes into direct relationship to truth, and tries to learn, and in any degree, succeeds in knowing—that is one necessary element of manhood. And the other is Love, the power of sympathetic intercourse with things and people, the power to be touched by the personal nature with which we have to do—love therefore, including hate, for hate is only the reverse utterance of love, the negative expression of the soul's affection; to hate anything is vehemently to love its opposite. Love thus, as the whole element of personal affection and relationship of every sort, this too is necessary, in order that a man may really be a man. These two together must be in all men. Not merely in the greatest men. It is not a question of greatness, but of genuineness and completeness. Just as the same chemical elements must be in a raindrop that are in Niagara, and, if they are, then the raindrop is as truly water as the cataract; so the power of learning truth and the power of loving man must be in you or me, as well as in Shakspeare or Socrates; and if they are, then we are as genuinely and completely men as Socrates and Shakspeare.

From this it will immediately follow, that the more perfectly these two constituents of human nature meet, the more absolutely they are proportioned to each other, and the more completely they are blended, so much the more ready will the human nature be for the fulfilment of every function of humanity. And if, as we have seen, one of the loftiest functions of humanity is to stand between the absolute truth and the world's needs, and to transmit the one in such way that it can really reach and help the other, then it will also follow that the more perfectly the knowing faculty and the loving faculty meet in any man, the more that man's life will become a transmitter and interpreter of truth to other men.

That sounds like a dry inference; but it is one of which our own dearest experiences have borne to all of us most precious testimony. If you look back to the men who have taught you most, and in the fuller light where you now stand, study their character, you will surely find that the real secret of their power lay here, in the harmonious blending of the knowing and the loving powers in their nature; in the opening of their nature on both sides, so that truth entered in freely here and you entered in freely there, and you and truth met, as it were, familiarly in the hospitality of their great characters. The man who has only the knowing power active, lets truth in, but it finds no man to feed. The man who has only the loving power active, lets man in, but he finds no truth to feed on. The real teacher welcomes both.

You know this in all who are really teachers. It is most clear of all in that highest of all the teacherships which the world has to show, which comes with its blessing to the beginning of every human life which is not by special misfortune poorer than it ought to be. Ask where a mother's power lies, and surely the answer must be that no being like the true mother stands between visions of the highest truths on one side, and a human soul on the other, and offers a nature in which the knowing power and the loving power are kneaded and moulded together into a perfect oneness, into a sacred and pure transparency for the transmission of the first facts of the universe, and God and Life to the intelligence of her child, who lives in her knowledge by her love. The purest mingling of all elements into one character and nature which we can ever see, is in the Christian mother, in whom the knowledge of all that she knows and the love which she feels for her child, make not two natures, as they often do in men, in fathers, but perfectly and absolutely one. She values knowledge not for its own sake, but for her child. She loves him not with the mere animal fondness with which the brute mother loves her child, but as the utterance and revelation of every truth to her. Thus her love and her intelligence are blended perfectly; and the result is that which we know, the wonderful power of the mother's life to bring the deepest, highest, farthest truths, and win for them their first entrance into the nature of her child.

The New Testament tells us of Jesus that He was full of Grace and Truth. Grace and Truth! These are exactly the two elements of which we have been speaking, and it must have been in the perfect meeting of those two elements in him that His mediatorship, His power to transmute the everlasting truths of God into the immediate help of needy men consisted. He was no rapt self-centered student of the abstract truth; nor was he the merely ready sentimental pitier of the woes of men. But in His whole nature there was finely wrought and combined the union of the abstract and eternal with the special and the personal, which made it possible for him, without an effort, to come down from the mountain where he had been glorified with the light of God, and take up instantly the cure of the poor lunatic in the valley; or to descend from the hill where he had been praying, to save his disciples half-shipwrecked on the lake; or to turn his back on the comforting angels of Gethsemane, that he might give himself into the hands of the soldiers who were to lead him to the cross. "While he thought upon the vision, the Spirit said unto him, Behold three men seek thee." Can any words more typically tell the life of Christ than those!

It is a truth which we have all learned from some experience through which we have been led, that any great experience, seriously and greatly met and passed through, makes the man who has passed through it always afterwards a purer medium through which the highest truth may shine on other men. Have you not seen it? Here is some man whom you have known long. You have seemed to have reached the end of all that it is possible for you to get from him, all that it is possible for him to do for you. Nothing has come through him from behind to you. You have seen him. You have seen a sort of glint or glimmer of reflection of God's light upon the surface of His life, as the sun might be reflected on a plate of steel. But nothing of God or God's truth has come through him to you as the sun shines through a lens of glass, pouring its increased intensity upon the wood it sets in flame.

But some day you meet that man, and he is altered. Tenderer, warmer, richer, he seems to be full of truths and revelations which he easily pours out to you. Now you not merely see him; you see through him to things behind. As you talk with him, as you look into his face, you see with new surprising clearness what God is, what man is, what a great thing it is to live, what a great thing it is to die, how mysterious and pathetic are sorrow and happiness, and fear and hope. You cannot begin to tell the change by merely thinking that the man has learned some new facts and is telling them to you, as a book might tell them from its printed page. The very substance of the man is altered, so that he stands between the eternal truths and you no longer as a screen, which shuts them from your sight, but as an atmosphere through which they come to you all radiant. You ask what has come to him, and you hear (if you are near enough for him to tell you his most sacred history), of some profound experience. He has passed through an overwhelming sorrow. He has stood upon the brink of some tremendous danger. He has spent a day and a night in the deep of some bewildering doubt. He has been overmastered by some sudden joy. It may have been one of these or another. The result has been in such a change of the very substance of the nature, that, whereas before it was all thick and muddy, so that whatever light fell upon it was either cast aside or else absorbed into it and lost, now it makes truth first visible, and then clear and convincing to the fellow-men who see truth through it.

And when you try to analyze this change, do you not find that it consists in an impregnation of the nature which has had this new experience with two forces—one a love for truth, the other a love for man? and it is in the perfect combination of these two in any life that the clarifying of that life into a power of transmission and irradiation truly lies. What man goes worthily through sorrow and does not come out hating shams and pretences, hungering for truth; and also full of sympathy for his fellow-man whose capacity for suffering has been revealed to him by his own. It is the perfect blending of those two constituents in the new nature of your tried and patient friend which have given him this wondrous power of showing God and truth to you.

What man goes bravely and faithfully through doubt and does not bring out a soul to which truth seems to be infinitely precious, and the human soul the most mysterious, sacred thing in all the world. Out of the union of those two persuasions has come the prophetship of this life which now you cannot look at without seeing the infinite behind it made clear by it.

Surely, if we can believe this, then the way in which God lets his children encounter great, and sometimes terrible, experiences is not entirely inexplicable. Surely if these souls which now are deep in sorrow, or are being cast up and down and back and forth in doubt, are being thus annealed and purified that they may come to be revealers, mediators between God and their fellow-men, then into our wonder at the existence of doubt and sorrow in God's world there comes a little ray of light. Who would not bear anything that could refine his life into fitness for such a privilege as that?

I had meant to speak of several of the special visions which, through the soul that is prepared for such an office, become transformed into influence and blessing to mankind. I can only indicate them in the slightest way. Suppose that God has let you see His goodness. A strong, unalterable persuasion that God is merciful and kind has been poured onto your life, into your mind. That fact itself, once known, absorbs your contemplation. If you and God were all the universe, the knowledge of His goodness would be everything to you. You would sit lonely in the empty world and fill your soul with gazing on the brightness of that truth. So you do sit to-day, as if you and God were indeed alone, and no one in the universe except you two. And then, as you sit so, there comes some sort of appeal from fellow-men. The three men are down at the door while you are dreaming on the housetop. Your child comes to you with some childish joy and wants its explanation; some puzzled neighbor cries across to you, from his life to yours, and wants to know if you have any clue to all this snarl of living. Somehow the cry awakens you, and you go down and put your truth into your brother's hands. At first it seems almost a profanation. The truth is so sacred and seems so thoroughly your own. But as you give it to your brother, new lights come out in it. For God to be good means something more when the goodness turns to new forms of blessing in the new need of this new life. O you who think you know that God is merciful because of the mercy which He has shewed to you, be sure there is a richness in your truth which you have not reached yet, which you will never reach until you let Him make your life the interpreter of His goodness to some other soul!

Or again perhaps the truth which you have learned, the vision which you have seen, is the sinfulness of sin—what a terrible thing it is for any child of God to disobey his Father. Overwhelmed with that knowledge, you sit and brood upon your sad estate. I think that all religious history bears witness that that conviction, if it remains purely a personal truth of our own life, certainly grows tyrannical and morbid and brings despair. As soon as it becomes a stimulus, inspiring us to go and help our brethren escape out of their sin, it becomes salutary and blessed. If I knew any soul to-day, haggard and weary with its consciousness of sin and danger, I think that what I would try to do to help it would be this—make it see in its own sinfulness the revelation of the sinfulness of all the world; then let it forget its own sinfulness and keep only the impulse that must come out of its sight of how horrible the world's sin is; then let it go, full of that impulse, and try to save the world. So it must find its own salvation.

So of the truth of immortality. Not as a personal privilege of mine, but as a token of the greatness and worth of the human soul, making every service which I can render to it more imperious and delightful—so do I come to understand the fact that man never dies with the fullest faith.

So of such a truth as the Trinity. Not as a puzzle or a satisfaction of the intellect, but as an expression of the manifold helpfulness with which the divine nature offers itself to the human, so it will be to me the richest and the holiest creed.

There are no limits to our doctrine. Every truth which it is possible for man to know it is good for him to know with reference to his brother men. Only in that way is the truth which he knows kept at its loftiest and purest. This is the daily meaning which I want to find in the picture of Peter sitting before his vision, on the house-top and the three men knocking in the street below.

There is a danger, which we all recognize, of selfishness in our religion. It comes in various forms. It makes one man say: "I am content, for I have seen the Lord." To that man the great host of his fellow-men who need his Lord as much as he, are nothing. He will leave them unheard in the street and sit within, wrapped in the complacency of his assured salvation. Another man says, "What business is it of any one except myself if I close my eyes and do not see the Lord? Does it hurt any one but me? Who has a right to interfere or urge me?" To both of these men is there not a message in the story of Peter which we have been studying this morning? To the first man it says: The seeing of your own vision is but half, and half without the other half grows weak and perishes. Your religion, kept solely for yourself, will certainly decay. Up, up, and go abroad and find the men who need your Christ, to whom you can bring Him, in giving Him to whom alone you can make your own faith in Him complete and strong.

To the other man it says, Indeed it is the business of other men than you, it is the whole world's business whether or not you are a Christian! Indeed it does rob other souls than yours, if you will not live spiritually and see the truth which God is showing to your soul. If there are men whom, being yourself a Christian, you might bring to Christ, then you rob not only yourself but them, if you refuse to come to Christ. The window which makes itself dark, darkens not merely itself, but also all the room into which the light might have shone through it.

I dare to hope that some generous nature may feel this appeal. Be spiritual, be religious, come to Christ. Cast off your sins, not for yourself, but for some soul which possibly may learn from you, what it could not learn in any other way, how good and strong and forgiving is the sinner's God.

It is a terrible thing to have seen the vision, and to be so wrapped up in its contemplation as not to hear the knock of needy hands upon our doors.

It is a terrible thing to hear the knock and have no vision to declare to the poor knocker.

But there is no greater happiness in all the world than for a man to love Christ for the mercy Christ has shown his soul, and then to open his whole heart outward and help to save his brethren's souls with the same salvation in which he rejoices for himself. May none of us go through life so poor as never to have known that happiness.

SERMON II.

The Mother's Wonder.

"Son, why hast thou thus dealt with us?"—LUKE II. 48.

THE mother of Jesus is the speaker, and it is of Jesus that she asks her question. On the way home from the temple at Jerusalem, where they had gone to worship, you remember, they missed the child Jesus from their company. On going back they found him in the temple, "sitting in the midst of the doctors, both hearing them and asking them questions." Then it was that His mother said unto him, "Son, why hast thou thus dealt with us? Behold thy father and I have sought thee sorrowing. And he said unto them, How is it that ye sought me? wist ye not that I must be about my father's business?"

"Why hast thou dealt thus with us?" It is a puzzled question. The boy, who had been an obedient child in her household, whom she had cared for in her own way and found always docile to her guidance, had suddenly past beyond her and done a thing which she could not understand. It seemed as if she had lost him. Her tone is full of love, but there is something almost like jealousy about it. He has taken himself into his own keeping, and this one act seems to foretell the time when he will take his whole life into his own hands, and leave her outside altogether. The time has past when she could hold him as a babe upon her bosom as she carried him down into Egypt. The time is prophesied already when he should go in his solitude up to the cross, and only leave his mother weeping at the foot. She is bidden to stand by and see her Son do his work and live his life, which thus far has been all of her shaping, in ways she cannot understand. No wonder that it is a clear, critical moment in her life. No wonder that her question still rings with the pain that she put into it. No wonder that when she went home, although he was still "subject unto her," her life with her son was all changed, and she "kept all these sayings in her heart."

I think that this question of the mother of Jesus reveals an experience of the human heart which is very common, which is most common in the best hearts and those who feel their responsibility the most. It is an experience which well deserves our study, and I ask you this morning to think about it with me in some of its examples. The Virgin Mary is the perpetual type of people who, intrusted with any great and sacred interest, identify their own lives with that interest and care for it conscientiously; but who, by-and-by, when the interest begins to manifest its own vitality and to shape its own methods, are filled with perplexity. They cannot keep the causes for which they labor under their own care. As his mother asked of Jesus, so they are always asking of the objects for which they live, "Why hast thou thus dealt with us?" Such people are people who have realized responsibility more than they have realized God. Just as Mary felt at the moment when she asked this question, that Jesus was her son more than that he was God's Son, so there is a constant tendency among the most earnest and conscientious people, to feel that the causes for which they live and work are their causes, more than that they are God's causes, and so to experience something which is almost like jealousy, when they see those causes pass beyond their power and fulfil themselves in larger ways than theirs. For such people, often the most devoted and faithful souls among us, it seems to me that there must be some help and light in this story of Jesus and his mother.

The first and simplest case of the experience which I want to speak of, is that which comes nearest to the circumstances of our story. It comes in every childhood. It comes whenever a boy grows up to the time at which he passes beyond the merely parental government which belonged to his earliest years. It comes with all assertion of individual character and purpose in a boy's life. A boy has had his career all identified with his home where he was cradled. What he was and did, he was and did as a member of that household. But by-and-by there comes some sudden outbreak of a personal energy. He shows some disposition, and attempts some task distinctively his own. It is a puzzling moment alike for the child and for the father. The child is perplexed with pleasure which is almost pain to find himself for the first time doing an act which is genuinely his own. The father is filled with a pain which yet has pride and pleasure in it to see his boy doing something original, something which he never bade him do, something which perhaps he could not do himself. The real understanding of that moment, both to child and father, depends upon one thing— upon whether they can see in it the larger truth that this child is not merely the son of his father, but also is the son of God. If they both understand that, then the child, as he undertakes his personal life, passes not into a looser, but into a stronger, responsibility. And the father is satisfied to see his first authority over his son grow less, because he cannot be jealous of God. It is a noble progress and expansion of life, when the first independent venture of a young man on a career of his own, is not the wilful claim of the prodigal: "Give me the portion of goods that falleth to me,"—but the reverent appeal of Jesus : "Wist ye not that I must be about my Father's business?"

Let this serve for an illustration. It is the scene which, recurring in every household, as a boy claims his own life, is constantly repeating the experience of the household of Nazareth. And now all responsible life, all life entrusted with the care of any of God's causes, has this same sort of correspondence with the life of the mother of Jesus. There can be no higher specimen of responsibility than she exhibits. She is entrusted with the care of Him who is to be the Saviour of the world. And that responsibility she accepts entirely. She is willing to give up everything else in life, to be absorbed and worn out in the task of supreme privilege which God has given her. There comes no trouble or lack in the degree of her readiness for labor or for pain. But the quality of her self-sacrifice shows its defect elsewhere. She is not able to see where the limits of her work must be. She is not able to stop short in her devout responsibility, when the task passes beyond her power, and her son begins to deal directly with his Father.

Compare with her, in the first place, that person with whom we are familiar in all the history of Christianity, whom we see about us constantly—the champion of the Faith, the man who counts it his work in life to maintain and protect the purity of the belief in Christ. It is a noble task for a man to accept. It is filled with anxiety. The faith for which the man cares is beset with many dangers. It costs him sleepless nights and weary days. He incurs dislike; he excites hostility by his eager zeal. To all this he is fully equal. The danger of many a stout champion of truth comes quite at the other end. There comes a time when God, as it were, takes back into His own keeping that faith over which He has bidden His disciples to stand guard. The truth begins to show a vitality upon which the believer has not counted. It puts itself into new forms. It develops new associations. No wonder that he is troubled. No wonder that, unless he is a large and thoughtful man, thoroughly reverent of truth as well as thoroughly devoted to the truths which he has held, he grudges truth in some way the larger freedom which it is claiming for itself, and almost opposes its development.

Take an example. A good man has for years counted himself a champion of the often denied and insulted justice of God. He has been ready to maintain it everywhere. Against all weak representations of God as a being all indulgence, he has asserted that God must punish wickedness. That truth he has supported, as he has conceived it, in its simplest, crudest form—physical, unending punishment. Suppose the day comes when that faith claims for itself a free and more spiritual meaning; when men's souls become aware that in the world to come, as in this world, the punishment of sin must be bound up in sin itself; when not the agonies of hell, but the degradation of the moral nature, stands out as the dreadful thing. No wonder that at first, the surprised believer is almost dismayed. His faith, over which he has stood guard so faithfully, seems to be slipping away from him. His faith seems to be playing him false. He is bewildered, as Mary was when Jesus for the first time began to show his personal will and ways. But by-and-by the time came when she rejoiced in it, no doubt. "Whatsoever he saith unto you, do it," she ordered the servants at the marriage in Cana. By that time she had learned to trust her Son far out of her own sight, to look to his own self-development with perfect confidence. And so the believer, and the champion of belief, comes in the course of time to rejoice when his belief outgrows him; when what he has to stand guard over is seen to be, not the special form in which a dogma has been conceived, but the spirit to which knowledge can come, and to which it must come always more spiritually and richly; not the truth, but truthfulness.

It does seem to me that this is what many a believer needs to learn to-day. His faith seems to be slipping away from him. Truths will not remain the definite and docile things they used to be. His doctrine opens into some deeper form. He turns to the doctrine he has held and says to it, "Why have you dealt thus with me?" "Why will you leave me?" And the answer is, "I must be about my Father's business." Truth is God's child. Truth must be what God wills, not what the believer wills. It is a blessed day for the believer when he learns this, and thenceforth only waits to see what new forms God will give his faith from year to year, and then is ready to follow it into whatever new regions God will send it forth to seek.

And this same truth applies to the care for the world's reformation and improvement, which different kinds of good men have. There are some men undertaking to reform the world who want to keep the whole plan in their own hands and never have its working outgo their wisdom. There are other reformers who believe themselves to be working in a great system which is far too large for them to comprehend, to which they can only give a helping touch at one point where it comes near their lives. The first kind of reformer believes that he understands it all, knows just how evil is to be eradicated, just how good is to be aroused and the world saved. The other reformer does not profess to know anything except that God is over all and that under God he has the privilege of helping this cause or that cause of righteousness in some special time of need, and at some special point which he can touch. The first is the reformer with a theory. The second is a reformer with a devotion.

And it is evident what will be the different effect on these two men, if, as so often happens, the progress of humanity seems to declare a will of its own, does not advance as we expected it to advance, lags where we look for it to hasten, or leaps to some great attainment where we expected it to proceed by slow degrees. The theoretical reformer, who thinks himself a master of human progress, and has imagined that he understood it all, is entirely lost as he sees the reform which he has thought could only come to pass in one way, attaining its accomplishment in another, and going on its way far off in some new direction, leaving him behind. The devout reformer, who has considered himself the servant of human good, is glad enough to see that human good is far larger than he can understand, and is content if he can lend his little skill to some corner of its many wants, and be carried on with it, working for it, to unknown results.

There are always people who are uneasy if hard times improve by other ways than they suggested. There are men enough in our land to-day who cannot be totally glad that slavery is abolished, because its abolition did not come about by their plan. There are men in the Church who begrudge the work she does, if it is not done by their own school of churchmen. What is the trouble with all these people? Is it not simple enough? They have the care of some one of God's children, some one of the causes which are born of Him, and which He loves, but they treat it as if it were not God's child, but only theirs. They are afraid if they see it growing strong in ways which they do not understand. When it dawns upon such a man that behind all the care which he has for any of the great interests of righteousness and the use which God is making of him in its behalf, God himself is holding that interest in the hollow of His hand, and with His infinite wisdom is preparing for it ways of success which His servant cannot begin to know, how calm and confident the servant's care for that good work must grow; how ready he must be to see the methods of the reform which he desires change utterly before his eyes, to see it taken utterly out of his hands and yet work on for it with all his might and soul. Here is the salvation of honest partisanship. You believe that only your political party can save the country. But if you believe that the salvation of the country is a care of God, you will stand ever ready to help whatever new party God may seem to entrust with one period of that ever unfinished work. You and I believe that our Church has a great work to do for Christ's Gospel in our country, but if we believe that Christ's gospel is something which is very near to the heart of God, we cannot possibly limit our sympathy to what our Church is doing. Even if our Church fails of its duty, we cannot possibly feel as if the gospel had failed. We shall have to rejoice, even while we work on with her, that God has other ways to do the work in which she does her part so feebly.

These cases are no doubt too general; they do not touch us very closely. Let us try to come nearer home. I think that the same principle applies to every work which any one of us tries to do for any of his brethren. I know that in this congregation there must be many who are anxious for the life of some one whom they love. A certain responsibility lies upon you for some brother's life. Somebody seems to have been given to you to care for. You did not seek the care. But here is some one who, because there is no one else to care for him and see that he goes right, has grown to be your care. That responsibility is no light one, you well know. It presses on you. You are anxious under it. Can our story help you? Surely it can. You say, "How? Is there not an unlikeness at the very outset of the story? Was not this one over whom the Virgin Mary watched, the Son of God?" But tell me: is not the man whom you are anxious for, the brother who is in the midst of his temptation, the friend who is out of work and growing idle, the beggar whom you are trying to reform out of his drunkenness, is not each of these too a son of God? And is it not true, and must it not enter into the very centre of your care for them, that they are under God's care just as truly as they are under your care; and that, while God uses you for their development, it is perfectly possible, it is every way to be expected, that He will develop them by means and in directions of which you never would have dreamed?

I think that it is hopeless for any man to undertake to render high help to another man's life who is not constantly aware of this. Mary learned two things about her Son that day in the temple, things which she had known before, but which became perfectly and permanently clear to her there. One was, that his life was mysteriously larger than her own. The other was, that God was over and behind her, caring for that life for which she had been caring. The largeness and mystery of her Son's life and the fatherhood of God to him, those two things she learned there, and thenceforth they were part of her life always. She never can have forgotten them again. They must have made all the future service that she rendered to him at once more faithful and more calm and more sacred. And my dear friend, you too must learn these truths about the life of any man whom you are trying to help, any man who seems to be committed to you by God, or you cannot really help him as he needs. You must know the mystery of his life and his sonship to God.

Ah, how God sometimes teaches us those things

about some one whom we are trying to guide and aid. We have undertaken our task very flippantly and narrowly. "Well, this is my man," we say, "I do not see who else can help him, and so I will. I will patronize him. I understand him; I see what is to be made out of him; I will make him this, and this,"—laying some fine plan down in our mind. "This is what he shall be," and so you take your scholar into your school; your companion into your company; what you call your friend into what you call your friendship. The time must come, if you are ever really going to be of deepest use to that man, when, out of something which he says or does, these two truths come to you about him, that he is larger in his nature, more mysterious than you can grasp, and that he is the son of God, led by his Father, over and above your care.

We talk about men's neglect of one another's lives, and certainly there is enough of it. They go their way saying of each other, in some utterance of their indifference, "Am I my brother's keeper?" We recognize how terrible it is because we see that, as of old, he who scornfully disowned his brother's care, really was his brother's murderer, so always he who thinks he has no duty of helping other men, certainly hinders them and does them harm. But beside all the pain at seeing how men disown the care of their fellows, there is another pain which is often yet more painful as we see how men who do attempt to help their brethren, help them all wrong, with such ignorant and clumsy hands that they do them more harm than good. Meddlesomeness, arrogance, foolish indulgence, wanton severity, wooden insistence upon a way of goodness which God never meant for the man whom you are trying to make good, opposition to good impulses because they happen to be in other lines than yours, fussiness, suspicion, jealousy, all of these evils come in, and others with them, to make sometimes worse than worthless the most sincere desire of some good man to help and guide his neighbor. Blind leading the blind everywhere! What, it seems to me, all these good people need, is this: the larger view of the life that they are anxious for. There is a mystery about this man which I cannot fathom. And this man is a child of God. You say, "I might feel that about, some inspired child whom I was privileged to teach. How can I feel it about this poor sot, whom I am trying to keep out of the grog-shop; or this poor trifler and lounger whom I want to bring to church; or this poor creature with the shattered nerves whom I must watch lest he should throw himself into the fire? Can I count his life mysterious, count him a child of God?" Unless you can, you cannot help him with any truly deep help. You may keep him unscorched and presentable, but the shattered, broken, wasted life at the centre, where its real exhaustion lies, will get no reinforcement from the man who has no reverence for it and no sense of God's love for it.

The moment that Moses forgot that the people he was leading were God's people, and smote the rock, crying, "Hear, O Israel, must I bring you water from this rock?" that moment his highest help to them was gone. He could give them water still, but the water which he gave as if it were his gift, and not God's, was an insult both to them and to God; and from that day his death began.

And if we ask what will be the characteristics of the ministry of any man, who, while he renders help to other men, feels these truths deeply about the men to whom he ministers, the answer will be clear. It will have the qualities which we can easily imagine to have been in the treatment of the child Jesus by His mother after her experience in the Temple. It will consist in general inspiration more than in special direction; and it will be more occupied in removing obstacles to growth than in dictating the forms and directions in which growth shall grow. The best advisers, helpers, friends, always are those not who tell us how to act in special cases, but who give us, out of themselves, the ardent spirit and desire to act right, and leave us then, even through many blunders, to find what our own form of right action is. And always the best thing you can do for any brother, I am more and more convinced, is to try to keep him from being a bad man, and so give God a chance to make him a good man in whatever way He may choose. This takes away the superior and patronizing tone which is the blight of many a man's most sincere desire to be useful. This leaves the humblest free to help the highest. The mouse may gnaw the lion's net, but he does not ask the freed lion to crawl into the wall with him and live a mouse's life. So you may help a strong man to shake off his vice, but when he is at liberty, leave him to God to learn what life God made him for, and be thankful if it is something a great deal larger and higher than your own.

There are small men to whom all this would be depressing. They do not want to do anything for other men unless they can take the whole work into their own hands and make it wholly theirs. For a larger man it is a great deal nobler and more ennobling to work with God and on a material of which God has shown to him the mystery. A weak Hebrew mother, with a poor stupid boy who never left the company with any true impulsive life to seek the God whom he belonged to, may well have pitied Mary, and thought her unhappy in her wilful child. But "Mary kept all these things and pondered them in her heart." She learned that it was nobler to bring her boy to God and see him take God for his Father, than it was to keep him to herself. And so you and I come to understand that the type of the truest relationship between man and man is not the Romish confessional, the spiritual directorship where one man gives his life into another's hands, but is the frank friendship of generous men, wherein each helps the other, but is always glad to know that he is really only helping God to help him; and so each always rejoices to see the other, under God, outgo himself.

But we must not stop here. There is a yet deeper and closer care laid upon a man than his care for his brother, and that is the care of himself, of his own soul. And there too the truth applies which we have won out of our story of Jesus and his mother. There too it is true that a man cannot execute his responsibility aright unless in that for which he is responsible he sees something mysterious, and a child of God.

A man's care for himself! How strange it is! How a man seems to separate his life; to stand off, as it were, and gaze at his own life with criticism and anxiety. It is the commonest of all experiences with all thoughtful people. "Know thyself," says the old proverb; as if the knower and the known were genuinely two, distinct from one another. "Keep thy heart with diligence," says Scripture, as if the heart and the heart-keeper were separate. The will and wisdom stand guard over the conscience and the character.

A man who is really thoughtful, who has risen to the capacity of such self-care, praises himself, and blames himself, with a more even-handed justice because with a more intimate and conscientious knowledge, than that with which he judges of the lives of other men. He is to himself like something outside of himself, with whose conditions nevertheless all his own fortunes are inextricably bound up. Therefore he lays out plans for his own treatment. He says: "I will make myself this or that." He says, "I will bring myself to my best in this or that way." And then, as he tries to carry out his plans, he becomes aware that on this self of his which he considered so entirely his own, in his own power, some other force besides his own is working. He finds himself the subject of some other will and wisdom, some other education than his own. His plans for his own life are overruled and interfered with. He meant to educate his self by self-indulgence; this other force, below his own, sweeps his self off into distress and deprivation. He meant to live in self-complacency; the deeper force plunges him into mortification and shame. It is as if the wind thought that it was ruling the waves which it tossed to and fro, but gradually became aware of the tide which underneath was heaving the great ocean on whose surface only the wind spent its force.

Is this a true picture of human life as the thoughtful man comes to know it? I think it is. Who is there of us that is not aware that his soul has had two educations? Sometimes the two have been in opposition; sometimes they have overlapped; sometimes they have wholly coincided, but always the two have been two. Our own government of ourselves is most evident, is the one which we are most aware of, so that sometimes for a few moments we forget that there is any other; but very soon our plans for ourselves are so turned and altered and hindered that we cannot ignore the other greater, deeper force. We meant to do that, and look! we have been led on to this. We meant to be this, and lo! we are that. We never meant to believe this, and lo, we hold it with all our hearts. What does it mean? It is the everlasting discovery, the discovery which each thoughtful man makes for himself with almost as much surprise as if no other man had ever made it for himself before, that this soul, for which he is responsible, is not his soul only, but is God's soul too. The revelation which came of old to the Virgin Mother about her child—Not your child only, but God's child too; yours, genuinely, really yours, but behind yours, and over yours, God's.

That is the great revelation about life. When it comes, everything about one's self-culture is altered. Every anticipation and thought of living changes its color. It comes sometimes early, and sometimes late in life. Sometimes it is the flush and glow which fills childhood with dewy hope and beauty. Sometimes it is the peace which gathers about old age and makes it happy. Whenever it comes it makes life new. See what the changes are which it must bring. First it makes anything like a bewildering surprise impossible. When I have once taken it into my account that God has his plans for my soul's culture, that these plans of His outgo and supersede any plans for it which I can make, then any new turn that comes is explicable to me, and, though I may not have anticipated it all, I am not overwhelmed, nor disturbed, nor dismayed by it. I find a new conviction growing in my soul, another view of life, another kind of faith. It is not what I had intended. I had determined that as long as I lived I would believe something very different from this which I now feel rising and taking possession of me. It seems at first as if my soul had been disloyal to me, and had turned its back faithlessly upon my teaching. I appeal to it, and say: "Soul, why hast thou thus dealt with me?" And it answers back to me: "Wist you not, that I must be about my Father's business? Did you not know that I was God's soul as well as your soul? This is something which He has taught me."

That is the real meaning, my dear friends, of many a case in which men say, " I do not know how I came to believe this truth. I never sought it. I never meant to believe it. I always said I never would believe it. But the belief in it has come about in spite of myself." It was the over-fatherhood of God. It was God claiming His own soul. Let a man see this, and he welcomes the convictions that have come to his soul thus direct from God, even more cordially than those which he has sought out and won with deliberate toil. What he has believed in spite of himself he believes even more strongly than what he has struggled to believe. He cannot be jealous of what God does for his soul. He is like a servant taking care of a child, with the father of the child standing behind and watching and making plans with a wisdom which the servant rejoices to know is wiser than his. Oh, if there were no higher guidance than what we can give to our own lives! Oh, if our souls never outstripped the plans which we make for them! Oh, if we never came to more truth than we are brave enough and wise enough to seek!

There are two different conditions in which a man receives without bewildering surprise the changes which come to him in life. One is the condition of the man who believes in no government of life at all. The other is the condition of the man who thoroughly believes that God is governing his life. To both of these men mystery is not merely conceivable; it is inevitable. To one it is the vague, dreary mystery of chance. To the other it is the rich, gracious mystery of loving care. To one it is the mystery of accident, the most awful and demoralizing atmosphere for a man to live in. To the other it is the mystery of personal life, which is the noblest end of thought which man can reach on any side. Neither of these men can be surprised. One of them cries, "It is another accident!" The other cries, "It is my father!" when any most unlooked-for thing occurs. Between the two there stands the man with his own tight self-made plan of living which he looks to see fulfilled, denying both mysteries, refusing to believe in accident and yet ignoring God. He is the man whose life is all battered and buffeted with surprises. He is like a man who sails the ocean and refuses to believe in tides. No wonder that after a long and dreary voyage, he drags at last a broken and wrecked life up on a beach which he never dreamed of when he started.

The other consequence of the great revelation of life, the revelation that the soul for which we care is God's soul, for which He is caring too, will be that the true man will have one great purpose in living, and only one. He will try to come to harmony with God, to perfect understanding of what God wants and is trying to do. Let me not be trying to make one thing out of this soul of mine while He is trying to make entirely another! Once more return to the story which has given us our suggestions for to-day. As Mary went back with her son, realizing out of his own mouth, that he was not only her son, but God's; as she settled down with him to their Nazareth life again, must not one single strong question have been upon her heart, " What does God want this Son of His to be? O, let me find that out, that I may work with Him." And as you go into the house where you are to train your soul, realizing, through some revelation that has come to it, that it is God's soul as well as yours, one strong and single question must be pressing on you too. " What does God want this soul of mine to be? O, let me find that out that I may work with Him." And how can you find that out? Only by finding Him out. Only by understanding what He is, can you understand what He wants you to do. And understanding comes by love. And love to God comes by faith in Jesus Christ. See then, what is the divine progress of self-culture. You let Christ give you his blessings. Through gratitude to Him you come to the love of God. By loving God you understand God. By understanding God you come to see what He wants you to be, and so you are ready to work with Him for your own soul. From the first touch of Christ's hand in blessing, on to the eternal work of laboring with God for our own sanctification, that is the progress of the Christian life.

The Son of Mary was a revelation to the mother

in whose care He lived. So a man's soul, his spiritual nature which is intrusted to his care, is a perpetual revelation to him. If you can only know that your soul is God's child, that He is caring for it and training it, then it may become to you the source of deep divine communications. God will speak to you through your own mysterious life. He will show you his wisdom and goodness, not in the heaven above you, but in the soul within you. He will make you His fellow-worker in that which is the most divine work of His of which we can have any knowledge, the training and perfecting of a soul. That is the privilege of every man who knows, and finds his life and joy in knowing, that the soul which lives within him, the soul which he calls his soul, is the child of God.

SERMON III.

The Church of the Living God.

A DOMESTIC MISSIONARY SERMON.

"The Church of the living God."—1 TIM. iii. 15.

I WANT to preach to you to-day about the Church. It has grown to be our habit on this Sunday morning, when we annually make our contribution for Domestic Missions, to speak especially and definitely about the Church; not, that is, directly of the personal Christian experience, but of the great corporate body of Christian life throughout the world, and especially of that particular organization in which we live and worship, and whose work in our own country we are to contribute to extend. If the Church is often thought about, and talked about, in a petty and mechanical and formal way, let us be very careful, if we can, to avoid formality and pettiness in our talk of her to-day. Let us try to make her seem what she really is, the Church of the living God, and the Home of living men.

Let us begin then with one of the most picturesque and striking and perhaps perplexing incidents which occur in the Church's life. A minister is called upon to baptize a little dying child. It is an infant of a day. A ray of light has come from heaven, and just flashed for an instant into the great flood of sunlight, and now is being gathered back again into the darkness out of which it came. The minister goes and baptizes the unconscious child. He does an act which perhaps to those who stand around, seems like the blankest superstition. "What does it mean?" they say. "Have a little sprinkled water and a few whispered words any influence upon this flickering flame of life which in a moment is to go out? If the child is to live elsewhere after its brief life here on earth is over, will this ceremony do it any good? If it revives and lives its life out here on earth, will it live any better for this hurried incantation?"

Meanwhile, to the minister, and to the Church of which he is a minister, that baptism of the dying child has a profound and beautiful significance. It is not thought of for a moment as the saving of the child's soul. The child dying unbaptized goes to the same loving care and education which awaits the child baptized. But the baptism is the solemn, grateful, tender recognition, during the brief moments of that infant's life on earth, of the deep meanings of his humanity. It is the human race in its profoundest self-consciousness welcoming this new member to its multitude. Only for a few moments does he tarry in this condition of humanity; his life touches the earth only to leave it; but in those few moments of his tarrying, humanity lifts up its hand and claims him. She says, " You are part of me, and being part of me, you are part of me forever. Your life may disappear from mortal sight almost before we have seen it, but, wherever it may go, it is a human life forever. It belongs to God, as, and because humanity belongs to Him." Humanity, recognizing itself as belonging to God, recognizes this infant portion of herself as belonging to Him, claims it for Him, takes it into her own most consecrated hopes, appropriates for it that redemption of Christ which revealed man's belonging to God, declares it a member of that Church which is simply humanity as belonging to God, the divine conception of humanity, her own realization of herself as it belongs to God.

Can there be any act more full of significance, more free from superstition? And is there not in this act, just because of the feeble unconsciousness of the child to whom it is administered, the most distinct indication of the nature of the Church into which he is admitted? There is no fact developed yet about the child except his pure humanity. We know nothing whatsoever about his talents, or his character. It makes no difference whether he is rich or poor. He may lie cradled in daintiest lace, or in most squalid rags. Beauty or ugliness, brightness or dullness, friendship or friendlessness, good blood or bad blood, are not taken into account; we baptize him, be he what he may, so that only he is a human creature, the child of human parents, the sharer of our human nature; we baptize him into the fellowship of consecrated humanity, into the Church of the living God.

Have we not then presented to us in this simple ceremony, which to one bystander may seem so insignificant and to another so superstitious, the deepest and broadest meaning of the Christian Church? It is the body of redeemed humanity. It is man in his deepest interests, in his spiritual possibilities. It is the under-life, the sacred, the profounder life of man, his re-generation. Every human being in very virtue of birth into the redeemed world is a potential member of the Christian Church. His baptism claims and asserts his membership.

And now suppose that Baptism were universal, and suppose that instead of being, what it is so often, even among Christian people, a formal ceremony, everywhere it were a living act, instinct with meaning, what a world this would be! Every new-born immortal welcomed by the whole spiritual consciousness of his race! There is some true sense, we may well believe, in which the physical life of humanity grows richer through its whole substance by the added life of each new body. Just in proportion as the spiritual is more sensitive than the physical, may we not hold that the spirituality of the whole race is richer for the access of this new soul? Baptism is the utterance of the rejoicing welcome. The whole world of spiritual capacity thrills with delight and expectation. The Church accepts its new member and undertakes his education. For what time he is to be in her, a part of her, before he goes to his eternal place to be a member of the Church in heaven, whether it be for a few short hours or for a long eighty years, the Church belongs to him and he belongs to the Church. If he does good work it is the Church's gain and glory. If he sins, and is profligate, it is as a member of the Church that he is wicked. The Church is spiritual humanity, and he, a spiritual human being, is, by that very fact, a Churchman.

I cannot tell you, my dear friends, how strongly this view takes possession of me the longer that I live. I cannot think, I will not think about the Christian Church as if it were a selection out of humanity. In its idea it is humanity. The hard, iron-faced man whom I meet upon the street, the degraded, sad-faced man who goes to prison, the weak, silly-faced man who haunts society, the discouraged, sad-faced man who drags the chain of drudgery, they are all members of the Church, members of Christ, children of God, heirs of the kingdom of heaven. Their birth made them so. Their baptism declared the truth which their birth made true. It is impossible to estimate their lives aright, unless we give this truth concerning them the first importance.

Think too, what would be the meaning of the other sacrament, if this thought of the Church of the living God were real and universal. The Lord's Supper, the right and need of every man to feed on God, the bread of divine sustenance, the wine of divine inspiration offered to every man, and turned by every man into what form of spiritual force the duty and the nature of each man required, how grand and glorious its mission might become! No longer the mystic source of unintelligible influence; no longer certainly the test of arbitrary orthodoxy; no longer the initiation rite of a selected brotherhood; but the great sacrament of man! The seeker after truth, with all the world of truth freely open before him, would come to the Lord's table, to refresh the freedom of his soul, to liberate himself from slavery and prejudice. The soldier going forth to battle, the student leaving college, the legislator setting out for Washington, the inventor just upon the brink of the last combination which would make his invention perfect, the merchant getting ready for a sharp financial crisis, all men full of the passion of their work, would come there to the Lord's Supper to fill their passion with the divine fire of consecration. They would meet and know their unity in beautiful diversity—this Christian Church around the Christian feast. There is no other rallying place for all the good activity and worthy hopes of man. It is in the power of the great Christian Sacrament, the great human sacrament, to become that rallying-place. Think how it would be, if some morning all the men, women and children in this city who mean well, from the reformer meaning to meet some giant evil at the peril of his life to the school boy meaning to learn his day's lesson with all his strength, were to meet in a great host at the table of the Lord, and own themselves His children, and claim the strength of His bread and wine, and then go out with calm, strong, earnest faces to their work. How the communion service would lift up its voice and sing itself in triumph, the great anthem of dedicated human life. Ah, my friends, that, nothing less than that, is the real Holy Communion of the Church of the living God.

And then the ministry, the ministers, what a life theirs must be, whenever the Church thus comes to realize itself! We talk to-day, as if the ministers of the Church were consecrated for the people. The old sacerdotal idea of substitution has not died away. Sometimes it is distinctly proclaimed and taught. What is the release from such a false idea? Not to teach that the ministers are not consecrated, but to teach that all the people are; not to deny the priesthood of the Clergy, but to assert the priesthood of all men. We can have no hope, I believe, of the destruction of the spirit of hierarchy by direct attack. It may be smitten down a thousand times. A thousand times it will rise again. Only when all men become full of the sense of the sacredness of their own life, will the assumption of supreme clerical sacredness find itself overwhelmed with the great rising tide. The fault of all onslaughts upon the lofty claims of the ministry has been here. They have vociferously declared that ministers were no better than other men. They have not bravely and devotedly claimed for all men, the right and power to be as good and holy and spiritual as any St. John has ever been in his consecrated ministry. When that great claim is made and justified in life, then, not till then, lordship over God's heritage shall disappear and the true greatness of the minister, as the fellow-worker with and servant of the humblest and most struggling child of God, shall shine out on the world.

Yet once more, here must be seen the true place and dignity of truth and doctrine. It is not knowledge anywhere that is the end and purpose of man's labor or of God's government. It is life. It is the full activity of powers. Knowledge is a means to that. Why is it that the Church has magnified doctrine overmuch and throned it where it does not belong? It is because the Church has not cared enough for life. She has not overvalued doctrine; she has undervalued life. When the Church learns that she is in her idea simply identical with all nobly active humanity, when she thinks of herself as the true inspirer and purifier of all the life of man, then she will— what? Not cast her doctrines away, as many of her impetuous advisers bid her do ; she will see their value, their precious value, as she never has seen it yet; but she will hold them always as the means of life, and she will insist that out of their depths they shall send forth manifest strength for life which shall justify her holding them.

The decrying of dogma in the interest of life, of creed in the interest of conduct, is very natural, but very superficial. It is superficial because, if it succeeded, it would make life and conduct blind and weak. But it is natural because it is the crude healthy outburst of human protest against the value of dogma for its own sake, of which the Church has always been too full. Let us not join in it.

Let us insist that it is good for man to know everything he can know, and believe everything he can believe of the truth of God. But while we will not pull down dogma, let us do all we can to build up life about dogma, and demand of dogma that service which it is the real joy of her heart to render to life. I will not hear men claim that the doctrine of the Trinity has no help or inspiration to give to the merchant or the statesman. It has great help, great inspiration. I will not hear men claim that it means nothing to the scholar or the bricklayer whether he believes or disbelieves in the Atonement. It means very much to either. Out of the heart of those doctrines I must demand the help and inspiration which they have to give. Then I must do all that I can to make the life which needs that help and inspiration hungry for them. I must do all that I can to make the world's ordinary operations know their sacredness and crave the sacred impulse which the dogmas have to give. I must summon all life to look up to the hills. I must teach the world that it is the Church, and needs and has a right to all the Church's privileges, and so make it cry out to the truths of the Trinity and Atonement to open the depths of their helpfulness, as they never have heard the call to open them when only theologians were calling on them to complete their theologic systems, or only a few special souls were asking them for special comforts or assistance. Here, in the assertion of the great human Church, is the true adjustment of the relations of Doctrine and Life! Doctrine kept active by life. Life kept deep by doctrine.

Ah, but you say, this does not sound like the New Testament. There certainly the Church and the world are not the same. They are not merely different; they are hostile to each other. There is a perpetual conflict between the two. Indeed there is! But what Church and what world are fighting together there? The Church is a little handful of half-believers. The world is a great ocean of sensuality and secularity and sin. Of course between those two there is an everlasting conflict, so long as each is what it is. The world distrusts the Church, in part at least, because it feels coming out from it no spiritual power. The Church dreads the world, which is always dragging it down from its imperfect loyalty and consecration. But he has listened very carelessly to the New Testament who has not heard in it the muffled, buried voices of another Church and another world, crying out for life! A Church completely strong in faith, not standing guard over herself, but boldly claiming all the world in all of its activities for Christ, and a world conscious of its belonging to divinity, counting its sin and intrusion an anomaly, a world ashamed and hungry, the world of which St. Paul dreamed, the groaning and travailing creation. How often as we read the New Testament, this deeper Church and this deeper world are dimly seen and faintly heard beneath this present faithlessness and sin. How, whenever they are seen and heard, we recognize, beyond a doubt, that they are the true Church, and the true world, and that every departure from or falling short of them is a loss of the Church's or the world's reality. And how, when the true Church and the true world stand before us, we see and know that they are not in conflict; that they are in perfect harmony; nay, far more than that, that they are identical with one another.

There is no fight so fierce and vehement as that which rages between two beings which ought to be perfectly one, but which, because each falls short of what it was designed to be, are now in conflict with each other. So long as the Church and the world are what they are there must be discord. We who are in the Church must keep watchful guard over her, and must dread and oppose the evil influences of the world. But at the same time we never must let ourselves forget that all this is unnatural. We must never lose out of our sight the vision, never lose out of our ears the music of the real Church and the real world struggling each into perfection for itself, and so both into unity and identity with one another.

Very interesting have been in history the pulsations, the brightening and fading, the coming and going of this great truth of the Church and the world ideally identical. That truth is always present in the words of Jesus. He told his disciples how they were to fight with the actual world, to be persecuted by it, even to be murdered by it. But he was always pointing abroad and saying, "The field is the world." The ideal Church, which was the real Church in his eyes, knew no limit but humanity.

By-and-by came the persecutions of the early Church, and they drove the Church in upon itself, and made the few believers think of themselves as outcasts and exceptions. The intensity of their personal experiences dulled and dimmed the thought of their being simply representatives of all humanity. The Church lived like a sect of souls with special privileges and illuminations.

The mediæval Church in its own way caught sight again of the idea of universality, but it was formal and selfish. It did not think of itself as fulfilling the life of the world, but of the world as existing for it, and to be practically swallowed up in its dominion. Still it had some notion of it and the world coming to identity with one another, though it was almost the identity of the wolf with the sheep which he has devoured.

With the Protestant Reformation came another intense assertion of the personal nature of religion, and the larger aspects, the world-meaning of the Church, was lost or lay in silence. Calvinism was too busy with the intense problem of the individual soul to think much of the great Redemption of the world, of all humanity.

But now, when in these latter days, there are so many signs that we are passing into a new region, beyond the strong immediate power of the Reformation which has prevailed from the sixteenth century till now, it is the relation of the Church to the active world, the conflict and the possible harmony between them, the message of the Church to the world, the turning of the world into the Church, these are the problems and the visions which are more and more occupying the minds of thoughtful vision-seeing men.

Such alternations and pulsations cannot go on forever. The hostility of the Church to the world, and the conformity of the Church to the world, neither of them is the final condition, nor shall the Church vacillate between them always. Gradually, slowly, but at last surely, this must come forth which we saw testified even in the hurried baptism of the little child who made this earth his home but for a single day, that the earth is the Lord's, and so that to be living in this earth is to belong to God; and that all human life is by the very fact of its humanity a portion of His Church.

I think that we can do the best work in the Christian Church only in the light of that truth cordially acknowledged. Because that truth is coming to more and more cordial acknowledgment, I believe that the Christian Church is becoming a better and a better place to work in every year. If I ask where in the Christian Church one can best live and work, I answer myself that it will be where that truth is most vital, where it makes most strongly the real power of the Church's life.

And this brings me to what little I want to say about our own Church, on this morning when we are to make our annual contribution for the extension of her work. We value and love our Communion very deeply. To many of us she has been the nurse, almost the mother of our spiritual life. To all of us she is endeared by long companionship, and by familiar sympathy in the profoundest experiences through which our souls have passed. When we deliberately turn our backs for a moment upon all these rich and sweet associations, and ask ourselves in colder and more deliberate consideration, why it is that we believe in our Episcopal Church and rejoice to commend her to our fellow-countrymen and fellow-men; the answer which I find myself giving, is that our Church seems to me to be truly trying to realize this relation to the whole world, this sacredness of all life, this ideal belonging of all men to the Church of Christ, which, as I have been saying, is the great truth of active Christianity. I find the signs of such an effort, in the very things for which some people fear or blame our Church. I find it in the importance which she gives to Baptism and in the breadth of her conception of that rite; for Baptism is the strongest visible assertion of this truth. I find it in her simplicity of doctrine. I find it in the value which she sets on worship; her constant summons to all men not merely to be preached to, but to pray; her firm belief in the ability and right of all men to offer prayer to God. I find it in her strong historic spirit, her sense of union with the ages which have past out of sight and of whose men we know only their absolute humanity.

In all these things I recognize the true, strong ten-

56 The Church of the Living God.

dency which our Church has to draw near to the life of the world, and to draw the world's life near to her. In this tendency all true Churchmen must rejoice. Her breadth of doctrine, her devoutness, and her clear hold upon the long history of human life, all these qualify her for a great work in bringing up humanity, and making it know itself for what it is, the true universal Church of the Living God, toward which all ecclesiastical establishments which have thus far existed in the world, have been attempts, of which they have been preparatory studies.

Can our Church do any such great office as this for the America in which she is set? There are some of her children who love to call her in exclusive phrase The American Church. She is not that; and to call her that would be to give her a name to which she has no right. The American Church is the great total body of Christianity in America, in many divisions, under many names, broken, discordant, disjointed, often quarrelsome and disgracefully jealous, part of part, yet as a whole bearing perpetual testimony to the people of America of the authority and love of God, of the redemption of Christ, and of the sacred possibilities of man. If our Church does especial work in our country, it must be by the especial and peculiar way in which she is able to bear that witness; not by any fiction of an apostolical succession in her ministry, which gives to them alone a right to bear such witness. There is no such peculiar privilege of commission belonging to her or any other body. The only right of any body lies in the earnest will and in the manifest power. The right to preach the Gospel to America lies in the earnest faith that the Gospel is the only salvation of the people, first as men, and then as Americans; whoever brings that faith has the right to preach; whoever does not bring it has no right, be the fancied regularity of his commission what it may!

In some sense there has been reason to fear, and there is still reason to fear, that what makes part of the strength of our Church, may also make part of its weakness. Its historic sense binds it, in a very live way, to the sources from which it immediately sprang, and tempts it to treasure overmuch its association with the great Church of another land, the Church of England. So long as it does that it can never truly be the Church of America. So long as it prefers to import customs and costumes, names and ways, instead of creating them here out of the soil on which she lives, she will be what she has been in very much of her history, what she is in many parts of the land to-day, an exotic and not a true part of the nation's life. The Episcopal Church's only real chance of powerful life, is in the more and more complete identification of herself with the genius and national life of America.

To do that, she must become a great moral power. No careful preservation of the purity of doctrine, no strictness of ecclesiastical propriety, can take the place of moral strength. It is by the conscience, that the Church must take hold of this people. It is in the conscience, that the nation is uneasy. In its uneasy conscience, it sees the vision and hears the voices of the life it might be living. To the conscience of the nation then, the Church that is must speak to tell the nation of the Church that it might be. The Church which forty years ago had bravely cried out at the sin of slavery, would be more powerful than we can imagine in America to-day. The Church which to-day effectively denounces intemperance, and the licentiousness of social life, the cruelty or indifference of the rich to the poor, and the prostitution of public office, will become the real Church of America. Our Church has done some good service here. She ought to do much more. Largely the Church of the rich, she ought to rebuke rich men's vices and to stir rich men's torpidity. She ought to blow her trumpet in the ears of the young men of fortune, summoning them from their clubs and their frivolities to do the chivalrous work, which their nobility obliges them to do for fellowman. She ought to speak to Culture, and teach it its responsibility. She ought to make real contributions to the creation of that atmosphere of brotherhood and hope and reverence for man, in which alone there is any chance that the hard social and economical problems of the present and the future can find solution. If she can do such things as these, she will be following in the steps of all the largest minded, deepest-hearted Fathers of the Church, all the way from St. Paul down. That is the true apostolical succession. That she must not boast that she has, but she must struggle more and more earnestly to win.

My friends, it is not possible for the true man to think of his Church without thinking of his country. I cannot be the Churchman that I ought without being a patriot. On this Sunday morning, when we plead for our Church, let the image of our country stand before us, with her chances, with her dangers, with her glories, with her sins! We are glad indeed that our Church is not the only church which is laboring for the land's salvation. We rejoice in all that our brother Christians of other names are doing; but we believe in the work which our Church has to do. We pray to God, O keep her simple, brave and earnest, free from fantasticalness and cowardice and selfishness, that she may do it. We look on, and far, far away we see the Nation-church, the land all full of Christ, the Nation-church, a true part of the World-church, issuing into glorious life, and swallowing up our small ecclesiasticisms, as the sun grandly climbing up the heavens swallows up the scattered rays which he sent out at his rising. And full of that vision, we are ready to do what we can to make our Church strong for the work which it must do in preparation for that day!

SERMON IV.

Standing before God.

"And I saw the dead, small and great, stand before God."
REVELATION XX. 12.

THE life which we are living now is more aware than we know of the life which is to come. Death, which separates the two, is not, as it has been so often pictured, like a great thick wall. It is rather like a soft and yielding curtain, through which we cannot see, but which is always waving and trembling with the impulses that come out of the life which lies upon the other side of it. We are never wholly unaware that the curtain is not the end of everything. Sounds come to us, muffled and dull, but still indubitably real, through its thick folds. Every time that a new soul passes through that vail from mortality to immortality, it seems as if we heard its light footfalls for a moment after the jealous curtain has concealed it from our sight. As each soul passes, it almost seems as if the opening of the curtain to let it through were going to give us a sight of the unseen things beyond; and, though we are forever disappointed, the shadowy expectation always comes back to us again, when we see the curtain stirred by another friend's departure. After our friend has passed, we can almost see the curtain, which he stirred, moving, tremulously for a while, before it settles once more into stillness.

Behind this curtain of death, St. John, in his great vision, passed, and he has written down for us what he saw there. He has not told us many things; and probably we cannot know how great the disappointment must have been if he had tried to translate into our mortal language all the ineffable wonders of eternity. But he has told us much; and most of what we want to know is wrapped up in this simple and sublime declaration, "I saw the dead, small and great, stand before God."

I think that it grows clearer and clearer to us all that what we need are the great truths, the vast and broad assurances within which are included all the special details of life. Let us have them, and we are more and more content to leave the special details unknown. With regard to eternity, for instance, I am sure that we can most easily, nay, most gladly, forego the detailed knowledge of the circumstances and occupations of the other life, if only we can fully know two things—that the dead are, and that they are with God. All beside these two things we can most willingly leave undiscovered. And those two things, if we can believe St. John, are sure.

"I saw the dead, small and great, stand before God." What is meant by "standing before God?" We are apt to picture to ourselves a great dramatic scene. Host beyond host, rank behind rank, the millions who have lived upon the earth, all standing crowded together in the indescribable presence of One who looks not merely at the mass but at the individual, and sees through the whole life and character of every single soul. The picture is sublime, and it is what the words of St. John are intended to suggest. But we must get behind the picture to its meaning. The picture must describe not one scene only, but the whole nature and condition of the everlasting life. The souls of men in the eternal world are always "standing before God." And what does that mean? We understand at once, if we consider that that before which a man stands is the standard, or test, or source of judgment for his life. Every man stands before something which is his judge. The child stands before the father. Not in a single act, making report of what he has been doing on a special day, but in the whole posture of his life, almost as if the father was a mirror in whom he saw himself reflected, and from whose reflection of himself he got at once a judgment as to what he was, aud suggestions as to what he ought to be. The poet stands before nature. She is his judge. A certain felt harmony or discord between his nature and her ideal is the test and directing power of his life. The philosopher stands before the unseen and majestic presence of the abstract truth. The philanthropist stands before humanity. The artist stands before beauty. The legislator stands before justice. The politician stands before that vague but awful embodiment of average character, the people, the demos. The fop, in miserable servility, stands before fashion, the feeblest and ficklest of tyrants. The scholar stands before knowledge, and gets the satisfactions or disappointments of his life from the approvals or disapprovals of her serene and gracious lips.

You see what the words mean. Every soul that counts itself capable of judgment and responsibility, stands in some presence by which the nature of its judgment is decreed. The higher the presence, the loftier and greater, though often the more oppressed and anxious, is the life. A weak man, who wants to shirk the seriousness and anxiety of life, goes down into some lower chamber and stands before some baser judge whose standard will be least exacting. A strong, ambitious man presses up from judgment room to judgment room, and is not satisfied with meeting any standard perfectly so long as there is any higher standard which he has not faced. Greater than anything else in education, vastly greater than any question about how many facts and sciences a teacher may have taught his pupil, there must always be this other question, into what presence he has introduced him; before what standard he has made his pupil stand: for in the answer to that question are involved all the deepest issues of the pupil's character and life.

And now St. John declares that when he passed behind the vail, he saw the dead, small and great, stand before God. Do you not see now what that means? Out of all the lower presences with which they have made themselves contented; out of all the chambers where the little easy judges sit with their compromising codes of conduct, with their ideas worked over and worked down to suit the conditions of this earthly life; out of all these partial and imperfect judgment chambers, when men die they are all carried up into the presence of the perfect righteousness, and are judged by that. All previous judgments go for nothing unless they find their confirmation there. Men who have been the pets and favorites of society, and of the populace, and of their own self-esteem, the change that death has made to them is that they have been compelled to face another standard and to feel its unfamiliar awfulness. Just think of it. A man who, all his life on earth since he was a child, has never once asked himself about any action, about any plan of his, is this right? Suddenly, when he is dead, behold, he finds himself in a new world, where that is the only question about everything. His old questions as to whether a thing was comfortable, or was popular, or was profitable, are all gone. The very atmosphere of this new world kills them. And upon the amazed soul, from every side there pours this new, strange, searching question: "Is it right?" Out of the ground he walks on, out of the walls which shelter and restrain him, out of the canopy of glory overhead, out of strange, unexplored recesses of his own newly-awakened life, from every side comes pressing in upon him that one question, "Is it right?" That is what it is for that dead man to "stand before God."

And then there is another soul which, before it passed through death, while it was in this world, had always been struggling after higher presences. Refusing to ask whether acts were popular or profitable, refusing even to care much whether they were comfortable or beautiful, it had insisted upon asking whether each act was right. It had always struggled to keep its moral vision clear. It had climbed to heights of self-sacrifice that it might get above the miasma of low standards which lay upon the earth. In every darkness about what was right, it had been true to the best light it could see. It had grown into a greater and greater incapacity to live in any other presence, as it had struggled longer and longer for this highest company. Think what it must be for that soul, when for it, too, death sweeps every other chamber back and lifts the nature into the pure light of the unclouded righteousness. Now for it, too, the question, "Is it right?" rings from every side; but in that question this soul hears the echo of its own best-loved standard. Not in mockery, but in invitation; not tauntingly, but temptingly; the everlasting goodness seems to look in upon the soul from all that touches it. That is what it is for that soul to "stand before God." God opens his own heart to that soul and is both Judgment and Love. They are not separate. He is Love because He is Judgment; for to be judged by Him, to meet His judgment is what the soul has been long and ardently desiring. Tell me, when two such souls as these stand together "before God," are they not judged by their very standing there? Are not the deep content of one, and the perplexed distress of the other, already their heaven and their hell? Do you need a pit of fire, and a city of gold, to emphasize their difference? When the dead, small and great, stand before God, is not the book already opened, and are not the dead already judged?

"The dead, small and great," St. John says that he saw standing before God. In that great judgment-day, another truth is that the difference of sizes among human lives, of which we make so much, passes away, and all human beings, in simple virtue of their human quality, are called to face the everlasting righteousness. The child and the greybeard, the scholar and the boor, however their lives may have been separated here, they come together there. See how this falls in with what I said before. It is upon the moral ground that the most separated souls must always meet. Upon the child and the philosopher alike rests the common obligation not to lie, but to tell the truth. The scholar and the plow-boy both are bound to be pure and to be merciful. Differently as they may have to fulfil their duties, the duties are the same for both. Intellectual sympathies are limited. The more men study, the more they separate themselves into groups with special interests. But moral sympathies are universal. The more men try to do right, the more they come into communion with all other men who are engaged in the same struggle all through the universe. Therefore it is that before the moral judgment seat of God all souls, the small and great, are met together. All may be good—all may be bad; therefore, before Him, whose nature is the decisive touchstone of goodness and badness in every nature which is laid upon it, all souls of all the generations of mankind may be assembled.

Think what a truth that is. We try to find some meeting ground for all humanity, and what we find is always proving itself too narrow or too weak. The one only place where all can meet, and every soul claim its relationship with every other soul, is before the throne of God. The Father's presence alone furnishes the meeting-place for all the children, regardless of differences of age or wisdom. The grave and learned of this earth shall come up there before God, and find, standing in His presence, that all which they have truly learned has not taken them out of the sympathy of the youngest and simplest of their Father's children. On the other hand, the simple child, who has timidly gazed afar off upon the great minds of his race, when he comes to stand with them before God, will find that he is not shut out from them. He has a key which will unlock their doors and let him enter into their lives. Because they are obeying the same God whom he obeys, therefore He has some part in the eternal life of Abraham, and Moses, and Paul. Not directly, but through the God before whom both of them stand, the small and great come together. The humility of the highest and the self-respect of the lowest are both perfectly attained. The children, who have not been able to understand or hold communion with each other directly, meet perfectly together in the Father's house, and the dead, small and great, stand in complete sympathy and oneness before God.

Another thought which is suggested by St. John's verse, is the easy comprehension of the finite by the infinite. All the dead of all the generations stand before God together. How such a picture sends our imagination back. We think how many men have died upon the earth. We think of all the ages and of all the lands. We think of all the uncounted myriads who died before history began. We see the dusk of the world's earliest memory crowded with graves. We let our minds begin to count the countless dead of Asia, with its teeming kingdoms; of this America of ours, with its suggestions of extinguished races. We remember the earthquakes, the battle fields, the pestilences. We hear the helpless wail of infancy, which, in all the generations, has just crept upon the earth long enough to claim life with one plaintive cry, and die. Where should we stop? We know that " All that tread the globe are but a handful to the tribes that slumber in its bosom;" and yet how crowded is the globe today. Not one must be left out! We heap up millions upon millions until we weary of the mere reiteration, and numbers cease to have a meaning. And yet not one must be left out! All must be there. All the dead, small and great, out of all the ages; out of all the lands! All the dead, small and great, are standing before God. Is there an effort more staggering than this, the effort to gather up in our imagination all the hosts of humanity, and believe in the true immortality of every one of them?

Here, I think, is where the faith of many men in their own immortality staggers the most. If only there were not so many of us! A man feels his own soul, and its very existence seems to promise him that he is immortal. And in his brethren, whose life he watches, he sees the same signs that for them too there is another life. But when he looks abroad, the multitude dismays him. There are so many souls. What world can hold them all? What care can recognize, and cover and embrace them all? If there only were not so many of us! The thought of one's own immortality sinks like a tired soldier on a battle-field, overwhelmed and buried under the multitude of the dead. Have not many of you felt this bewilderment? I think that it is one of the most common forms in which perplexity, not clear and definite, but vague and terribly oppressive, lays itself upon a human soul. What can we say to it? How can we grasp and believe in this countless army of immortals who come swarming up out of all the lands and all the ages? There is only one way. Multiply numbers as enormously as you will, and the result is finite still. Then set the finite, however large, into the presence of the infinite, and it is small. Its limitations show. There is no finite, however vast, that can overcrowd the infinite; none that the infinite cannot most easily grasp and hold.

Now, St. John says, that he saw all the hosts of the dead stand "before God." We too must see them stand before God, and they will not oppress us.

For God is infinite, and a thousand million draughts come no nearer to exhausting infinity than ten would come. Here must be the real solution of our difficulty, in the infinity of God. You say, "I can have five friends and understand them, and discriminate between them, and love them all; but give me fifty friends and you swamp me in the ocean of their needs. I have not intelligence, nor care, nor sympathy enough to comprehend them all." But make yourself infinite, and then the difficulty disappears. Unnumbered souls may stand before you then, and you can open a vastness of nature which shall take them all in, and be to each one just as much a friend as if there were no others; yet being all the while the comprehending and including presence which embraces all.

Be sure that if you will begin not by counting the multitude of the dead, and asking yourself how any celestial meadow where you can picture them assembled can hold them all, but by lifting yourself up and laying hold on the infinity of God, you will find range enough in Him for all the marvellous conception of the immortality of all men. Every thought of man depends upon what you first think of God. Make your thought of God large enough, and there is no thought of man too large for you to think within it.

Take, then, these three ideas, and I think that we can see something of what it must have been for souls to stand, as John the Evangelist in his great vision saw them standing before God. They had gone up above all the small and temporary standards, and laid their lives close upon the one perfect and eternal standard by which men must be judged. No longer did it matter to them whether they were rich or poor, whether men praised them, or abused them, or pitied them. The one question about themselves, into which all other questions gathered and were lost, was whether they were good, whether they were obedient to God.

And then, along with this, there had come to them a true and cordial meeting with their brethren. No child of their Father was too lofty or too low for them to be truly his brethren, when they stood, small and great, together before God.

And yet, again, in presence of the Infinite, they had comprehended their immortality. They had seen how, within that life to which their lives belonged, there was room for a growth which might go on to all eternity.

No wonder that as St. John looked upon that vision it filled all his soul with joy. No wonder that he hastened back to tell it to the men and women who were yet upon the earthward side of the thick curtain of death. "I have seen the dead," he cried. "Those who have gone from us into the darkness, all our friends who have gone so silently, so sorrowfully, holding fast to this life as long as they could, going into the mystery upon the other side only when they must, sending back no word out of the darkness into which they went—I have seen them all! I actually looked upon them. Among the millions who have gone like them out of all the lands, I saw them. They were standing before God. They are living.

They are far more living than you are who are left behind them here." Must not the remembrance of such a sight have filled his soul with joy? Must it not have been present with him afterward, whenever he saw a new soul depart to join the vast company whom he had seen standing before God?

There is the difference between his view of death and ours. He saw what souls go to. We are so apt to see only what souls go from. When our friend dies we think of all the warm delights of life, all the sweet friendships, all the interesting occupations, all the splendor of the sunlight which he leaves behind. If we could only know, somewhat as John must have known after his vision, the presence of God into which our friend enters on the other side, the higher standards, the larger fellowship with all his race, and the new assurance of personal immortality in God; if we could know all this, how our poor comfortless efforts of comfort when our friends depart, our feeble raking-over of the ashes of memory, our desperate struggles to think that the inevitable must be all right; how this would all give way to something almost like a burst of triumph, as the soul which we loved went forth to such vast enlargement, to such glorious consummation of its life! We should be able to forget our own sorrow, or at least to bear it gladly, in our thankfulness for him, as the generous farmer-boy might see his brother taken from his side to be made a king, and toil on himself all the more cheerfully at his humble and solitary labor, thinking of the glory to which his brother's life had come.

It is well, then, with those to whom John's vision is fulfilled. Blessed are the dead who die in the Lord, and stand immortal before Him.

And now one question still remains! Is the fulfilment of the vision of St. John for any man to wait until that man is dead? Can only the dead stand before God? Think for a moment what we found to be the blessings of that standing before God, and then consider that those privileges, however they may be capable of being given more richly to the soul of man in the eternal world, are privileges upon whose enjoyment any man's soul may enter here. Consider this, and the question at once is answered. Already, now, you and I may live by the standards of the eternal righteousness, and we may claim our brotherhood with the least and the greatest of our fellow-men, and we may so lay hold on God that we shall realize our immortality. The soul that has done all that, is now standing before God. It does not need to push aside the curtain, and to enter into the unknown world which lies behind. While the man is living here, walking these common streets, living in closest intercourse with other men, he is already in the everlasting presence, and his heaven has begun.

But now these are the very things which Jesus Christ promises to give, and which he has given to multitudes of men. All who will come to Him and serve Him are brought thereby to the loftiest standards of righteousness, to the broadest and deepest human fellowship, and to such a true knowledge of God that their own immortality becomes real to them.

Is it not true, then, that Christ does for the soul which follows him, that which the experience of the eternal world shall take up and certify, and complete? Already in Him we begin to live the everlasting life. Already its noble independence, its deep discrimination, its generous charity, its large hopefulness, its great abounding and inspiring peace gathers around and fills the soul which lives in obedience to Him. Already, as He himself said, "He that believeth on the Son hath everlasting life."

And yet, while we need not wait till we are dead for the privilege and power of "standing before God," yet still the knowledge of that loftier and more manifest standing before Him, which is to come in the unseen land, of which St. John has told us, may make more possible the true experience of the divine presence which we may have here. Because I am to stand before Him in some yet unimagined way, seeing Him with some keener sight, hearing His words with some quicker hearing which shall belong to some new condition of eternity, therefore I will be sure that my true life here consists in such a degree of realization of His presence, such a standing before Him in obedience, and faith, and love, as is possible for one in this lower life.

When the change comes to any of us, my friends, how little it will be, if we have really been, through the power of Jesus Christ, standing before God, in our poor, half-blind way upon the earth. If now, in the bright freshness of your youth, you give yourself to Christ, and through him do indeed know God as your dearest friend, years and years hence, when the curtain is drawn back for you, and you are bidden to join the host of the dead who stand before God eternally, how slight the change will be. Only the change from the struggle to the victory, only the opening of the dusk and twilight into the perfect day. "Well done, good and faithful servant, thou hast been faithful over a few things. Enter thou into the joy of thy Lord."

SERMON V.

Brotherhood in Christ.

"*Simon, called Peter, and Andrew his brother; James the son of Zebedee, and John his brother.*"—MATTHEW X. 2.

IN the list of the apostles of Jesus there are two pairs of brothers. We cannot tell, of course, what were the reasons which directed the Master's choice among the fishermen of Galilee of those who were to preach his Gospel and to be the first pastors of his Church; but certainly it is significant and suggestive that twice in the small number of the twelve it should have happened that the natural tie of brotherhood was emphasized by a common call to the new life and a common work in the same service. It suggests the relationship which may exist between our common human kinships and those loftier and diviner influences which are always seeking admission to the life of man.

Simon and Andrew, James and John—they had grown up together in their simple homes beside the Sea of Galilee, passing on from childhood into youth, from youth into manhood, under the same influences, keeping, as brothers will keep, that openness between their lives which came of the same early memories. You know how brothers, however far they drift apart, have always doors between their lives which keep them in communication. The doors may be long blocked up with the great burdens of later life which have been piled against them; the locks may have grown rusty and the keys may have been lost; yet still the doors are there, and the wall never is quite as thick and solid as are the walls which divide other lives. The doors may still some day be opened, and even while they remain closed, there come sounds through them of what is being done upon the other side. Surely such relations, never completely closed, existing between human creatures all over the world, must have something to do with the diffusion through human life of any great influence of thought or feeling.

The world is covered with a network of brotherhoods. The first and simplest relationships run on and out in every direction, and multiply themselves till hardly any man stands entirely alone. This network of brotherhoods, like every evident fact of life, sets us to asking three questions—first, what is its immediate cause? second, what is its direct result? and third, what is its final reason? These are the three questions which the thoughtful man asks about every fact.

And with relation to this fact the answer to the first two questions is very plain. The cause of this interwoven network, this reticulation of life with life, is the whole system of nature by which each human being takes its start from another human being, and is kept, for a time at least, in associations of company and dependence with the being from whom it sprang and with the other beings who have the same source with it. And the direct result of such relationships is also plain. They are full of mutual helpfulness and pleasure. As to the third question, the answer is not so entirely clear and certain. But, as we watch and think, it seems to me that we are at least led to wonder whether one final cause or purpose of this interlacing of life with life, by natural and indissoluble kinships, may not be just this, the providing, as it were, of open communications, of a system of shafts or channels piercing this human mass in every direction, crossing and recrossing one another, through which those higher influences, which ought to reach every corner, and every individual of the great structural humanity, may be freely carried everywhere, and no most remote or insignificant atom of the mass be totally and necessarily untouched.

We have only, I think, to picture to ourselves what would be the case if there were no such great system of natural relationships covering the earth, somewhere in which every human being found his place; and then we see how reasonable it is to think that the great system which actually does exist, may have been created for this purpose which I have described. Suppose that every human being stood alone. Suppose that every atom, however it may have come into existence, lay next, indeed, to other atoms, but with no lines of brotherhood or any natural relationship between them. Can we not feel at once how different the world would be? Every truth or power which was to fill the mass would have to be communicated separately by a special act to every particle. Some little transmission there might be from surface to surface, but none from heart to heart, of these atoms which were strung upon no cords of brotherhood. If the whole mass of mankind were to be infused with the knowledge of God's existence, every separate man would have to be convinced with his own evidence, and the evidence which persuaded his brethren would have no convincingness for him. I can imagine only one result. Good influence, right thought, true feeling would seem almost of necessity to be obliged to lie in pools here and there upon the great expanse of human life, wherever it found the most sensitive and susceptible minds; great districts of humanity being totally unreached, instead of the great broad fields, being watered through and through. Truth would flash here and there from a splendid diamond nature on which it chanced to strike, and be but one thin ray of intense light. It could not be a suffused radiance varying always in depth and richness, but lighting every man and carried everywhere along the atmosphere in which all priests kept brotherhood with one another.

Our truth is this then—that the natural relations which exist between man and man, the relations of brotherhood, sisterhood, parenthood, childhood, and all the other kinships of mankind, have one at least of their purposes, and one of their most sacred purposes, in this—that they are God's great system along whose lines He means to diffuse his truth and influence through the world. They are a structure of channels, honeycombing the mass of human life, along which the water of life may flow. Look at Christ's Incarnation. In Him we know that God came into the world. And see how it was that God, in Him, appealed to and diffused Himself through human life. He sets himself right into the midst of a human family. First out through that sacred channel which lies forever open between a mother and her child, a channel through which the currents which flow motherwards are no less strong than the currents which flow childwards, through that channel first his influence flows, and flows so spontaneously that it flows even while it is yet unconscious of itself. His mother is his first disciple—his first Christian. Then it is evident, from what the very fragmentary records tell us, that his power found out the other open channels which connect a man's life with his brothers' lives, and flowed in them. "Neither did his brethren believe on him," we read at first, as if their unbelief in him was strongest because his appeal to them had been the closest and most urgent. But by-and-by the "Lord's brethren" stand high among his disciples, as if when they did believe in him their belief was the most natural and real of all. Around his cross more than one of the mourners was of his kindred. Is it not evident that the great system of the universal brotherhood in which all men are children of the same Father, was reached by the

power of the Son of God through the smaller system
which had its centre in the household of the carpenter?
And if we look at Christ's larger method, at the way
in which his work went on after it had gone beyond
that earliest stage among his personal kindred, the
same thing still appears. His truth ran abroad in
the channels which were made by the natural relations of mankind. It was a fulfilment of the method
of the Old Testament, in which again and again the
Jew was commanded concerning the words which
God had spoken unto him: "Thou shalt teach them
unto thy children." So Jesus makes the father's faith
a reason for the sick child's restoral to health; so he
fills the home at Bethany with his pervading presence; so he sends the recovered lunatic of Gadara
back to his home, to spread among his friends the
story of his healing. So he bids his disciples make
way for the mothers bringing him their children; so
he finds in household life an image of the Everlasting Father's willingness to hear his people's prayer.
True, he is always recognizing that the ultimate power
of his religion is individual. He declares that sometimes, in its assertion of itself, it will break up family
life and set the son at variance against the father,
and the daughter against her mother. But all that
is expressly declared to be unnatural. It is the
rending of a family life which is not worthy of the
great influence which it has to transmit. It is the
bursting of a channel which has grown too weak to
carry the tides of the religious life. The whole great

scheme of Christianity, with its family Sacrament of Baptism; with its family conception of the government of God; with its Table of the Lord; with its graces, which are all transfigurations of the family affections; this Christianity began by using, and has always used, the network of natural brotherhood which it found enveloping the earth as a means for the diffusion of its truth and power. Its Christ is no philosopher, dropping seed-thoughts into single hearts, thinking only of individual character, or at most only of artificial combinations, of states built up elaborately and with complicated laws. He is the Son of Man, entering into the heart of the humanity to which he intrinsically belongs, beating his truth into its life-blood and making his power run in the channels of its primitive affections.

It is not only Christianity, nor only religion, that thus makes use of the network of natural relationship with which the earth is covered. Every higher and more spiritual influence, every interest which claims more of man than his mere physical appetites, avails itself of this same first fact of related human life, this fact that no man stands alone, but each is bound by some kind of kinship in with all the rest. This is the way in which knowledge spreads itself. Along the lines which tie the father to the child, and the older to the younger brother, runs the communication of facts and the contagion of the enthusiasm of learning. Taste spreads itself through a family circle as the sun spreads its light through an atmosphere where every particle is brother to every other.

Patriotism is not a fire which each new citizen has to go and light for himself at the central altar of his country's principles. It is caught in the warm air of loyal homes. It kindles unconsciously where hearts lie close together in the first relationships of man. Suppose that some new truth came to-day to take possession of humanity; suppose that some great practical philosophy desired to occupy the world; can we imagine for it any practicable way but this, that it should spread along these lines which it would find already marked out for it, the lines in which influence is used to run, the lines which God's hands have hollowed from life to life, from soul to soul?

And now if we have seen the principle, let us ask ourselves what its results will be. If religion spreads itself among mankind along the lines of man's natural affections and relationship, the results which we may look for will, I think, be two. First, the exaltation and refinement of those affections and relationship, themselves; and, second, the simplifying and humanizing of religion.

We all know how the natural relations between human creatures all have their downward as well as their upward tendency, their animal as well as their spiritual side. The lusts of Power and Pride and Cruelty and Passion all come in to make foul and mean that which ought to be pure and high. What is there that can keep the purity and loftiness of domestic life? What is there that can preserve the color and glory of the family, like the perpetual consciousness, running through all the open channels of its life, that they are being used to convey the truth and power of God? The father who counts himself one link in the ever developing perpetuation of truth among mankind, handing on to his children what has been already handed down to him; the brother who without struggle or effort feels all that he believes flowing through this life into the open life of the brother by his side; are not these the men in whom brotherhood and fatherhood keep their true dignity and never grow base, jealous, tawdry or tyrannical? Everything keeps its best nature only by being put to its best use. The relations of kinship are no exception to this rule. It is when, underneath the pleasant courtesies and intimacies of the home, there is all the time going on a diffusion and distribution of religion, of the highest motives and the highest thoughts; it is then that the home beams, even on the surface of its life, with its richest beauty.

And, as the home, pervaded by this diffusion of religion, comes to its best beauty, so religion too is at its best, when it is flowing through the channels which were made for it to run in. Religion, we know, is apt to grow unhuman. Either vaguely speculative, or hardly dogmatic, or fantastically formal, it loses the fulness and completeness, the healthiness and entire vitality which are the conditions of its best work. And the more solitary you make religion, the more it becomes in danger of such degenerations. It is in its contact with the healthy relations of human life that religion keeps its own true healthiness. It is as given from the father to the son, that religion truly reveals its authority and beneficence. It is as passing from brother to brother, along the channels of their commonest intercourse, that religion loses its cloudiness and becomes full of sincerity, honesty and common sense. Wherever religion deserts these primary and perpetual channels and becomes monastic, the brooding solitary experience of single souls, transmitting itself through the artificial relationships of priest and penitent, instead of through the normal relationships of life, in every such case religion becomes fantastic and diseased. It is the tendency of the unnatural associations of mankind to sacrifice the individual to the community. It is the privilege of the natural relationships of man, at once to secure social life and to foster individuality. That is the invariable difference between the companionship of the cloister and the companionship of the family. Religion, as it flows through one, grows complicated and unhealthy. Religion flowing through the other, gains ever new simplicity and health.

I know, my dear friends, well enough, that when I talk thus I am talking ideally. I am talking of these first relations of men to one another as they are when they are at their best. They are not always so. And when they fail of their best it is always true that the very quality in them which made them capable of special good, makes them the means of greatest evil. I have spoken of the way in which the network of natural affection, stretched all over the earth, may carry everywhere the truth and power of Christ. But you know well enough that every channel which is made to carry good influence, may be taken possession of by wickedness and made its instrument. The pipes which were laid to bring pure water into the city may bring in corruption. The veins which ought to run cool with the blood of health may be turned into rivers of fire and fever. The great system of popular education which ought to fill the land with sound learning, may be itself the means by which ignorance and error may be carried into countless homes. And so it is with all that other system of which I have been speaking. Through the same natural affections by which religion ought to be spread abroad, it is possible enough that infidelity, and vice, and worldliness may get a prevalence which they could gain in no other way. What is it that perpetuates the blighting influence of fashion? What are the channels through which are spread abroad, all over a community, the false standard of wealth, the base idea of manliness which poisons countless hearts? Are they not the same God-created channels through which the holiest influences were meant to flow? "Simon, called Peter, and Andrew his brother; James, the son of Zebedee, and John his brother." Many and many a time their brotherhood is the power of a common curse, instead of a common blessing. Many and many a home there is to-day where fatherhood and childhood, brotherhood and sisterhood, the self same channels still through which God meant that truth and righteousness should flow, are bearing pollution to innocent hearts, and temptation to weak hearts, and discouragement to sad hearts; pain instead of joy, hopelessness instead of hope.

I know all this. Who can live in the midst of this network of brotherhood and not know it? But yet all this misuse and perversion of the principle only makes the principle more plain. Every sight of corruption running freely through the channels which connect life with life, only shows how open those channels are, and makes an earnest man more anxious to rescue them for their best use.

What shall we do then? What shall you do, who feel with every breath you draw how other lives are living in open communication with yours, how their very life-bloods flow together in one common system? What shall you do, who are anxious that what is best in each should come to all the rest; that you should be able to give to your brethren the faith which is so strong in your own heart, and get from them the faith by which they live? What shall you parents do, who want to make your children love the Lord you love? What shall you brothers do, who want to make your brothers know the truth you know? What can you do to make the channels of your family life and of your natural relationship to one another, carry the influences which you want to give, and bring back to you the influences which you want to receive? It is not hard to tell, although it may be very hard to do. First, you can try to keep the whole character of your intercourses fine, and pure, and high. Look into countless families that you know—perhaps if I dared I might even bid some of you look into your own—and ask yourself whether, supposing some one member of that family to be truly religious, the atmosphere of the home is lofty enough and pure enough to furnish the proper medium by which that one member's religion may freely pass into the lives of all rest. Fire will leap through heated air; and the most deep of all emotions, the most eager of all desires, the emotion of the love of God, the desire to serve and know Christ, will pass most readily from heart to heart where all emotion is pure and lofty, and where all desire is unselfish and enthusiastic. But in homes where all the air is full of selfishness, where the whole tone is sordid, where every member is jealously watching that no other gets advantage over him, where brotherhood means suspicion, and fatherhood petty tyranny, and childhood restless impatience to be free, what chance is there for the divine fire of the higher life to leap through a heavy atmosphere like that? "I have been a Christian all these years; and look at my children—not one Christian among them all;" so the perplexed, disappointed father or mother talks. But when you open the door of that household's history, you feel the reason of the failure in an instant. As the door opens there comes pouring out on you a turbid wrangle of family quarrels, or a chatter of perpetual frivolity, or perhaps, what perhaps is worst of all, a great, dull, heavy cloud of well-fed stupidity, and ignorance, and mental stagnation, which is all that family life within those walls has ever meant. Through such a darkness as that, what wonder that the little candle-light of the father's or the mother's piety, weak enough itself, has never had the strength to pierce. No! The first thing to be done, in order that the natural relationships may be made the channel for religious influence, is that they should be kept pure with unselfishness, and open with intelligence, and fine with sympathy. Then when any religious influence seeks to pass from life to life, it will find already built a channel that is worthy of it and fit to carry it.

But there is something more definite than that. It is a very wide law and a very beautiful one, that the best way to make a thing fit for the use for which it was first made is to put it to that use. The best way to make the dusty trumpet clear is to blow music through it. The best way to make the sluggish mind capable of thinking is to think with it. And so the best way to make the natural relationships capable of carrying religious influence is to give them religious influences to carry, so strong and ardent that they shall force and burn their own way through whatever artificial obstructions may have stopped up the channel through which they were meant to go. Again I hear a Christian parent complaining that his religion has not told upon his children to make them Christians; but, when I ask, I find that there never has been one direct effort to make it tell; never, in all the years while they have lived together, one word or act, which definitely and specifically, tried to send the father's religion through the open channel that was between them, from the father's life into the child's. Everything else, every other truth and interest and treasure, has been offered and urged over and over again, but not one word or act has ever urged or even offered religion.

I know what will be said at once, and I think I understand it. I know how often it is hardest to speak about the most sacred things to those who are the nearest and the dearest to us. I understand that shrinking which keeps the brother's lips closed from urging on his own brother the truth and the persuasion which he will urge freely enough on any other man. The glib and ready Sunday-school teacher goes from his class to his home, and in the presence of his own children he is silent as a stone. In that phenomenon, which is so familiar and often so perplexing, I think we can see the mixture of two feelings, one of which is bad, the other good. The bad feeling is the sense of shame which comes when we think of pressing the love of God and the service of Christ upon the minds and consciences of those who are always living with us, and who know what poor, weak, wicked and unfaithful things our own lives are. The good reason for our silence is more subtle. It is, I think, the feeling which comes to us almost everywhere, but comes to us most strongly in the presence of those whose hearts lie nearest to our own, that for the conveyance of the most sacred influences words are the most clumsy and unsatisfactory of means; that life is the only testimony by which the power of Christ in one man's heart can thoroughly bear its witness to the heart of any other man. It is natural enough that this consciousness should be most clear and strong just where the possibility of heart bearing direct testimony to heart becomes most evident, in the home where hearts ought to lie nearest and openest to one another. I know how these two reasons, and perhaps some others, make it very hard sometimes for the father to talk to his child, or for the brother to talk to his brother, about the most sacred things. And yet I know how often just one word is needed to break through the obstruction and reserve, and let all the wealth of God's grace which has been gathering in one humbly consecrated heart, pour forth into another which is waiting empty and hungry all the time. At least we are all bound to be sure that it is something nobler than mere pride or shame that is keeping us from saying to our brother what may be his word of life.

But, after all, the word is only one method; the simplest, the most immediate, the most natural, but not the only nor the richest method by which men send influence forth to their brethren. If, honestly, the urgent word does not seem to be the true way to reach the lives which God has set the closest to our own, the truth remains that he who really seeks to send abroad the Gospel, and who lives that Gospel in the centre of some one of the networks of brotherhood with which God has covered the earth, and who cares for other souls beside his own, and is on the watch for every feather with which the arrow of his influence can possibly be winged, will surely find the ways he seeks, however impossible it is to tell before what they will be; and cannot fail to discover at last that God has blessed through him the lives which are no less dear to him than his own.

With that assurance, full of responsibility and full also of encouraging hope, I leave the truth which I have tried to preach to you. Go to your homes and question them! O Zebedee! O mother of Zebedee's children! ask yourselves whether your household is kept open by pure, refined, unselfish, elevated living, by a continual sense of God, by ever present prayer, so that the best of light and strength which God has given to any one tends freely to become the strength and light of all. Why are John and James so often not together in the company of Christ? What does it mean that so often Simon Peter lingers in darkness, while Andrew is in the full sunshine of the Master's service? Go home and question your household life about these things, and claim for your home that blessing for which God made our homes; the blessing of persuasive grace; the blessing of a brotherhood and sisterhood in the divine life, ever echoing and fulfilling the brotherhoods and sisterhoods which make the richness and beauty of our human living; and ever picturing and anticipating the perfect brotherhoods and sisterhoods in the great world-family of God.

SERMON VI.

The Giant with the Wounded Heel.

"And I will put enmity between thee and the woman, and between thy seed and her seed. It shall bruise thy head, and thou shalt bruise his heel."—GENESIS iii. 15.

THE scene in the story of which these words are written is fixed deep in the imagination of mankind. We read it in our childhood, and it is never afterwards forgotten. As we go on, seeing more and more of life, life and this story of the Book of Genesis become mutually commentaries on each other. Life throws light on the story and the story throws light on life.

Let us take one passage from the story now, and try to hold it in the light of life and see its meaning brighten and deepen. God is represented as talking to the serpent who has been the tempter of mankind. The serpent, the spirit of Evil, has forced his way into the human drama. He has compelled the man and woman to admit him to their company. He cannot now be cast out by one summary act. He has come, and he remains. All that takes place in human history takes place in his presence. Upon everything he tries to exercise his influence. He is everywhere and always, and always and everywhere the same.

To this serpent, this spirit of evil in the world, God is speaking. What is it that he says? He might tell the monster that the world belonged to him. "Since man has let you in, he must abide the issue. He is yours. There is no help for it, and you must do with him as you will." On the other hand he might with one sweep of his omnipotence bid the hateful reptile depart. "Begone; for man belongs to me; and even if he has given himself to you, you can have no power over him at all, for he is mine." The words which are written in our text are different from both of these. What does God say? There shall be a long, terrible fight between man and the power of evil. The power of evil shall haunt and persecute man, cripple him and vex him, hinder him and make him suffer. It shall bruise his heel. But man shall ultimately be stronger than the power of evil, and shall overcome it and go forth victorious, though bruised and hurt, and needing recovery and rest. He shall bruise its head.

Is there not in these words which the awful voice of God is heard speaking at the beginning of human history, a most clear and intelligible prophecy of human life? It separates itself at once from the crude theories which men have made on either side. It is not reckless pessimism nor reckless optimism. It is God's broad, wise, long-sighted prophecy of man, harassed, distressed and wounded on the way, but yet in spite of wounds and hindrances finally getting the better of his enemy and coming to success. With that promise of God—promise and warning together—sounding in his ears, man started on the long journey of existence, and has come thus far upon his way.

We want to ask ourselves how far that prophecy has been fulfilled, how far it has justified itself in history. We grow all out of patience with men's crude and sweeping and unqualified epitomes of life. One man says "It is all good," and will see none of the evil and sin and misery which are everywhere. Another man says "It is all bad;" and for him all the brightness and graciousness and perpetual progress go for nothing. One man calls humanity a hopeless brute. Another man calls humanity a triumphant angel. God in these words of Genesis says," Neither! but a wounded, bruised, strong creature, not running and leaping and shouting, often crawling and creeping in its pain, but yet brave, with an inextinguishable certainty of ultimate success, fighting a battle which is full of pain but is not desperate, sure ultimately to set his heel upon his adversary's head." Certainly there is a picture of man there which, in its most general statement, corresponds largely with the picture which history draws, and with that which our own experience presents. Let us look a little while first at the truthfulness of the picture; then at the way in which it comes to be true, and then at the sort of life which it will make in men who recognize its truth. The fact, the reason, and the consequence. Those are the natural divisions of any subject. Let them be the divisions of ours.

I look first at the institutions which mankind has formed for doing his work in the world. Institutions are nothing but colossal men. They are the great aggregations of humanity for doing those universal works which it is the interest not merely of this man, or of that man, but of all men to have done. Church institutions, state institutions, present the workings of human nature on a large scale, and so give excellent opportunity to study the fundamental facts of human life. And when we look at the great institutions of the world, what do we see? Everywhere, whether it be in Church or state, essentially the same thing. Noble principles, vast, beneficent agencies, gradually conquering barbarism and misery, making men better, making men happier, but always miserably hampered by wretched little sins of administration; stung in the heel by the serpents of selfishness, and sordidness, and insincerity and narrowness. Civilization, which is simply the sum of all the institutions which are shaped out of the best aspirations of mankind—it is simply amazing when we tell over to ourselves what the powers are which keep civilization to-day from putting its heel square and fair upon the head of barbarism, and finishing it forever. Popular government perverted by demagogues; Commerce degraded by the intrusion of fraud; the Church always weakened by hypocrisy; Charity perplexed by the fear of imposture and the dread of pauperism. Why, is not the image of institutionalism, embodying great principles, full of the consciousness of great ideas, and yet hindered and halting everywhere through the blunders and weaknesses of its administration—is it not just the picture of the giant with the bruised heel, the great strong creature, limping dubiously along the road over which he ought to be moving majestically to assured results?

Look again at society—that great mother and mistress of the thoughts and lives of so many of our old and younger people. It has its devotees and its denouncers. How few of us have ever seriously set ourselves to ask what is the real value and meaning of that social life which occupies so large a portion of the activity of civilized humanity? In its idea it is beautiful. Eagerness to take pleasure in the company of fellow-men—eagerness to give pleasure, by whatever contribution we can make—a wish to share with others all their gifts and ours—these are most true and healthy impulses. The society which is instinct with these impulses is the enemy of solitude; it puts its foot on selfishness; it makes men brothers; it kills out morbidness and self-conceit. Society is doing this—" What! our society?" you say, " this false, and foolish, and corrupt, and selfish, and frivolous uproar which takes possession of our city every winter, and runs its round of excitement, and jealousy, and dissipation, until Lent sets in?" Yes, even that! Sorely bruised in the heel it is, wounded and crippled in a melancholy fashion; a poor enough image of that divine communion of the children of God, which is the real society of men and women—

but yet a thing to be cured and cleansed, not to be cast away, not a thing for any man to turn his back upon and be a misanthrope, but for all men and women to do what they can to rescue and to fill with the spirit of a nobler life.

Then, think again of learning. We have a perfect right to indulge our enthusiasm over man as a studying and learning creature. Man seeking after knowledge is felt at once to be man using very noble powers. It is man doing the work for which a very noble part of him was made. We think of the ready and cheerful self-sacrifice of the scholars, great and little, not merely of those who have been rewarded for the surrenders which they made by the applause of a delighted world, but of the scholars whose self-sacrifice has lain in obscurity, who have eaten their crusts in silence, and not even recompensed themselves with groans. We think of all that man's untiring pursuit of knowledge has attained; of the great conquests which have been rescued out of the kingdom of ignorance. We let our imagination run forward and picture in delighted bewilderment the future triumphs of the same divine audacity, man's brave determination to know all that is knowable. And then, while we are glowing with this large enthusiasm, what is this which comes to interrupt and chill it? What are these petty jealousies and hates of learned men? What is this pedantry? What is this narrowness which neglects and despises, and even tries to hinder other learning than its own? Close on the large ambition comes the miserable discontent, the carping criticism, the discouragement, the love of darkness. The worm is in the wood of the brave ship that sails so proudly out to sea. The rust is on the arrow which is sent flying through the air. What is the Poet's complaint, that "knowledge comes but wisdom lingers," except a declaration that here too the full completeness of a great process is prevented, the serpent is stinging at the heel which ultimately must be set upon the serpent's head and crush it.

And what shall we say about religion? The future of mankind is a religious future. It is man as religious, that is to rule the world. What changes of form religious thought may undergo, who can pretend to say? But that religion shall perish, none of us believes. And if religion continues, she must reign. We cannot imagine for her a merely subordinate or passive life. She must reign, reign till she has put all enemies under her feet. Indeed I do not know how any man can really believe in religion today, who does not believe in the destiny of religion to be the mistress of the world. I cannot believe in God without believing that he is the rightful Lord of everything; for that is what "God" means. A God who is not rightful Lord and Master, is not God. We say this with entire certainty, and then, we look up to see religion conquering the world. We do see what we look for. But we see something else besides. How the great conqueror is harassed and tormented. What petty annoyances and trouble, she is beset with. Look at the crudeness, and the mercenariness, and mechanicalness with which men, even her own friends, misconceive her most spiritual truths. Look how her theories break down in human action. Behold the hypocrisy, the selfishness, the bigotry, the fanaticism, the untruthfulness, the formality, the cowardice, the meanness of religious people! Wounded in the house of her friends, is this great majestic Being who is some day to rule and save the world. And outside of her friends, among her enemies, men insult her and oppose her as if she were their worst foe, and not, what she really is, their only hope. The work which she is bound to do will none the less be done, but it will be done under perpetual opposition and persecution, done with torn and bleeding hands and feet.

Thus hurriedly I think over the great powers which are helping the world, and everywhere the case concerning all of them seems to be the same. All of them are doing good work. All of them are destined to ultimate success. Of none of them do we despair. But every one of them is working against hindrance and enmity and opposition. Not one of them goes freely and fearlessly to its victory. It is the combination of these two facts that gives the color and the tone to human history. From every century comes forth the same report. Great powers, sure to succeed, yet ever hindered at their work; never abandoning hope, yet moving timidly because they know, that sure as their final victory may be, their immediate lot is wounds and insult. Is it not exactly the old prophecy. The serpent

The Giant with the Wounded Heel. 101

whose head is ultimately to be crushed, now ever wounding the heel which is finally to be its destruction. Could any image picture human history so well?

Turn now away from this large look across the fields of history, and think how true the picture of the Book of Genesis is to our personal life. I might open the closed and sacred pages of any man's experience. Here is a man who for his thirty, forty, fifty years has been seeking after goodness, trying to conquer his passions and vices, and be a really good man. What will he say of his struggle as he looks back upon it? Let him stand upon this Sunday hillock, a little nearer to the sky perhaps than on the week-days; let him stand here and say how life looks to him as his eye runs back. You know the hindrances you have met. Paul's story has been your story. When you would do good evil was present with you. You never sprang most bravely from the low ordinary level of your living, that a hand did not seem to catch you and draw you back. You never felt a new power start up within you that a new weakness did not start up by its side. Terrible has been this quickness of the evil power, giving you the awful sense of being watched and dogged. Awful has grown this certainty that no good impulse ever could go straight and uninterrupted to its victorious result, and yet, is it not wonderful how you have kept the assurance that good and not evil is the true master-power of your life! The resolution has been broken. It has been wounded.

It has limped and halted. It has stood for months, perhaps for years, in the same place and made no progress, but it has never died. There is no man here who has not failed; but is there any man here in all this multitude who has given up? Not one! Every man here, when he looks forward, means some day to enter into the gates of salvation, to leave his sins behind him and live the life of God. In such a hope, in the light of such a resolution only, is life tolerable. Everything that hinders and delays that resolution is an accident and an intruder. The resolution itself is the utterance of God's purpose for the life.

I think the same is true about our faith. To believe is the true glory of existence. To disbelieve is to give ourselves into the power of death, and, just so far, to cease from living. And you are living and not dead. You do believe. You are quite sure of spiritual verities. God is a truth to you. Your soul is your true self. Christ, the spiritual perfectness of manhood, the true Son of God, is really King of the world. This spiritual faith you would not part with for your life. It is your only hope. You look forward to the day when it shall have conquered and cast out every doubt in you, and reign supreme. But now, how doubt besets you! Now, how a denial comes like its shadow on the heels of every faith! Who is this man whom in your loftier and more hopeful moments you discern, far off, on some bright distant day, entering into the open portals of a perfect faith, and leaving doubt dead outside the door forever? Is he the victor of an easy fight? Does he come springing up the shining steps with muscles only just tried enough to feel themselves elastic from the long struggle? Indeed, not so! The man —yourself—whom you see finally victorious, comes crawling to the temple of entire faith, dragging after him the wounded heel which Doubt, for long years before at last he died, stung, and stung, and stung again. Wonderful is that faith in faith, a thing to be thankful for to all eternity; wonderful is that faith in faith by which the soul dares to be sure, even in the very thick of doubt, that in belief, and not in unbelief, is its eternal rest and home.

I have spoken of the prophecy of Genesis as if it referred to that total seed of the woman which is all humanity. I have no doubt that it does so refer. But it has also always been considered to have reference to that special representative humanity which was in Jesus Christ. To him it certainly applies. What is the story of that wondrous life which, centuries afterward, Christ lived in Palestine? It is the story of a life wounded again and again by an antagonist whom at the last it overthrew. Christ's victory was perfect on the cross. There, finally, he conquered the world, he conquered sin. There he went up upon his throne, and Sin and Death were under his feet. But how did he come to that throne? Behold him staggering, wounded, bruised, beaten, all the way from Pilate's brutal judgment hall to Calvary. Remember what the years before had been. All the time he had been conquering the world and sin, and yet all the time sin and the world had been apparently conquering him. At the tomb door of Bethany, he stands and groans and weeps. Death has cut deep into his affections. His friend is dead. We may well believe that he hesitates and almost doubts. Then he lifts up his head and cries, "Lazarus, come forth!" and as the dead man comes to life, is it not true in that moment that the bruised heel of the woman is set upon the head of the serpent which has bruised it? Is not the old prophecy of Genesis, in that moment, perfectly fulfilled?

May I not then rest here my statement and assertion of the fact? Is it not true that everywhere the good is hampered and beset and wounded by the evil which it is ultimately to slay; true also that the good will ultimately slay the evil by which it was wounded and beset? These two facts, in their combination, make a philosophy of life which, when one has accepted it, colors each thought he thinks, each act he does. The two facts subtly blend their influence in every experience. They make impossible either crude pessimism or crude optimism. No man can curse that world in which the best of men, and the best of manhood, is steadily moving onward to the victory over the serpent. No man can unqualifiedly praise the world where that onward movement of the best is always being wounded and retarded by the serpent, over which it is to triumph at the last. But surely it gives certainty to our own observation of the history of man; surely it gives dignity to what has seemed to be the mere accident of confusion in our own lives, when we find them both prophesied on the first page of the world's Book. Yes, that which puzzles you or me, that which so often seems to make life meaningless and cruel, at least it is no chance and thoughtlessness by which it comes, for it is written in the very prospectus and prophecy of human life.

It would be possible, I think, also to show that it is written, or at least the possibility of it is written in the very necessity of things. On that I must not linger. I have dwelt so long upon the fact, that I must say but a few words of the cause and the consequence.

Of the cause I may say only this, that there is one conceivable state of things which in its operation must produce just that phenomenon which we have been studying at such length this morning. That state of things is a vast general purpose for the best good of mankind, submitted for its execution to the wills of men. Granted a God who means all good for his creatures, and who, as a part of his benevolent designs for them, calls their free agency to help in bringing about his purposes, and what shall we behold? Indubitable evidences that the good is stronger than the evil; a great, slow, steady progress of the good, forever gaining on the evil; and all the time reactions and detractions, rebellions of the evil against its conquest by the good. A stream with grand majestic onward flow, whose broad strong bosom is not smooth, but flecked all over with eddies, little twists and turns, in which the water for a time is running the wrong way. A stately figure of humanity, slowly pressing down its heel upon the serpent's head, yet with its face full of disturbance and of pain, because the serpent on whose head the heel is set is always stinging with the very venom of despair the heel that crushes it.

Tell me, my friends, if this is what would come if there were a great divine purpose in the world necessarily submitted for its execution to the will of man: then, since this has come, since this is the very picture which our eyes behold, shall we not let ourselves believe that the cause which I have described does indeed lie behind this wonderfully interesting, pathetic, fearful, hopeful life we live? A great divine purpose, dependent for its detailed execution on the will of men! Let me believe that, and then I know what means this ineradicable hope and this perpetual discouragement. Let me know that, and then I understand both why the good does not conquer now, and why the good must conquer at the last.

Our last question still remains. What sort of human life will this world tend to make in the mean time, or what will be the truest and most fitting life to live in a world such as this which we have seen our world to be. For man is capable of many lives, and is able to answer to the world in which he lives with its appropriate response.

Two qualities, I think, must certainly appear in the man who has thoroughly caught the spirit and is susceptible to the best influences of this world.

One quality I call watchful hope, and the other I call anxious charity. We need our adjectives as well as our nouns when we describe the true temper in which a man must live. The nouns describe the fundamental confidence which must arise from the conviction of a divine purpose for the life of man. The adjectives depict the sense of danger which comes from the knowledge that this divine purpose is committed for its execution to the unstable wills of men. Hope and charity, these must both spring up from the soul of faith. If God has truly a purpose for our lives, who dare be hopeless? If God has really a purpose for our brotner's life, who dare despair of him? Ah, we do only half believe it. Therefore our hope is such a colorless and feeble thing; therefore our charity so doubts and hesitates. But they are in us still. They must be in us just in proportion to our faith in God.

And yet the hope must be a watchful hope, the charity must be an anxious charity. Neither can fling itself out broadcast and without reserve. Hope is aware of danger ; charity is full of fear; in this world where God has done all God can, and yet leaves the last decision of his own destiny in the hands of man.

A watchful hope! An anxious charity! Are not these very clear and recognizable qualities? Do they not make a very clear and recognizable character? They make a character which has stamped the life of humanity wherever it has really known and felt the conditions of its life.

One sometimes thinks how it would be if to each star which floats in space the life which its inhabitants are living should impart a color, which other stars might see as they pass by it in the never resting chorus of the planets. Can we not picture to ourselves with what a special hue the long spiritual experience of the men who live upon it must have clothed this earth of ours? A sober glory, a radiance of indescribable depth and richness; and yet a certain tremulousness as of a perpetual fear; no outburst of unquestioning, unhesitating splendor, but a restrained effulgence, hoping for more than it dare yet to claim, pathetic with a constant, age-long discontent.

Whether our sister stars discover it or not, we know it well; we who live here and see the highest typical life of man upon the earth. Do we not know how all the best and holiest men live in a hope so great that its own greatness clothes it in a mystery which is almost doubt, as the sun clothes itself in sunlight which is almost a hiding of the splendor it displays. We cannot describe it to ourselves or one another, but how well we know it; that watchful hope and anxious charity; that sober, earnest, cheerful, and careful richness which have filled the lives and shone out of the faces of the best men the world has seen, and given its profoundest meaning to the name of Man!

When we look up to Christ and catch the color of His wondrous life, is there not there the confirmation and supreme exemplification of all this? In him are watchful hope and anxious charity complete. This story of his life is no wild shout, flung forth out of the cloudless sky, but a rich, solemn, deep, beautiful music, wherein the sense of danger always trembles and sways beneath the constancy of an unalterable certainty of God.

If we are saved by Christ, it will be into the life of Christ that we are saved, into the inextinguishable hope and into the watchful fear together. Not intoxicated by the hope and not discouraged by the fear, we shall go on our way expecting both parts of the old prophecy to be fulfilled in us, as they were both fulfilled in Him. Expecting to be stung and bruised by the serpent, but sure ultimately, if we let God give us all His strength, to set the bruised and stung heel on the serpent's head. That life may we all have the grace to live.

SERMON VII.

The Sea of Glass mingled with Fire.

"And I saw as it were a sea of glass mingled with fire, and them that had gotten the victory over the beast" . . . stand on the sea of glass, having the "harps of God."—REVELATION XV. 2.

WITH all the mysteriousness of the Book of the Revelation, one thing we are sure of; that in it we have the summing up of the moral processes of all time. There may or may not be a more special meaning discoverable in its pictures, but this there certainly is. Many people find great pleasure in tracing out elaborate analogies between its prophecies and certain particular events in the world's career. "Here," they cry, pointing to some particular event of contemporary history, "do you not see that this is what these chapters mean?"—"Yes," we may generally answer, "they very possibly do mean that, but they mean so much besides that. They mean that, and all other events in which the same universal and eternal causes were at work. These special examples fall in under them, but do not certainly exhaust their application. They are much larger and include much more. They take in the whole circle of great spiritual and moral principles."

The Sea of Glass Mingled with Fire. 111

In this way I look at, and shall ask you this afternoon to study with me, the verse which is our text. I take it to represent, in a highly figurative way, the result of all moral contest. We may call that our subject.

It surely is no unimportant one. It is a subject that ought to touch all of us very closely, to waken our interest and deep anxiety. I am not to speak to you of imaginary or unreal conditions, not of unheard of depths of sin, or unimagined heights of holy rapture, but only of moral contest, of this struggle with suffering and wickedness, of trial, of that state which every earnest man who is conscious of his own inner life at all knows full well. What is to be the end of it all? How is it all coming out? These are the questions for which I find some suggestion of an answer in the pictorial prophecy of St. John.

They who had gotten the victory over the Beast stood on a sea of glass, mingled with fire. What is the meaning of this imagery? I confess that I do not pretend to know in full what is intended in the Revelation by this term "The Beast." But on the principle which I just stated, I think it certainly means in its largest sense the whole power of evil in all its earthly manifestations; everything that tempts the soul of man to sin or tries his constancy with suffering. Others assert more personal meanings for the name. One very large school says that it means the Church of Rome; another set of commentators used to make " the Beast " to be Napoleon the Third. Perhaps the name may well include them both, in so far as both stand for badness and mischief in the world; but for our present purpose at least, it will be well not to meddle with any of that sort of partial, precarious interpretation, but to hold what certainly is true, that "the Beast," in its largest sense, means all that is beastly, all that is low and base and tries to drag down what is high and noble; all sin and temptation; and so that "they who have gotten the victory over the Beast," are they who have come out of sin holy, and out of trial pure, and out of much tribulation have entered into the kingdom of heaven.

These are to walk upon "a sea of glass, mingled with fire." What does that imagery mean? The sea of glass, the glassy sea, with its smooth transparency settled into solid stillness without a ripple or the possibility of a storm, calm, clear, placid—evidently that is the type of repose, of rest, of peace. And fire, with its quick, eager, searching nature, testing all things, consuming what is evil, purifying what is good, never resting a moment, never sparing pain; fire, all through the Bible, is the type of active trial of every sort, of struggle. "The fire shall try every man's work of what sort it is." "The sea of glass," then, "mingled with fire," is repose mingled with struggle. It is peace and rest and achievement, with the power of trial and suffering yet alive and working within it. It is calmness still pervaded by the discipline through which it has been reached.

This is our doctrine—the permanent value of trial —that when a man conquers his adversaries and his difficulties, it is not as if he never had encountered them. Their power, still kept, is in all his future life. They are not only events in his past history, they are elements in all his present character. His victory is colored with the hard struggle that won it. His sea of glass is always mingled with fire, just as this peaceful crust of the earth on which we live, with its wheat fields, and vineyards, and orchards, and flower-beds, is full still of the power of the convulsion that wrought it into its present shape, of the floods and volcanoes and glaciers which have rent it, or drowned it, or tortured it. Just as the whole fruitful earth, deep in its heart, is still mingled with the ever-burning fire that is working out its chemical fitness for its work, just so the life that has been overturned and overturned by the strong hand of God, filled with the deep revolutionary forces of suffering, purified by the strong fires of temptation, keeps its long discipline forever, roots in that discipline the deepest growths of the most sunny and luxuriant spiritual life that it is ever able to attain.

How wide this doctrine is. The health of the grown man is something different from the health of the little child, because it has been reached through so many strains and tests and dangers. His strong body carries within it not only the record, but the power of all that it has passed through. His bones are strong by every tug and wrench and burden they have borne. His pulse beats even and true with the steady purposeful power which it has learned from many a period of feverish excitement. His blood flows cool, his eye is clear with the simple and healthy action which they have gathered out of many a time of danger that has come since the rosy untried health of babyhood. He is stronger by the accumulated strength of trial. His sea of glass is mingled with fire.

So take the strong man who has won a large property through many disappointments and reverses, and compare him with the baby of fortune who has just dropped by inheritance into money which he never earned. Compare the rich fathers who have made the fortunes with the rich sons who spend them. Is there no keener and more intelligent sense of the value of money in one than in the other? Sometimes indeed the sense is only keener and not more intelligent. Sometimes the father is a miser, while the son is a pattern of judicious liberality. These differences are personal; but always, either for good or bad, the old contest, the long, hard days of patience, the courage, the perseverance which earned the fortune color its whole possession and use. The repose of old age is full of the character that came from the early struggle. The sea of glass is mingled with fire.

Or shall we take the man whose life has known bereavement, who has passed sometime through those days and nights which I may not try to describe to you, but which come up to so many of you as I say the old word, death? Days and nights when he watched the slow untwisting of some silver cord on which his very life was hung, or suddenly felt the golden bowl dashed down and broken of which his very life had drank. The first shock became dulled. The first agony grew calm. The lips subsided into serenity. But was there not something in him that made him greater and purer and richer than of old; something that let any one see who watched the change, that it was "better to have loved and lost than never to have loved at all." A whole new quality, that rich quality which the Bible calls by its large word "patience," the power of his trial, was in his new serenity, until he died. His sea of glass was always mingled with fire.

So it is with the world; so it is with nations. A people that has fought for its life, that has had its institutions and ideas subjected to the fiery ordeal, can never be again what it has been. It is not simply older by so many years, but deeper and truer by so much suffering. Besides the mere value which men learn to put into what they have had to fight for, however worthless it may be in itself, the nation that has been saved by struggle, if it has faith enough to believe that it was really saved by struggle and not by accident, by the strength of its ideas and not by the chance turning of the weathercock of battle, must always, in whatever times of peace may follow, deal with its ideas with greater reverence for the strength that has come out of them in war. Under its safest security it will always want to feel still the capacity for the same vigorous self-defence if it should ever again be needed. Thus its sea of glass will always be mingled with fire.

These are all illustrations of our doctrine. But

the trouble will be that, however much we recognize the general rule, the exceptions to it, the variations in the effect of trial upon character, will be so numerous as to perplex us. We meet with so many people whose character seems not to be elevated or fired, but depressed and smothered by suffering. They come out of adversity apparently with a great loss of what was noblest and most attractive in them before. Men who were smooth and gracious in health, become rough and peevish in sickness. Men who were cordial and liberal in wealth, turn proud and reserved and close as poverty overtakes them. If trial kindles and stirs up some sluggish natures, on the other hand it quenches and subdues many vigorous and ardent hearts and sends them crushed and self-distrustful to their graves. It seems sometimes as if trouble, trial, suffering were in the world like the old fabulous river in Epirus of which the legend ran that its wonderful waters kindled every unlighted torch that was dipped into them, and quenched every torch that was lighted.

But however much difficulty this may give us in single cases, it falls in well with our general doctrine. For it makes trial an absolutely necessary element in all perfected character. If so much character does really go to pieces at its first contact with suffering and struggle, then all the more, no matter how terrible the waste may be, we see the need of keeping struggle and suffering as tests of character. We see that to sweep them away would be both an insult and a cruel harm to the nature which was meant to meet them, to crush and conquer and analyze them, to assimilate their strength out of them as a plant assimilates the nutriment out of the hindering ground through which it has to fight its way up into the sunshine, and to grow strong by struggle. You may just fling your seed upon the surface, and it will easily come to a sort of sickly germination. It has no earth to fight its way through, but then it has no earth to feed on, either; and the first of it is almost the last of it too.

We cannot exaggerate the importance of the change which comes to pass in a man's life when he once thoroughly has learnt this simple truth. Disappointments of every sort, sorrows, sufferings, trials, struggles, restlessness and dissatisfaction, false friends, poor health, low tastes and standards all about us— who shall enumerate the million forms, new to each man's new appreciation, in which life is to each man dark and not bright, bitter and not sweet? Who shall catalogue the troubles of human life? But who shall tell the difference between two men who live in different aspects of all these things? Are they intrusions, accidents, thwartings and disappointments of the will of God? Or are they (this is what our doctrine says they are) Messiahs, things sent, having like the ships that sail to our ports from far-off lands of barbarian richness, rare spices and fragrant oils and choice foods that we cannot find at home, whose foreign luxuriance forces its odorous way through the coarse and uncouth coverings in which their wealth was packed away in the savage lands from which they came? Are they prolific sources of spiritual culture, contributing what our best happiness could not have except from them, the energy and vitality which there is no way of stirring up in human nature but by some sense of danger, the fire to mingle with the glass.

In sick-rooms, in prisons, in dreary, unsympathetic homes, in stores where failure brooded like the first haze of a coming eastern storm, everywhere where men have suffered, to some among the sufferers this truth has come. They lifted their heads up and were strong. Life was a new thing to them. They were no longer the victims of a mistaking chance or of a malignant devil, but the subjects of an educating God. They no longer just waited doggedly for the trouble to pass away. They did not know that it ever would pass away. If it ever did it must go despoiled of its power. Whether it passed or stayed, that was not the point, but that the strength that was in it should pass into the sufferer who wrestled with it; that the fire should not only make the glass and then go out, leaving it cold and hard and brittle. The fire must abide in the glass that it has made, giving it forever its own warmth and life and elastic toughness. This is the great revelation of the permanent value of suffering and struggle.

But some lives still grow old, some men live strongly and purely in this world, you say, and then go safely and serenely up to heaven, who have no struggle anywhere, who never know what struggle is. What shall we say of them? How are they

The Sea of Glass Mingled with Fire. 119

ripened and saved? How does the fire get into their sea of glass? Ah, my dear friend, first you must find your man. And you may search all the ages for him. You may go through the crowded streets of heaven, asking each saint how he came there, and you will look in vain everywhere for a man morally and spiritually strong, whose strength did not come to him in struggle. Will you take the man who never had a disappointment, who never knew a want, whose friends all love him, whose health never knew a suspicion of its perfectness, on whom every sun shines and against whose sails all winds, as if by special commission, are sent to blow, and who still is great and good and true and unselfish and holy, as happy in his inner as in his outer life? Was there no struggle there? Do you suppose that man has never wrestled with his own success and happiness, that he has never prayed, and emphasized his prayer with labor, "In all time of my prosperity, Good Lord, deliver me!—"Deliver me!"—that is the cry of a man in danger, of a man with an antagonist. For years that man and his prosperity have been looking each other in the face and grappling one another. Whether he should rule it or it should rule him, that was the question. He saw plenty of men whose prosperity ruled them, had them for its slaves, bound them, and drove them, and beat them, and taunted them, mocked them with the splendid livery it made them wear, which was only the symbol of their servitude to it; that dreadful prosperity of theirs which they must obey, no matter what it asked of them, to which they must give up soul and body. He was determined it should not be so with him. He wrestled with his prosperity and mastered it. His soul is not the slave of his rich store or of his comfortable house. They are the slaves of his soul. They must minister to its support and culture. *He* rules *His*, and that is a supremacy that was not won without a struggle, than which there is no harder on the earth.

So that even here there is no exception. There is no exception anywhere. Every true strength is gained in struggle. Every poor soul that the Lord heals and frees goes up the street like the man at Capernaum, carrying its bed upon its back, the trophy of its conquered palsy. There are no glassy seas which will really bear the weight of strong men but those that have the fiery mingling. All others are counterfeits, and crack or break.

There are several special applications of our doctrine to the Christian life, which it is interesting to observe.

I. It touches all the variations of Christian feeling. In almost every Christian's experience comes times of despondency and gloom, when there seems to be a depletion of the spiritual life, when the fountains that used to burst and sing with water are grown dry; when love is loveless, and hope hopeless, and enthusiasm so utterly dead and buried that it is hard for us to believe that it ever lived. At such times there is nothing for us to do but hold with eager hands to the bare rocky truths of our relig

The Sea of Glass Mingled with Fire. 121

ion as a shipwrecked man hangs to a strong ragged cliff when the great retiring wave and all the little eddies all together are trying to sweep him back into the deep. The rough rock tears his hands, but still he clings to it. And so the bold bare truths of God and Christ, of responsibility and eternity, unclothed for the time of all the dearness that they used to have, how sometimes we have just to clutch and hold fast by them in our darkness to keep from being swept off into recklessness and despair. Then when the tide returns, and we can hold ourselves lightly where we once had to hang heavily, when faith grows easy and God and Christ and responsibility and eternity are once more the glory and delight of happy days and peaceful nights, then certainly there is something new in them, a new color, a new warmth. The soul has caught a new idea of God's love when it has not only been fed but rescued by Him. The sheep has a new conception of his shepherd's care when he has not merely been made "to lie down in green pastures," but also has heard the voice of him who had left the ninety and nine in the wilderness and gone after that which had wandered astray until he found it. The weakness of our own nature and the strength of that on which we rely: danger and its correlative, duty; watchfulness, and its great privilege, trust, come in together, and are the new life of the soul, the active power in its restored peace, the fire in its glassy sea.

The same applies to doubt and belief. "Why do things seem so hard to me?" you say; "why does every conceivable objection and difficulty start up in a moment, just as soon as I attempt to lay hold upon the Christian's faith? Why is it so easy for these others to believe, so hard for me?" One cannot answer certainly until he knows you better. There is a willful and an unwilling unbelief. If it is willful unbelief, the fault is yours. Man must not certainly complain that the sun does not shine on him, because he shuts his eyes. But if it is unwilling unbelief; if you really want the truth; if you are not afraid to submit to it as soon as you shall see it, and it is something in your constitution, or in your circumstances, or in the side of Christian truth that has been held out to you that makes it more difficult for you to grasp it than your neighbor; then you are not to be pitied. You have a higher chance than he. To climb the mountain on its hardest side, where its rough granite ribs press out most ruggedly to make your climbing difficult, where you must skirt round chasms and clamber down and up ravines, all this has its compensations. You know the mountain better when you reach its top. It is a realler, a nobler, and so a dearer thing.

If there be such here, let me speak to them. The world has slowly learnt that Christianity is true. If you learn slowly, it is only the old way over again. The man who learns slowly learns completely, if he learns at last at all. If you can only keep on bravely, perseveringly, seeking the truth, saying I must have it or I die; saying that till you do die; dying at last, if needs be, in the search; then I declare not only that somewhere, here or in some better world, the truth shall come to you; but that when it comes the peace and the serenity of it shall be made vital with the energy of your long search. Yours shall be that faith with which a pure, truth-loving soul may stand unashamed before the throne of God, and hear his work called "Well-done," and blessed and consecrated to perpetual value. You will believe better even in heaven for these earthly difficulties bravely met. For perfect truthfulness must find the truth at last, or where is God?

As we look out, the applications of our doctrine widen everywhere. What is the whole history of the world under the Gospel of forgiveness, from its first to its last, but one vast application of it. Here are men whose condition as perverted, mistaken, sinful beings makes it absolutely necessary that the dispensation that shall save them must be one not of mere culture and development but of rescue and repentance. Let the great future of those men be what it will; let the sublimest regions of calm unbroken holiness be reached in some celestial sphere; let truth and godliness become the atmosphere and the unconscious life-blood of the perfected man, still the perfected man must carry somewhere in the nature which holds high converse with the angels and worships with affectionate awe close to the throne of God, the story of its sin and its escape. Redeemed, its great redemption must forever be the shaping and the coloring element of all its glorious life.

"Worthy is He who hath redeemed us"—that song the purest lips and the most exalted heart never will outgrow.

Simon Peter is forgiven, re-adopted, becomes the preacher of the first sermon, the converter of the first Gentiles, the founder of churches, the writer of epistles, the champion of faith; but he is always, to the last, the same Simon Peter who denied his Master and struggled with himself in all the bitterness of tears, upon the crucifixion night. Paul mounts up to the third heaven, hears wonderful voices, sees unutterable things, can give in bold humility the autobiography of the eleventh chapter to the Corinthians, but he never ceases to be the Paul who stood by at the stoning of Stephen, and had his great darkness rent asunder by the bright light that he saw upon the road from Jerusalem to Damascus. You and I, brethren, come by Christ's grace into sweet communion with God, but the power of our conversion—does it ever leave us? Are not we prodigals still, with the best robe and the ring and the shoes upon us, and the fatted calf before us in our father's house, conscious always that our filial love is full of the strength of hard repentance which first made us turn our faces homeward from among the swine? And so the saved world never can forget that it was once the lost world. All of a history such as its has been accumulates, and none of it is lost. It will forever shine with a peculiar light, sing a psalm among its fellows that shall be all its own. The redeemed world—all the strong vitality which that name records, will be the fire that will mingle with the glassy serenity of its obedient and rescued life.

Here then we have the picture of the everlasting life. What will heaven be? What will be the substance on which they shall stand who worship God and praise him in the ages of eternity? I find manifold fitness in the answer that tells us that it shall be a "sea of glass mingled with fire." Is it not a most graphic picture of that experience of rest always pervaded with activity; of calm, transparent contemplation, always pervaded and kept alive by eager work and service, which is our highest and most Christian hope of heaven? Let us be sure that our expectations regarding heaven are scriptural and true. Heaven will not be pure stagnation, not idleness, not any mere luxurious dreaming over the spiritual repose that has been safely and forever won; but active, tireless, earnest work; fresh, live enthusiasm for the high labors which eternity will offer. These vivid inspirations will play through our deep repose and make it more mighty in the service of God than any feverish and unsatisfied toil of earth has ever been. The sea of glass will be mingled with fire.

Here too we have the type and standard of that heavenliness of character which ought to be ripening in all of us now, as we are getting ready for that spiritual life. As men by the grace of God gradually win the "victory over the beast," they begin already to walk upon the sea of glass mingled with fire. Let this be the lesson with which we close our thoughts upon our text. Surely, dear friends, there is a very high and happy life conceivable, which very few of us attain, and yet which our religion most evidently intends for all of us. Calm and yet active, peaceful and yet thoroughly alive, resting always completely upon truth, but never sleeping on it for a moment, working always intensely, but serene and certain of results, never driven crazy by our work, grounded and settled, yet always moving forward in still but sure progress, always secure, yet always alert—glass mingled with fire.

That life which we dream of in ourselves we see in Jesus. Where was there ever gentleness so full of energy? What life as still as his was ever so pervaded with untiring and restless power? Who ever knew the purposes for which he worked to be so sure, and yet so labored for them as if they were uncertain? Who ever believed his truths so entirely, and yet believed them so vividly as Jesus? Such perfect peace that never grew listless for a moment; such perfect activity that never grew restless or excited; these are the wonders of the life of Him who going up and down the rugged ways of Palestine, was spiritually walking on "the sea of glass mingled with fire."

As more and more we get the victory over the beast, we too are lifted up to walk where he walked. For this all trial, all suffering, and all struggle are sent. May God grant us all much of that grace through which we can be " more than conquerors through him who loved us," and so begin now to " walk with him in white," upon " the sea of glass mingled with fire."

SERMON VIII.

The Beautiful Gate of the Temple.

" The Beautiful gate of the temple."—ACTS iii. 10.

PETER and John went up to the temple together, and as they went they passed through "the gate of the temple which is called Beautiful." This gate must have been very beautiful indeed. It was the outer gate of the temple, that which opened upon the temple area from the broad and splendid street which led from the city to the sacred place. As the entering worshipper passed through this gate, the glory of the splendid structure displayed itself before him. He saw the open courts, the vistas of the galleries, the sweep of stairs, the brilliant walls of the temple of Herod. Entering by the Beautiful gate, he saw the whole in all its beauty. And the gate itself was worthy of the view on which it opened. It was made entirely of the precious Corinthian brass, and its workmanship surpassed that of every other gate in all the temple. There was a certain satisfied sense of fitness here. The gate which opened on the sublime and beautiful prospect was beautiful and sublime itself. The worshipper entered on the glory of the temple through a portal that foretold the coming glory by its own.

The architecture of the old Jewish Temple may serve us for a parable to-day. The truth that it suggests will be the harmony between a noble undertaking and a beautiful beginning—that every true temple ought to have a beautiful gate. The importance of beginnings is the veriest common-place of practical virtue. That first step which costs, we know, cannot be too costly, if it starts the enterprise aright. And when we look at the fairest things that have been, or that have been done ever in the world, we are much struck by seeing how often the entrance has been at least worthy of, and, alas, how often it has surpassed with its beauty, the court to which it gave admission. The whole world had its beautiful gate in those days of innocence and perfect happiness which passed in Eden before man's sin and the sorrow that it brings began. Christianity commenced its career with the perfect Life of Jesus, and then the simple beauty of the Apostolic Church, to which our later eyes are ever looking back. So every human life starts in the beautiful mystery of childhood. So every nation begins its career in the romance of some mythology, or the idealized memory of some heroic man to whom it owes its being. So every man's labor in his profession opens with the days of study and theory, when the idea of his profession is beautiful and clear before him. So every best friendship and life-long love starts in a glamor of admiration that almost worships the image of the coveted friend.

We might dwell upon several of these, but let us think only of the wisdom and love of God who has put the beauty of youth at the entrance of every human life. Through that Beautiful gate every man comes into the temple. The temple is beautiful itself. Life is filled with joy and sacredness. But how few lives are more beautiful than the youth that leads to them! And how the noblest lives are promised in their youth by fair anticipations of their coming beauty! And then think again that the highest life always is religious. The best glory of the most full existence is in the overfilling of its fulness with the love and fear of God. And that sets us to asking whether to the beautiful temple of a mature religious life there is also a beautiful gate. Is there such a thing as a child's religion worthy of, and admitting to, the broad thoughtfulness and happy devotion of the mature religion of the grown man and woman, as there is a child's body and a child's mind, with their own beauty, worthy of and introducing to the physical and mental life of later years?

This brings us to our subject. I shall not ride the parable to death. I shall not weary you with Gates and Temples. I only wanted by the old passage in the Book of Acts to suggest our theme. I want to speak of the child's religion. The child's religion, as introductory to the religion of maturity, but yet as a distinct reality which has a substantial existence of its own. It surely is a subject which has its interest for everybody. The parents who care for their own children, the teachers to whose care the children are immediately intrusted, the Church which has its commission to all the world, and evidently must not leave the children out, the lover of his kind who looks for its religious progress—where is the man who can say or think that he need have no interest in the possibility and character and means of children's religion? Here are the children all among us, and yet we often talk to one another, as if nobody under twenty had anything to do with the great things which are of such unspeakable importance after we have come of age. Here are the children all among us, and many a time a minister stops in his sermon and feels disheartened—almost dismayed—when he thinks how he is going on year after year, saying almost never a word in church, to tell the children that the Christ he talks of is not a gray lecturer, giving grown men lectures on hard dry truths, but a kind friend, young with the divine youth of eternity, and wanting them to come to him. Here are the children among us, and we open our Sunday-school and make it bright for them, and do get very close to them there with the love of God, but all the while we feel (and the children are quick and sensitive enough to feel it too), that the Church does not more than half know what to do with them; its theories and machineries are made for grown up people. It wishes the children would hurry and grow up, so that it might know how to talk to, what to do with, what to make of them. They belong to the Church, and yet do not belong to it. Here are the children all around us, and yet we have to begin to speak of a child's religion by saying something about the very possibility of such a thing.

And the first thing that we must say, when we are asked whether it is possible for a child to be religious, must be this, I think; that the religion of childhood is not only possible, but is the normal type of religion; is that which Christianity most contemplates, and that which, when Christianity shall have really entered into her power, all men shall accept as the very image and pattern of religion. We might as well ask whether a child's life is possible. The child is the embodiment of life, life in its freshness and first glory. As unnatural and exceptional as is the birth of a man full-grown—an Adam or an Eve without a childhood—to the true idea of living, so unnatural and exceptional to the true notion of religion is the thought of a grown up man being converted, beginning his religious life with the stiff movements and faded affections of mature years. The New Testament is our book of authority; but the New Testament is always leading men astray, because they deal with it unreasonably, because they do not take into account the times in which it was first written. And so the current idea of the churches, which has only just begun to be dislodged, that adult conversion is the type and intended rule of Christianity, comes largely from the fact that the first preachers of Christianity had of necessity to be largely occupied with men who had known nothing of Christianity in their youth. Peter and Paul had to go to grown up men, and ask them to begin the Christian life. But surely that was not to be the perpetual picture of Christian culture. Christ was too human for that. God had written through all his creation, in the interweaving of young life with old, his intention that one continuous culture should run through the whole scale of the human creature's development. Christ had been too evidently a child; the incarnation had too evidently taken all of life into its benediction, for the children ever to be wholly counted out. The great Erasmus once wrote a piece in Latin for a boy to speak which had this last thought beautifully put: "We commemorate," so he taught the young declaimer with his bright eye and his glowing face to say, "we boys commemorate the boy—*pueri puerum*—we commemorate our Master Jesus, the chief ideal of all, but yet peculiarly the chief of us—that is, of boys." The evident design of God's creation, the comprehensive form of the incarnation, the clear presence in children of the power of and the need of religion, these are the forces which, in spite of every tendency of the grown people to make children wait till they grow up, has always kept alive a hope, a trust, however blind, that a child's religion was a possible reality; that a child might serve and love and live for God.

But even where this has been granted, the old feeling that religion belongs to adult people, still has power, and defeats the best results of that faith in the religious possibilities of children which has been

The Beautiful Gate of the Temple. 133

persistently uttered in the Church's sacrament of baptism, and which has in modern times founded the Sunday-school, and created the vast religious literature of childhood. The old feeling still is strong enough, while it allows the possibility of children's being religious, to insist that their religion must be of the sort that has taken shape for adults alone. Read many of the children's religious books, listen to many of the children's sermons, and you will understand in a moment why they have not wrought their fruit and filled our churches with young Samuels and Timothys and Marys. They attempt to impose upon the child the religion that belongs to the man. They take the elaborate self-conscious experience to which men have been forced by the stresses of their life, and they bid the children look at those experiences and imitate them, and so be religious. The result is that nine-tenths of the children do not get hold of religion at all, and accept the easy heathenism to which they seem consigned; while the other tenth get hold of it only too much, and are the self-conscious little saints, the priggish and pedantic Christians whom it is so sad to see and so easy to caricature. So it comes about that, though it is the type of truest Christianity, a really healthy Christian life in a child is a rare sight. There have been some men, of whom one can hardly express himself too strongly, who have gone through the country preaching what they call children's revivals, taking that type of the beginning of a new life which belongs to thieves and murderers, and gray old reprobates, who by the grace of God are casting off the vices of a horrible lifetime, and repenting of the most brutal sins—an experience full of convulsion and agony, who try only too successfully to create a counterfeit of that experience in the children whom they want to convert. It is a real disbelief in the reality of a child's religion, and so an attempt to make the child assume the man's. It is the modern echo of that medieval marvel which was called the children's crusade, when their leaders took the children of Europe and led them as their fathers were going to the conquest of Jerusalem, and wasted their little lives by hundreds all along the weary and disastrous way.

But even where the sad extravagance and blunder of the children's revival is not attempted, and could not be tolerated, still I am sure that we are making a corresponding error when we try to force truth in the hard scholastic shapes into which men have cast it on the minds of the young. Every theologian must own that his theology is harder than the New Testament. It is the New Testament and not his theology that he ought to teach the child. The child's mind is natural and not artificial. Our theological systems are artificial and arbitrary, not natural. And the child, while he can make nothing of the balancing of persons in the scholastic doctrines of the Trinity, will know quicker than you or I the meaning of the equal divine love of Father, Saviour and Spirit. Though his mind will make nothing of the notion of a scheme of an atonement, he will understand wonderfully that Jesus lived and died for him. Though he will cast off the notion of an angry God, wreaking vengeance on his creatures forever and forever, he will understand that sin is dreadful, and must bring, of its own essential nature, dreadful consequences ; and that of those consequences none but he who knows the measure of the sin can see the end. Who can say what a power children may some day have over religious thought, in bringing back Christianity, as we long to see it brought, from a scheme of complicated and artificial arrangements to be the free utterance of the heart of God to man?

And so we come to this; that while men believe in the possibilities of children's being religious, they are largely failing to make them so because they are offering them not a child's, but a man's religion, men's forms of truth and men's forms of experience. The child makes nothing out of either. The one power that he has and longs to use is the power of personal loyalty and love. He wants Christ. When through the systems here and there the personal Christ steps forth, the true character of the child's religion always suggests itself, as the child runs to him.

I have already said that there was something in the Epistles that had worked to the discouragement of children's piety; but there is nothing of that in the Gospels. The Gospels come after the Old Testament, like spring after winter. There is child-life in the Old Testament, but it is crushed and buried. When Jesus appears, the children come singing Hosannas, and asking him to bless them, as the ground laughs with its flowers when the sun gets high.

And then our next question comes. If there is such a thing as a child's religion, and if men have made great mistakes because they did not understand it, then, what is it? What is the true character of the religion of a child? Certainly, to be sweet and real, it must be the possession by God of the faculties and qualities that belong especially to childhood. And it is not hard to enumerate some of those qualities at least. The first and most prominent of them all is the faculty of genuine, unqualified, unhesitating admiration. The grown man has to find out his ideals with difficulty. The world is tarnished to him. He has to abstract himself, and it is by a labored effort that he culls out from under its stained and battered surface the unseen and beautiful idea and promise which is at the heart of everything. But a child has no such effort. To him the world is beautiful, and he sees everything easily in its perfection. While the grown man is ready first to criticise, and only afterwards to discover what there is good and beautiful in the faulty thing, the child is struck first with admiration, and only reluctantly discovers that what he admires is not wholly good. Now this difference surely must tell upon the kind of religion that we are to look for in the earlier and the later life. There is a religion which finds the world unsatisfying, and so turns longingly, wistfully, pathetically, wearily to God. There is another religion which finds the world wondrously beautiful and good, yet always suggesting something more beautiful and better than itself, and this religion too turns to God, but glowingly, springingly, hopefully. The first religion starts from a sense of sin and comes to God for forgiveness. The second religion starts in a thankful joy, a sense of promise, and comes to God for fulfilment. The first starts with disgust at self, and so comes to love for God. The second starts in admiration of God, and so comes to forgetfulness of self.

It is needless to say that both these religions meet in the fullest religious experiences; but it is evident which of them most naturally belongs to the experience of a child. You cannot teach a child that hatred of himself, you cannot fill him with that sense of sin that sends the worn and weary sinner with his load of sins staggering up to cast them down before the cross. The attempt to create such experiences in children either kills them with morbid misery or makes them dreadful little hypocrites. But this power of admiration in the child promises its own religion, of its own natural kind. His are the years in which one can really believe in ideals. God can stand out before him, awful, yet dear; for to the child to whom all is mysterious, nearness and awfulness do not destroy one another as they do to us older folk. No doubt of God's faithfulness, no questioning of His ways comes in to cloud the perfectly unspotted adoration. How good it is that there are years at the beginning of every life when it is the most easy thing to believe in an absolute right and goodness. How strange it is that we should not use those precious years for the attainment of their own appropriate and beautiful religion. We grudge children their ideals. There are the much abused Sunday-school books which many good people unite to condemn. They are bad enough, many of them; but that which is made the special object of abuse in them. that they describe unnaturally perfect boys and girls, is not necessarily a fault. If the perfect children they describe are only healthy and not sickly in their virtue, they just meet and cultivate that belief in the possibility of perfection which is instinctive in a child's heart, and which in a man's is so often, so soon, buried deep under the accumulated conviction of the reality of sin. The present tendency of those who write children's books is to describe not the perfect child, but children as they are. The old-fashioned way was truer to the child's idealizing nature. For the first feature of a child's religion will be this, which we cannot ignore, that a child will come to God far oftener and far closer from love of the good than from hatred of the evil.

And then another thing in a child's religion is the perfect healthiness of his traditionalism, of his belonging to a certain sect and holding to certain opinions. So many grown people seem to have mixed up as much of evil as of good in their adherence to the faith of their fathers. They cling to it controversially. Their love for it is mixed up with jealousy and spite and pride. A child knows nothing of all that. His denomination, his creed, is like his nation, or his home. It is his because he was born there. It is dear to him with the unquestioning sense that he belongs to it and it to him. Alas, that our sectarian lines are drawn so narrow that very often a child cannot keep this simple home feeling as he grows up; alas, that so often as the child goes on to develope his own appropriate type of Christian faith and feeling, he finds that the sect in which he was born will not hold his special aspect of the truth, and so has to go abroad and break the ties of earliest sympathy in order to be the Christian that the Lord meant him to be. Alas, that we are all such sectarians, whatever we may call ourselves, and that the great idea of a whole Christian Church is as yet so little realized. But these are troubles which the man grows into. The child may freely glory in his own Church, and yet be no sectarian; may accept his creed from the lips of others, and yet be no dogmatist. And so a second feature in the child's religion will be this—a healthy traditionalism, a warm, true love for the Church he is brought up in; not an abstract and general, but a clear, localized religion. The true parent, the true teacher, will try not merely to make the child love God, but to make him love his own church, as the place where he knows God, and where he finds God always.

And then again, as a child is able to love his own church without any of the evil effects of sectarianism, so he is able to love the organizations and habits of the Church, without the evil effects of formalism. The child's nature is poetic. This is seen in the ease with which it feels the symbolic character of symbolic things. Its symbols are real symbols; they really stand for something besides themselves, something unseen. Now formalism comes largely from the sheer loss of the poetic sense. The stupidity of ritualism is the prosaic way in which its symbols have lost their meaning, and become valuable in and for themselves. This is the way in which many people make a Fetish of the Church. The Church is the most poetic of all things, so long as men see her with poetic eyes, so long as her outward shows stand for spiritual truths; but there never was anything so wretchedly prosaic as the outward shows and ways of the Church, her visible sacraments and tactual successions, when they have ceased to be merely representative of spiritual verities and are valued for themselves. Now, is it saying too much to claim that a child with his nature full of poetry is able to take and use the ceremonies and external things of the Church and keep their meaning, as many men cannot? He needs them. It is all very well for you to say that you can worship without a liturgy, and without the company of a congregation. You think you can. You have faith in your power for abstracted and solitary devotion; but it is not right for you to assume that your child can do it. This is why, as I think, all the children of a parish such as this, even those who are best taught at home, ought to be gathered into the parish Sunday School, which for many purposes is their church. Apart from what they learn there, it brings them into a true conscious partnership in the church and its workings, makes itself their church, fills them with its spirit, lets them understand its life, and look on it as their home. This is why I wish all the children of our church were there.

Only one thing more let me say about the character of the child's religion. Is it not true that the simplest and primary form of the presentation of the Gospel is the one which is preserved most truly and necessarily in the teaching of children? The Gospel came first into the world as good news. It was a simple, glorious story, told in the purest and directest way. It was a message, a revelation, God's love to man, God's pity and salvation for man, told by the roadside and the wellside, told in the temple courts, told from the cross. But how that first conception of the Gospel gets blurred and lost. To us grown men, the Gospel is a philosophy of life, a system to be argued about, almost anything but a message coming right down from God to man. But the child's nature is all receptive of stories, open for messages on every side. The child is a little Athenian, always listening for some new thing. All the world about him is mysterious, ever breaking out into tidings of itself. And so the child is ready, if it can be rightly told him, to hear, above all the other messages that come to him out of this ever opening and surprising world, the best and highest news of all, the Gospel, simply as glad tidings of the love of God and the salvation of the world by Jesus.

I must not mention more; but put together in

your own mind these characteristics of a child's religion which we have recounted, and see if you have not a recognizable and beautiful conception as their result. It is no monstrous thing. It is no priggish and unpleasant aping of what is possible only for maturer life. It is a true child who loves God and sees everything beautiful in Him, who loves the Church and finds its ways and forms full of significance and pleasure, and who hears and accepts as part of the story of the world which it is gradually learning to know, the story of how God loved that world, so that He came into it and lived here and died here, to help every man to live in holiness and to save every man when he fell into sin. There is no child for whom that religion is not possible. Brave, true, frank, gentle, joyous, what is there better than this in the labored religion of our later days? It is not only a promise, it is a present reality. The boy is not only a little man, he is a boy, with his own present capacity of character. He is even now "a member of Christ, a child of God, and an inheritor of the kingdom of heaven."

We have said something of the possibility and of the character of a child's religion. And now we want to go on and say a little of the methods of it; how is it to be created in all its beauty in these children whom you know? Ah, first of all, let us feel for our comfort and humility that the power to create it rests far back of our feebleness. They are God's children. We stand over the little stalk and say, "How shall I make this flower grow?" Think how

God must listen to us as we say that. God who made the growing power of that little flower, and ripened it in the flora of worlds that perished before our history began. No education can be true or fruitful which forgets the perfect education of which it is but a minister. No man can care wisely or well for any one he loves, who dares forget that God is caring for that friend of his, whether he be old man or little boy, with a wisdom and love incomprehensible. I cannot but think how many families and schools it would at once fill with happy earnestness and relieve of nervous anxiousness to be pervaded with this remembrance continually. So often grown people here pass out of childhood and become incapable of dealing with children. But God is always young and always sympathises with the children whom He sends into the world.

Bear this in mind, and then before us opens the work of helping under God in the training of his children. It is not easy. The child's nature everywhere shows its imperfectness. It is hard to open it for what it ought to receive, and it is hard to close it against what it ought to reject. It is like the beautiful gate with which we are comparing it, for Josephus tells us about that gate, that it took the strength of twenty men to open it or close it. I am not going to undertake a general treatise on the Christian education of children. There are only two suggestions which I want to make and urge with all the force I can upon those to whom the training of children is intrusted.

The first is this; the absolute need of perfect truthfulness in children's religious training. Nobody, I think, can look at the strange state of religious thought in this day, without seeing at once the importance and the difficulty of making truthfulness first and absolute when we try to teach children religious truth or to excite them to religious feeling. Religious truth has passed in many people's minds into new forms. Men hold other conceptions than they held twenty years ago. I do not argue now whether the newer theology is more or less true; but many an earnest thinker to whom the truth has come with a freshness and a force to his own soul in some new shape, will still, as he undertakes to teach children, tell them not what he believes, give them not the fresh food on which he knows that his own soul is nourished, but spread before them traditional statements of orthodoxy which are ordinarily reputed safer, but which he himself really does not believe. He has not full faith in his truth. He is willing to rest himself, nay, he is gladly resting himself upon it daily for salvation; but when he comes to teach the children, he draws back, and from a curious mixture of timidity and care for them and spiritual faithlessness, he puts before them some dead husks instead of the live truth on which he feeds. Are there not many parents and teachers whose views of the Bible as God's Book, of the Lord's Day as His festival, of the Atonement as the free expression of His love, of the Resurrection of the body and the life in heaven, are free, rational, scriptural and vital, who will yet teach their children as they were taught, in hard, mechanical and untrue statements of those great Christian verities? It keeps the religious education of our nurseries and Sunday-schools too often behind the best religious conviction of the time. It is not right. I do not ask that every crude speculation should be immediately thrust upon the minds of trusting children, who will take it in all its crudeness for a settled conviction; but I do believe that he who is set to teach children about God, should show to them the best and fullest that the Lord has shown to him, and not another something which he does not believe, but which for some reason he has come to think is best for them at present.

See what are the evils of such strange conduct. In the first place, it is insincere in the teacher. That is reason enough against it. In the second place, it will be ineffective, for a man cannot teach with his whole heart what he only half-heartedly believes. The bright eyes of the children will see through him. And, in the third place, it is doing fearful wrong to the children's future, who must find out some day that what they have learned is not true, and so must give it up; and in giving up your feeble and false version of it, will stand in terrible danger of giving up the Christian religion altogether.

No, give the children the best that God has given you. Teach them nothing that you do not believe they can carry on, growing to them with their growth, through all this life, into the life beyond.

There is a difference between a child's religion and a man's religion, but remember always it is not a difference of false and true. The child's religion must be like the clothes with which the Israelite children started out of Egypt, which, according to the old legend, grew as they grew till the boys and girls were men and women. To have a partial religion grow into a perfect religion, is one of the most natural and healthy processes of human life. To change a false religion for a true one is the most necessary, but most violent struggle of the human soul.

There is a class of books and teachers—the ordinary Sunday School talker, is often of that sort—who, it seems to me, does very much, partly from timidity, partly from laziness, partly from sensationalism, to keep a certain unreality and insincerity in the religious teaching of the young. Everywhere but in religion, in history, in science, each new and truer view, as soon as it is once established, passes instantly into the school books of the land. Am I not right in saying that there are great convictions about scripture and the Christian faith which are heartily accepted by the great mass of thinking Christian people now, which are not being taught to the children of to-day? If that is so, as I fear it is, then this new generation has got to fight over again the battle that our generation has fought, and fight it, too, less hopefully, because there will have been less of sincerity in its education. It is always a better and safer process to outgrow a doctrine that we have been sincerely taught, than to abandon one that had no real hold upon our teacher's mind. In the first case we keep much of the sincerity, even if we let the doctrine go. In the second case, when we let go the doctrine, there is nothing left. Is there not here the secret of much of the ineffective religious teaching of the young, of the way they cast our teaching off when they grow up? No! my dear friends, all of you anywhere who are called to teach, with larger faith in truth, with larger faith in God, with wise love for his children, I beg you to make truthfulness the first law of your teaching. Never tell a child that he must believe what you do not believe, nor teach him that he must go through any experience which you are not sure is necessary to his conversion and his Christian life.

And then the other principle that I wanted to remind you of, was the necessity of a larger element of suggestiveness in the best training of a religious nature. A child is not a block of marble, to be hewn out into what you will. A child, and especially a child considered as a religious being, is a plant which you are to set into the right soil of truth, and then watch as it developes its own special nature. And every child is a separate and peculiar plant, different from every other. What shall the teacher do then? Not say, "I will make of this child before me, this or that," but " I will quicken every activity with its own spiritual stimulus. I will break off the chains and get every obstruction of sin and slothfulness out of the way, and help this child to be what God made him to be, whatever it is." A teacher who says that, brings truth always so fresh to each young life that it can be eaten and turned into that life's own forms of action; not hard and fossilized, so that it must always be kept in just the shape in which it is first given. He will not be surprised or disappointed when he sees his pupil developing a type of Christian life different from his own. If it is only real, and pure from all conceit, and truly full of Christ, he will be delighted to watch it, and rejoice more to have given an impulse to a movement which shall far outrun himself, than he ever could have rejoiced to train a hundred scholars into mere echoes and repetitions of his imperfect individuality.

This power of suggestiveness runs everywhere. More is accomplished in this world always by the suggestions of motive and force than by the impositions of form and rule. He who believes in suggestion has trust in the vital powers of things. The whole world is waiting to start into far higher action than anything yet, if one could only touch its springs. This is the beauty, this must be the quiet satisfaction of the lives of those obscure and patient workers who build nothing themselves, but who suggest the need and wish of building to other minds greater than theirs. Think of being the schoolteacher of Shakespeare, or Milton, or Pascal; and yet only a few antiquarians know the name of either. Surely there are last that shall be first. Surely this power of suggestiveness must always be the teacher's wisest and best.

Let me rest with these two ideas. You see at once how both of them, truthfulness and suggestiveness, are words of personal character. In all teaching, but most of all in religious teaching, the personal nature of the teacher is supreme.

"I am thy God that teacheth thee," Jehovah said. Only in deity are met perfectly those qualities that make the perfect Being, "apt to teach." We are under teachers in God's school here. But what a light all this throws upon that which seems so terrible to us on earth, the sad and awful mystery of a child's death. What is it when a child dies? It is the great head-master calling that child up into his own room, away from all the under-teachers, to finish his education under his own eye, close at his feet. The whole thought of a child's growth and development in heaven instead of here on earth, is one of the most exalting and bewildering on which the mind can rest. Always the child must be there. Always there must be something in those who died as children to make them different to all eternity from those who grew up to be men here among all the temptations and hindrances of earth. There must forever be something in their perfect trust in the Father, something in the peculiar nearness and innocent familiarity of their life with Jesus, something in the simplicity and instinctiveness of their relation to the truth, something pure even among all the perfect purity which we shall all have reached, something wiser than the wisest, showing that even there there is a revelation that can be given only to the babes.

Something more perfectly triumphant and serene to mark forever the perfected life of those who never sinned, and whose whole education has been in the full sunlight of their Father's presence. There will be seen forever what we have tried so dimly to depict to-day, the possibility and beauty of a child's religion.

We hear much in these days of the precocity of children. Never were they so forward. Never were children treated so like men and women. Never did they get ideas so freely from the freest contact with the life about them. It may be bad or good; whichever it be, it marks a critical time and multiplies the responsibility of those who in any capacity are teachers now. Josephus tells us that once in the seige of Jerusalem this golden gate which we have made the image of childhood, vastly heavy and hard to move, "was seen to be opened of its own accord about the sixth hour of the night." And he says that some thought it was a good omen, "as if God did open then the gate of happiness." But others thought it very bad, "as if the gate was open to the advantage of their enemies." So in this critical time of ours, not the least critical sign is this: that the golden gate stands open wide; that childhood is exposed and sensitive to new impressions and ideas. Is it for good or evil? Certainly, not necessarily for evil, if with a deep trust in God and a true love for His children, those to whom the care of the gate is given can only do their duty. The wider open the gate the better, if only the truth can be poured in. The more receptive the children's life the better, if only they who train the children can thoroughly believe that there is a manly and beautiful religion of which the child is capable, and work with God to bring their children to it. When that conviction takes possession of the Church, then the Church shall indeed have her children in her arms. Then Isaiah's vision of the complete New Jerusalem shall be fulfilled. "Thou shalt call thy walls salvation, and thy gates praise."

SERMON IX.

Disciples and Apostles.

A FOREIGN MISSIONARY SERMON.

"And when it was day he called unto him his disciples, and of them he chose twelve, whom also he named Apostles."—LUKE vi. 13.

I WANT to speak to you to-day of Foreign Missions. I hope and I believe that it is not an unwelcome subject. It would be very melancholy, I think, if after all these years in which we have pondered and studied together the Gospel of our Saviour, and learnt in all the changing experiences of life something of its precious value, we should still find our hearts grudging the single Sunday of the year which is given to the special consideration of our duty to make the whole world sharer in that Gospel which we claim to love. Rather this Sunday ought to seem the flowering Sunday of the year. To-day we ought to seem to come into the very heart of the Gospel. The other Sundays may well seem beside it to have been lingering upon the borders of our faith. To-day we come directly to its centre, and, with true confidence in both, claim our Saviour for the world and claim the world for our Saviour. May such a mind and spirit be in us to-day.

I have turned for a text to one of the critical times in the life of Jesus. It was not a time which made much noise. The act which Jesus did was very quiet. It did not come with observation. Only afterwards, as time went on, did it appear how important the event really was. But when we look at it to-day we can see that it marked the advance of the whole work of Jesus, from its first into its second stage; from the condition of a local school, into the ambition of a world-wide religion. It is all told in a few words. Jesus "went out into a mountain to pray, and continued all night in prayer to God. And when it was day he called unto him his disciples, and of them he chose twelve, whom also he named apostles." It was the time when out of the heart of the discipleship came the apostleship. And what do these words mean? Disciple, of course, means learner. The idea rests entirely between two persons, the teacher and the scholar. It involves nothing but the receiving of knowledge by some one docile mind. But Apostle means missionary. Its idea is utterance, or sending forth. It sees and feels the great wide world. It looks out to the very horizon of humanity. It takes truth not as a lesson, but as a message. What the disciple has drunk into his own satisfied soul, the apostle is to carry abroad, wherever there are men to hear it.

When then Jesus turned his disciples into apostles, you see what an event it was. It was really the flowering of that Gospel which he had been pouring into them through all their discipleship. The plant fills itself with the richness of the earth. No noise is made. The whole transaction lies between the plant and the rich earth that feeds it through its open roots. All is silent, private, restricted. But some day the world looks, and lo! the process has burst open. Upon the long-fed plant is burning a gorgeous flower for the world to see. The long supply of nourishment has opened into a great display of glory. The earth has sent its richness through the plant to enlighten and to bless the world. The disciple has turned to an apostle.

Notice, when Jesus took this great step forward, he did not leave behind his old life with his disciples. He chose out of the number of his disciples twelve, whom also he named apostles. They were to be disciples still. They did not cease to be learners when he made them missionaries. The plant does not cease to feed itself out of the ground when it opens its glorious flowers for the world to see. All the more it needs supply, now that it has fulfilled its life. And so this great epoch in the Christian Church was an addition, not a substitution. John, James, and Peter, were all the more devout disciples of the Master, filled themselves all the more eagerly with his truth and spirit, after they had become his apostles and were telling his truth to other men.

And notice yet another thing. It is out of the very heart of the discipleship that the apostleship proceeds. It is the very best, the choicest, as we say, of the disciples, that are chosen to be apostles. This is apparent to any one who reads the story. Jesus calls all his disciples together, and out of them he chooses twelve. It is no inattentive idlers hanging on the outskirts of the group who listen to him, that he thinks good enough to go and carry his message. It is they who have listened to him longest, and most intelligently, and most lovingly. It is Simon and Andrew his brother, James and John, Philip and Bartholomew, Matthew and Thomas; it is men like these, the very heart and soul of the discipleship whom he selects and calls apostles. And so it always is. Always it is the best of the inward life of anything, that which lies the closest to its heart and is the fullest of its spirit, which flowers into the outward impulse which comes to complete its life. It is the most truly thorough learning which by-and-by begins to be dissatisfied with its own learned luxury, and to desire that all men should have the chance of knowledge. It is the most true refinement that believes in the possible refinement even of the coarsest man. It is most intelligent appreciation of the blessings of free government which looks beyond the narrow walls of national pride and desires freedom and good government for all the world. I hold it to be one of the most beautiful and re-assuring facts in all the world that the purer and finer any good attainment grows, the more it comes into the necessity of expansiveness. It is the crude and half formed phases of any good growth which are selfish and exclusive. It is the half cultivated people who guard their feeble culture by arbitrary lines of separation. The heart of any good thing is catholic and expansive. It claims for itself the world. It longs to give itself away, and believes in the capacity of all men to receive it. This noble and true and beautiful truth, whose illustrations are everywhere, was it not declared by Jesus, when out of the choicest heart of the group of his disciples, he selected his apostles?

Most deeply is this truth illustrated in the history of man's idea of God. It is the purest and loftiest and divinest thought of God that is most generous and world-embracing. Men dream of gods that are scarcely higher or better than themselves; gods stained with passion and with selfishness, and those gods do not care for men. The Lotos-eater pictures his gods like himself. He sees them in their selfish repose.

"On the hills together, careless of mankind.
For they lie beside their nectar, and the bolts are hurled
Far below them in the valleys, and the clouds are lightly curled
Round their golden houses, girdled with the gleamy world;
Where they smile in secret, looking over wasted lands,
Blight and famine, plague and earthquake, roaring deeps and
 fiery sands,
Clanging fights and flaming towns, and sinking ships and pray-
 ing hands.
But they smile, they find a music centred in a doleful song
Steaming up, a lamentation and an ancient tale of wrong,
Like a tale of little meaning, though the words are strong."

So sing the Lotos-eaters; then listen to Isaiah's song about his God: "He saw that there was no man, and wondered that there was no Intercessor;

therefore His own arm brought salvation." By as much more as He is purer and holier, by just so much more is He larger, less able to rest in His own satisfaction, more compelled to go and help the poor sons of men; and so it is out of the heart of the holiest conception of deity that the Incarnation comes.

Shall we not then set down as absolutely fundamental in our study of the Christian Church, this relationship between the disciple life and the apostle life, that is, between the inward and the outward impulse? In the life of every parish this relationship ought to be recognized. The failure to recognize it is what makes so many of our parishes very far from what they ought to be, keeps them uneasy with a constant doubt of themselves, and a continual sense that they are suspected by the world outside. What is a church or parish for? What is the meaning of this little company gathered out of a great community, which meets in this building, for instance, statedly, Sunday after Sunday, year after year? No doubt they are, in the first place, learners, disciples, students together of the truth of God, listeners at the lips of the Master for his revelations. But unless there is continually issuing from the heart of their discipleship a true apostleship, unless the best souls among them keep fresh and live the outward impulse, the consciousness that their church and they exist not for themselves alone but for the world, how their church life grows dead.

Those of you who have loved the church longest and most dearly, will bear me witness that there is always an inward, self-enclosing tendency to be resisted by every congregation. Very often the more the congregation wakes up to earnest life, this inward tendency asserts its strength. Given its full sweep, it would make the congregation a club, existing for high ends indeed, but existing for its own benefit alone. It would make the pew as exclusive and private a piece of property as the parlor. It would judge the way in which its work was being done by the way in which those few selected people were becoming wiser and better men and women. If it admitted outsiders at all, they would come in simply as spectators of that process of culture which was going on. It would be a church of disciples. It is a constant effort, I say, requiring continual watchfulness both in minister and people, to see that an earnest church does not come to this, to see that it is kept apostolic, with the outward consciousness always alive. knowing that it exists not for its pewholders, but for the community; for just as many of the human race as it possibly can reach; knowing that its pewholders will get the best good out of it the more completely they can feel, the more manifestly they can show, that they feel that it is in no real sense their church. It is first God's church, and then the church of all or any of God's children. I cannot help saying how truly I believe that this apostolic consciousness is present in this congregation. God grant it may increase and deepen till our church shall never cease to feel, through all the satisfaction of its own life, the life of every poor godless creature on the rich streets or the wretched streets of Boston, as a mother never loses the feeling of her reprobate son, half round the world, though for the moment she can do nothing for him.

But if we look not at a congregation, but at the best and most growing human lives, I think that this relationship between their outward and their inward tendency falls into a certain sort of system, which is continually repeated. It is a sort of pulse, which we can feel beating as we stand with our finger on the heart. Every life which comes to its best begins with a sort of loose expansiveness; it is drawn inward till it reaches an almost selfish concentration; then it opens with a larger and finer movement to embrace mankind. This, it seems to me, is the normal and healthy course of any character. There is an illustration in the history of these twelve men who were with Jesus. Think what they must have been before they knew their Master. The open life of free and thoughtless young men, they must have lived, easily making friends, easily entering into everybody's superficial interests because they had only superficial feelings of their own, liking to be liked, and full of ready sympathies. Then they met Jesus. They were drawn away to him. By him they were drawn in upon themselves. To know him, and to know their own deeper lives in him, became their longing. They must have been missed from their old haunts in Capernaum. They must have passed their old companions almost like strangers on the street. Their lives were folded in upon themselves, and upon him who was at the centre of each. But by-and-by a new power began to work at the enfolded heart. He who had drawn them in upon himself, began to send them abroad. Another kind of love for their old friends, and all the world whom those friends represented, came to them. They began to be seen again upon the streets. They began to find out once more their old companions. Only now they are preaching. Now they are telling every one of the new life. Now the power of expansiveness is not their own careless good fellowship; it is the eager soul-craving grace of Jesus Christ. They have been drawn in from the world upon him, that he might send them out, full of himself, into the world.

That is a picture of every Christian life which works itself out to its completeness. There is the first easy instinctive human brotherhood; there is the drawing in and retirement of the nature on itself, with any strong experience, most of all with the strongest of all experiences, the occupation of the soul by Christ; then there is the large expansion of the strengthened soul, as it longs for the complete society, the brotherhood with man in God. It is the beating of the great spiritual pulse. It is the systole and diastole of the heart of a whole man's history. It is the succession of man's fellowship with man, man's discipleship to Christ, man's apostleship to men for Christ, succeeding one another.

Here is a man in our company who to-day, with light-hearted, careless indifference, is the easy friend

of everybody whom he meets. He welcomes all who
give themselves to him; he gives himself to anybody;
because to give and take is such a shallow thing that
it makes no impression. His intercourses are of that
surface sort which do not get down to where men
are really different from one another, and so he easily
consorts with whomsoever he may meet. He feels
no deep needs in himself, and so anybody satisfies
him. And now to that man comes some revelation.
Perhaps he enters the deep water of some great sorrow or some overwhelming joy. Perhaps he is swept
into the irresistible current of some absorbing study.
Perhaps, greatest of all, that in which all the others
find their only worthy completion, he is drawn into
the bosom of the realized love of God by the strong
arm of Christ his Saviour. What is, what must be
the first sign of that great thing which has come to
pass? A silence falling on the noisy communicative-
ness, a turning inward that they may watch the wondrous work within the soul of those eyes which have
been wholly busy in seeing the quick kaleidoscopic
changes of the things outside, a loosening of every
other grasp, that the hold on the new friend may be
complete. Men will stand round and lament almost
as if they mourned for the dead. "How he has gone
from us! How his life, which used to lie all plain and
open, is hidden. And where? We cannot tell! He
says, With Christ in God. We do not know. But
evidently he is gone from us." So they stand round
him and lament. But by-and-by, strangely but certainly, they become aware that he is coming back to

them; and coming far more richly, with far more close and generous and tender giving of himself to them, than in those old and careless days. Behold now all that he has is theirs. He loves them with a new love. He honors them with a new honor. He looks into their faces as if he saw behind each of them another face, which shone through theirs and gave to their sordidness its dignity and value. Where he used to open his arms to them, now he opens his heart. Where he once gave them his counsel, or his purse, now he gives them himself. Out of the retirement has come a new companionship. The pulse of the life has once more beat outward, and to the contraction this new expansion has succeeded.

It may be that this pulsation will go on and repeat itself again and again. It may be that some new revelation of truth will draw the soul once more in upon itself, but the glory of the true Christian life will be that it always reacts more vigorously outward for every new self-feeding upon Christ. This is its legitimate and healthy movement. Discipleship and apostleship are the pulsations of the Christian heart. They feed each other. Nay, why may we not look higher still, and when in the mysterious vision, which yet for all its mystery is true, we see Jesus standing forth full of the holiness of eternity, and saying, "Lo, I come," in answer to a needy world's cry for help, why should we not recognize that for the divine as well as for the human, for God as well as man, there is a necessity that the inward completeness should utter itself in outward communication; that the best which the soul is in itself, should be turned towards and poured upon whatever other soul may need it anywhere?

And now we have only to pass up from the individual to the race, and see how the same law which we have been tracing applies there too. There too we have these same three stages in the intercourse of man with man, and in their succession lies the history of the Christian Church, which can never be, ought never to be, considered as something apart from the history of humanity at large, but simply as the heart of human history, its centre, its ideal, working out in type or pattern what must ultimately be the destiny of all. What are the stages? First there is the natural aggregation and companionship of man, the instinct for society, that which makes tribes and states and families, that which inspires the self-sacrificing fellowship of which savage history gives us some glimpses, and of which poets love to sing, glorifying far off barbarian islands as if the romance and the heroism of friendship belonged to them, and almost necessarily died out as soon as their barbarian simplicity was invaded by civilization. No doubt this is not wholly poetry. No doubt there is a certain spontaneousness of human intercourse which belongs most naturally to the rudest and simplest conditions of life. With culture comes reserve. With the teaching of spiritual religion comes the emphasis of the single life and the clear demarkation of that group among mankind which is called the Church. The world lingers long in this stage. The Church accepts exclusiveness and limitation as her law and principle of life. But gradually, as she fills out her life more and more, she becomes aware of a new impulse. She begins to press on her own borders. She begins to see in the distance a new fellowship of man, a great deal clearer because a great deal deeper and more reasonable than the old. The easy brotherhood of savage life shows but poorly beside the great fellowship in Christ which is to fill the New Jerusalem. To the bringing about of that fellowship the Church by-and-by consecrates itself, accepting the missionary impulse as the only complete fulfilment of its life.

I am sure, my dear friends, that this is the only true conception of the relationship between the notion of culture and the notion of missions in the Christian Church. The notion of culture is preparatory to the notion of missions. The men and women in a Christian land, in a Christian congregation, who are consciously growing wiser, braver, purer, stronger by their share in the worship of a Christian Church, are on the way to a great unselfish conception of life, in which the bravery, comfort, purity and strength of their brethren anywhere in the world, shall be dear to them by the same motive of love to Christ and desire for the progress of his kingdom, which makes their own soul-life dear. Unless their spiritual culture finds its culmination in that craving for the spread of truth and the saving of men's souls, it is a thoroughly unsatisfactory thing. And yet, what do we see? Merely to look at it on the smallest scale, I have seen people standing outside of this congregation of ours, restrained from full entrance into the circle of its life by the natural, the inevitable necessities which limit the range of any one congregation, complaining of the exclusion, unreasonably finding fault with the exclusiveness of those who were its members. By-and-by, in time, the way is opened for them to become part of our body, to have their regular place among us, and all the incidental privileges of our organization. And more than once I have seen those very persons become the most exclusive, the least willing to welcome some new comer to the fellowship into which they themselves have found their way. It is the everlastingly recurring tendency to rest in the stage of discipleship and to refuse to cross the line into apostleship. There could be no better description than that of the indisposition of the faithful, constant, devout and thoughtful worshipper to believe in, to give his heart and his money to foreign missions. Discipleship, but not apostleship for him! And yet the one is wofully incomplete without the other. The one trying to live without the other, shows an inherent lack in the fundamental qualities of faith in God and faith in man, which are what the Christian religion really means.

This is the real sadness of the position which one often hears taken by the earnest, devout and conscientious members of the Church at home. They say that they do not believe in foreign missions. The sadness is not simply that in Africa or China darkness is to be left in some little region where they might send light. It is that they declare the imperfectness of their own faith; that they frankly say that either they do not believe that God can do for other men what he is doing every day for them, or else they do not believe that those other men are capable of receiving from God those blessings of the higher life which they are taking from him constantly—the lack of faith in God or the lack of faith in man. And yet to have those two faiths, and to grow richer in them constantly, is what it means to be a Christian. It is not the desire to enforce the argument of a Foreign Missionary sermon, it is the sincere and deep conviction of my soul, when I declare that if the Christian faith does not culminate and complete itself in the effort to make Christ known to all the world, that faith appears to me to be a thoroughly unreal and insignificant thing, destitute of power for the single life, and incapable of being convincingly proved to be true.

But I have dwelt long enough, perhaps too long, upon this general plea for the essential apostleship of Christianity. I want to address myself, in the few moments which I may yet occupy, to the peculiar aspect which the mission of our religion to the world presents in these especial modern times in which we live. A great deal of what is said concerning Foreign Missions always seems to me to take for granted a state of things which has long passed away, and to ignore the condition into which the world and Christian thought have passed to-day, and into which they are more and more fully entering. Men who

are earnestly, almost blatantly, progressive in other
things, are centuries behind the times in this. For
the world has changed. With its new rapidity of
communication, with the intermingling of its races,
with the careful study of one part by another part,
with the disposition of the weaker races to seek relations of protection and dependence with the stronger, it is simply impossible that every nation, every
race should keep its own religion uninvaded, uninflu-
enced by any other. The practical issue of all the
present tendency of human life must be that the best
thought of the world will overcome the worse
thought. There must come a natural selection of
religions, a survival of the fittest among faiths. No
longer can a range of mountains restrain two ideas
of God away from any contact or comparison with
one another. No longer can an ocean shut a bar-
barous superstition out of all knowledge of a bright,
pure, enlightened belief, that blesses men upon the other side. The winds that pulsate with all other messages, will not be silent concerning the good news
which all hearts need. The waters that are no longer walls but bridges, will be trodden by the invisible
feet of Faith. To dream to-day of that which old
Rome dreamed, when, looking over her vast domain,
she saw each subject race keeping its own faith, provided only that all the gods and oracles would teach
unquestioning loyalty to Cæsar; to think that it is
possible that all the nations of the earth should live
under their separate religions, provided only that
each religion should uphold the modern king-ideas

of personal rights, of open trade and of international obligations, that is the most hopeless backward vision that lingers behind the closed eyelids of any blind conservatism. The early Christians set out from Cæsarea and walked with simple, trustful feet right through that vain dream of old Rome. The modern Christian is found halting and helpless before the far more empty vision that haunts our half-awakened Christianity.

And if the world has changed, so too has Christianity itself undergone changes which ought, to any man that understands them, to illuminate the possibility of the conversion of the world to Christ. What are they? Compare the religion in which you were brought up, O my religious friend of forty years, and tell me! There surely is a difference. You will not talk to your children wholly as your parents talked to you. The notion of conversion is a more intelligible thing. The tests of the new life are more distinctly those which may be known and read of all men. The conception of personality in religion, of the necessary difference of every man's religious life from every other's, has won an almost exaggerated prominence. And in the stress of criticism and of unbelief, the Christian faith has been compelled to realize herself, to know what truly is a part of her and what is accidental. She is like a ship at sea, in hard and furious weather, which has taken in everything that is ornamental, which she carried easily and almost thought she could not sail without when the skies were fair, and is sailing now through the tempest with all herself, but nothing but herself; strong in her restored simplicity to go through storm and hurricane. This is what the Christian faith is to-day, and is more and more becoming, the simple loyalty to Jesus Christ, the cordial wish to see every man's and every race's faith develope into its own type of life, the knowledge that each man's new life is his old life, his ideal life; that every man's conversion is but the re-entrance into the first plan of God, for which he was made. My friends, there never has been a religion so made for all the world as that. Our own dear faith has never, since she stood tiptoe with St. Paul upon the shore of Troas, ready to cross over into Europe, has never since then stood so ready for her work, "with loins girt up to run around the earth." It is the meeting of these two conditions of our century that makes the friend of missions hope. The opening world, the simplifying faith! Stanley penetrates to the centre of the dark continent, and when he comes out he has left there, in the hands of King Mtesa, the despotic ruler over two million people, as a kind of epitomized Bible, a board on which the fascinated, half-converted savage has had written in Arabic, that he may daily read them, the Ten Commandments of Moses, the Lord's Prayer, and the command of Jesus, "Thou shalt love thy neighbor as thyself." The opened world—the simplified faith! Surely this of all times is not the time to disbelieve in Foreign Missions; surely he who despairs of the power of the Gospel to convert the world to-day, despairs of the noontide just when the sunrise is breaking out of twilight on the earth.

I think again that it is wonderful how many people who understand perfectly what the Gospel is, in the work that it does for them, are all wrong in their conception of what the Gospel has to do for the world, and so have false conceptions about the whole possibility of missions. They talk as if what the religion of Jesus had to do, was to go a perfect stranger into a dark land, with whose people it had before had no concern, to cast out everything that they had ever believed, to falsify all their hopes, to begin their life all over. Perhaps they thought the same thing once about themselves. Perhaps they stood for years untouched by Christianity, because Christianity seemed to them to be the utter destruction of all that they had ever been, or thought, or hoped. They could not understand it. It was all strange and foreign to them. But by-and-by Christ really came, and lo, he was the revealer of that old life. He purified that old self; but it was it still, purified and saved, that he set up to be the burden of their thanksgiving. The old hopes were enlightened; the old ignorant prayers were fulfilled. It was as when the Apostles went out and cried up and down Judea, "The Messiah has come," and Judea understood itself. It was as when Paul stood on Mars Hill, and cried, "Whom you ignorantly worship, Him declare I unto you;" and the altar to the unknown God burst for the first time into the bright blaze of an intelligent sacrifice. And that is what the Christian religion, fulfilling its missionary duty, has to do for all the world. It is the great interpreter of the religious heart of man. Its manifested God speaks, and the divine voices throughout all the world become intelligible. Its message is declared, and countless oracles that were all blind, win a clear meaning. Its sacrifice is held up, and the heathen altar drops its veil of superstition, and discerns its own long lost intention. Its Son of Man goes with his gracious footsteps through the hosts of heathen barbarians, and their sonship to God leaps into consciousness and life. Not as the rival, but as the mother of them all, so does she stand, harmonizing them with her presence and drawing all that is good and true of them into herself.

If that be her function and her right, then it is no unreasonable and bootless task. It is what Jesus did for Judaism. It is what Peter did for Cornelius. It is what some faith must some day do for all the partial and corrupt and rival faiths of men. I could not believe in my own dear faith, the sweet, pure, strong faith of Christ, if I did not believe that to her and to no other belonged that glorious privilege.

Ah, my dear friends, my people, there is the final truth about it, from which we cannot get away. We cannot believe in our Christ for ourselves, unless we believe in him for all the world. The more deeply we believe in him for ourselves, the more certain we shall be that he is the Saviour of the world. A deeper personal faith, a more complete discipleship, that is what you want. Have that, and the apostleship must come. If there is any part of your life not wholly consecrated to him, if there is any of his love which you have not appropriated, if there is any undone duty, which, as you do it, will open for you a new door into his heart, if there is any word, by speaking which you can commit yourself more utterly to him; just as surely as in any of these ways you deepen your own spiritual life and make Jesus more your Saviour, just so surely you will believe in Foreign Missions, and long to tell all men that he is their Saviour too.

SERMON X.

The Earth of the Redemption.

A FOREIGN MISSIONARY SERMON.

" The heavens, even the heavens are the Lord's: but the earth hath he given to the children of men."—PSALM CXV. 16.

TO-DAY we stand upon the summit of our privileges and look abroad upon our duties. It is as if we sat with Jesus by the well at Sychar and heard him say, "Lift up your eyes and look on the fields, for they are white already to the harvest." We are to think of Foreign Missions. And the words which have suggested the line of thought which I want to ask you to pursue, are these striking words of David.

The heavens and the earth are set in contrast with each other. The heavens with their sun and moon and stars, their wandering winds, their majestic domes and pinnacles and fields of cloud, their mysteries of rain and dew, of frost and snow; and then the earth, with its familiar cities and forests and corn-fields, its homes of men and women, its seas and rivers, its sports and toils, its friendships and kinships, these stand over against each other. And their contrast is in this—that while the heavens are out of the reach of man, the expression and result of forces which he cannot control, the earth is what man makes it. He is the changing power here. He turns the rivers where he will, and makes the forests give place to gardens, and builds the cities where the lions used to roar. Over his head all the while stretch the great mysterious heavens, sometimes all calmness, sometimes all tumult, sending their influences down to him, but out of reach of any influence of his. "The heavens, even the heavens are the Lord's. The earth hath he given to the children of men."

It is the familiar contrast which is always present and always having its effect upon our life. The earth and life upon the earth are never the same things that they would be if the great heaven did not stretch, mysterious and unattainable, above them. Man, great as his power grows upon the earth, is always kept aware of how limited his power is. There is always the heaven above him, which is not his, but God's. And this becomes a figure of the limit of man's power everywhere. Not to create first principles or truths, nor to change them in any way, but only to apply them, to set them at work upon the material of life, this is the limited prerogative of man. Not to call into being the highest powers, but only to open the lower regions of nature to their influence, as the farmer opens the earth to the sunshine and the rain, this is our human work.

So David's verse has in it the lofty description of the great philosophy of the universe, to the knowledge of which mankind gradually arrives, that the source of all power is beyond man's reach, and that the place of man is just to furnish in his faithful and obedient life a medium through which the power that is in the heavens may descend and work upon the earth.

For evidently when David says that God has "given the earth to the children of men," he cannot mean that it has been given away from those eternal plans and purposes of goodness which God must always keep with reference to all His creation. If we had any such thought as that we should only need another verse of the same David to set us right. In the twenty-fourth psalm he sings, "The earth is the Lord's and the fulness thereof; the round world and they that dwell therein." In whatever sense then it is true that God has given the earth to man, it is not true in any sense which would imply that it had ceased to be God's world, that He had given it away from Himself, out of His oversight or out of those purposes of righteousness and holiness which are in the very substance of His nature. It is God's world still. It has been given to man not absolutely, but in trust, that man may work out in it the will of God; given—may we not say?—just as a father gives a child a corner of his great garden, and says, "There, that is yours; now cultivate it." Still there lies the father's great garden with its orderly beds and rich flowers, which is the child's pattern in all that he tries to do. Nay, to the father's great garden the child must go to get the slips and seeds for his own soil; and when the summer comes it is by the standard of the father's great garden that the success or failure of the boy's gardening must be judged. That is the way in which God has given the earth to man; not to be played with for our own pleasure, but to be worked for Him.

You know how full the parables of Jesus are of this idea. "A certain householder planted a vineyard, and let it out to husbandmen." "A man travelling into a far country, called his servants and delivered unto them his goods." "Give me the portion of goods that falleth to me," says the younger son to the father. "And he divided unto them his living," runs the story. Everywhere the notion is of entrustment.

Here is the fundamental difference in the lives of men. Man finds the world in his hands. He can do with it what he will. Oh how obedient it is, how docile, and how plastic! He makes the fields his slaves, and bids them fill his barns and load his table. He makes the hills his treasuries and calls upon their silver and their gold to glorify his life. He says to the river, "Feed me," to the ocean, "Carry me;" to the subtle powers of the air, "Give me your light." Everywhere the world is his. But everywhere the difference of men lies here, in whether this mastery seems to be absolute, or whether it seems to be a trust. Absolute mastery means self-indulgence. Its reckless fruits are everywhere, in arrogance and insolence, in "the lust of the flesh, the lust of the eyes and the pride of life." The mastery of trust means humility, conscientiousness, elevation, charity, the fear of God and love of man. These are the two great types of strength which fill the earth—the Cæsars and Napoleons claiming the earth for themselves, and subduing it to their proud wills—the Pauls and Bonifaces and Xaviers and Elliots and Livingstons, claiming the earth for holiness, and subduing it to the will of God.

And now it is in connection with this higher and true view of the giving of the world by God to man that the coming of Christ into the world gains its true meaning. "God was in Christ reconciling the world unto himself." What do these words of the great apostle mean? Think of it! Here was God's world given to man to keep, to use, to work for God. Here was man, always falling into the temptation to think the gift of trust an absolute gift. And here the Giver came with clear assurance of himself; making the men who saw him know that it was he; touching the earth which was his own with a wise power that called out from it capacities which the poor tenant never had discovered; not taking it back out of man's keeping, but making himself man, so that all men might see what it might really mean for man to keep and use and work the earth of God; so God came to his world.

Could anything be more effectual than that? It was as if the maker of a great instrument had given it into the keeping of a pupil of his who, losing the knowledge of what mysterious and mighty harmonies were hidden in the subtle mechanism, had degraded it to low employment and played upon it only dancing ditties and sensuous melodies. By-and-by the master comes into the pupil's house. He lays his fingers on the keys. He wakes the organ's sleeping heart. The wakened instrument responds, and for a moment men hear the great revelation of its nature. There is the redemption of the organ. Just exactly such was Christ's redemption of the world. It was a true man; all the truer man because it was God in man; it was the Father in the Son who showed what earth, used in the fear of God, might be. In him there could be no doubt of what sort had been the giving of the earth to the children of men of which David had sung so long ago. It could not for one moment seem to have been a gift to man's self-indulgence and selfishness. It certainly had not been a giving of the earth away from God. It had been given to the divine in man, to that in man which had in it the nature of divinity, and which was capable, by obedience, of becoming infinitely near to God. It was the gift of trust from a Father to his child, in which the given thing is all the more the Father's when it has been given to the child who is true part of the Father. That this is the real nature of God's gift of earth to man, was the assertion of the incarnation and of all the life of Jesus.

I hope you see that this is no slight distinction. It lies at the bottom of all man's life upon the earth. Shall he make the earth the kingdom of God, or the kingdom of his own selfishness? Christ stands in the midst of all the tumult of human history and says to men, "After this manner pray ye. Our Father who art in heaven. Thy kingdom come. Thy will be done on earth as it is in heaven." The divine character of human life is asserted wherever that prayer is prayed. The brutal vices and the cultivated frivolities of men, the cruelties, and wrongs, and injustices of man to man, the stupefying of men's souls by self-indulgence, the lusts and hatred which make so much of the earth so wretched, all of these are declared to be intruders; not merely ungodly but inhuman; not the natural but the unnatural development of man's life upon the earth, wherever the true nature of God's gift of earth to man is set forth by the life and word of Jesus.

It is within this great general purpose that all the special personal works which Christ does for men are included. He forgives the sins of souls that are penitent. It is that they may be able to take the world which God has given them and live in it as His, full of the profoundest gratitude which a soul can feel. He comforts sufferers in sorrow. It is that by one more avenue they may understand his love, and so bring loving hearts to the understanding of this earthly life, and find it full of him. He sets before men the promise of eternal glory. It is that this life may be glorified by the anticipated radiance of the perfect life to which it leads. Forgiveness, consolation, the promised heaven, none of them has its complete and final purpose in itself. The ultimate purpose of all is present character; the man, here and now, living the redeemed life in the redeemed world, offering in all his godly use of it the world which God has given him to God. This was what Christ asserted and made possible.

And now, what has all this to do with foreign missions? Do you not see? The world is God's world, given by Him to man for man to use in obedience to God. Man has taken the world, but he has largely forgotten that it is his in trust, and has used it largely as if it were absolutely his. Yet everywhere misgivings and vague reminiscences of the true nature of the gift remain. These constitute the never fixed but never wholly perishing religious life of man. Now into this world God comes in Christ to redeem it to Himself, as I have been trying to describe. That coming takes place at one certain point. We can see I suppose two reasons for that. One reason was that if it were to be a genuine Incarnation, an actual utterance of the divine life in a special human body, there was a natural necessity that for that body there should be a fixed locality upon the earth. There must be a Holy Land. There must be a Bethlehem, and a Jerusalem where the actual feet of the Incarnate God should walk. The other reason, no doubt, was that this new wonder was to follow the principle of all God's wonderful communications, like the communication of light and the communication of truth, which never flash in simultaneous splendor through a whole atmosphere at once, but always pass by degrees, however rapidly, from particle to particle in a communicating medium which itself is glorified and educated by the passage. At one point then this Revelation comes, this Christ appears. But evidently that one point is but an incident. The fact which he comes to establish, the consciousness which he comes to renew, is one that belongs to all the earth. It is as true among the snows of Greenland and in the jungles of the tropics as upon the rocky plateau of Moriah and the green shores of Tiberias, that the earth is man's only as man is God's. The tidings must of necessity fall upon the earth as the sun must of necessity strike the planet first upon some one most exposed mountain top, but the mountain top knows that the sun is not for it alone, but for the world; and instantly it is calling to the other hill tops and to the deep valleys. Or, shall we say, in homelier metaphor, it is as if a father sends his message to the household of his children, and one child takes the message at the door, not the best child by any certainty, not by any certainty the child most capable of understanding what the message means, but just perhaps the child who stands the nearest to the door. And then the moment that that child has it in his hand, he knows that it is not for him alone, and calls out to his brothers, "Come and hear." That is the simple genesis of foreign missions, and its principle always remains the same. The circle widens from its first centre. New circles with new centres form, but still so long as there is any child in the whole house who has not heard the father's message, the impulse and the sense of duty live. The desire to let the whole redeemed world know of its redemption, moves in the heart of every man vividly conscious of the redemption in himself.

And what will be the result of such a telling of the true nature of God's gift of the world to man? We cannot fail to know beforehand. That part of the world which wants to use the world selfishly and basely, will reject the story, and perhaps will kill the man who tells it. That part of the world which has been dissatisfied with its attempt to make the world a mere scene of self-indulgence, but which has not been able to conceive for it any great consistent purpose, will be dazed and bewildered by such a vast story as this which the incarnation tells, that all man's life, and the earth where it is lived, belongs to God. But wherever any preservation of the world's first idea has been kept, it will be brought out to meet this declaration in which it will recognize at once a kinship to itself. Men and religions in whom has lingered and struggled some knowledge of the sacredness of human life and of the possibility of man, how they will gather around the missionary truth of Christ and say, "Yes, we have been sure that somehow we and our earth belonged to God: behold how we have tried to utter that assurance. This is what our poor altar means. Nay, this is what these very idols meant at first, which have since then become such wretched stumbling blocks. We know that we and our earth have belonged to God. Has he indeed come to claim us? Tell us about it." Is it not just what I said? Brother asking of brother what is the message which the Father has sent to the whole family, but which has fallen into one child's hands before the rest!

I think there can hardly be conceived a picture of any more gracious and beautiful relation between man and his fellow-man than is involved in such a thought of missionary work as this. There is no arrogance about the missionary preacher or the missionary nation that so thinks about the missionary work. It is not Moses standing superior to the cringing multitude, insulting their thirst with the parade of his power to give or to refuse the water: "Hear now, ye rebels, must we bring you water out of this rock?" Such missionary insolence and contempt for the heathen there may sometimes have been. This is not that. Rather it is the exquisite and noble honor for the souls it speaks to, which fills all the rest of the history of Moses beside that one unhappy outbreak. You remember the profound respect with which the great messenger of God again and again speaks of His Israel. "For they are thy people and thine inheritance." So he pleads with God. So must Christendom think and speak of heathenism; so it will think and speak of heathenism when it has caught the true idea of the message of redemption which it has to carry.

We have been talking about the work which Christendom has to do for heathenism, as the carrying of a message; and we speak of it rightly so. Only, in order to get the fullest understanding of this matter, we must remember what God's messages are, and what it is to carry them. One of the lessons which we learn in our own Christian life at home is that God's messages are not mere facts, to be given and received by the mere statement of their terms. God's messages which he has sent to us, have always been full truths, which were not ours until our whole nature had received them. Only when they had possessed each part of us, our hearts, our tastes, our consciences, our intellects, did they become really ours. Now we must know that in the same complete way we are to give to the heathen what God has given us. Only as full grown truth, not as mere bare fact, we are to give the gospel to the heathen. Preaching the gospel to the heathen is not standing upon the beach of a dark continent and crying into the darkness the story of the Lord. It is nothing less, nothing easier, than laying upon all the heathen nature, upon body and soul and mind and conscience and ordinary habits, all together, the truth of the redeemed world as it has been laid upon all our nature in all our Christian culture. That is the reason why the missionary colleges in China and in India, and the medical missions with their hospital where the poor bring their sick bodies to be healed, and the missionaries' homes with their living pictures of Christian family life, are as true and legitimate a part of our missionary power as are the churches where the missionaries preach. Philanthropy and education have come in these modern times to take a very prominent place in missionary operations, not because

The Earth of the Redemption. 185

they were needed in addition to religion, but because they were part of the complete religion, because the full truth of Christ must reach the whole nature of man through the whole nature of man, or the true Gospel was not preached. What wonder also if sometimes, since, as we have seen, the Gospel looks for recognition to a consciousness already present in the soul of man, it should be able to attain that recognition the more readily, if knocking first at the outermost and easiest doors of physical necessity and intellectual curiosity, it seeks through them a gradual approach to the chamber where the power of the deepest faith resides, and so philanthropy and education should be at first most prominent in the missionary work. It is so with the heathen man among us here, and there is no reason why it should not be so also with the heathen man across the sea.

There are two principal objections which in these days rise in men's minds, with every thought of Foreign Missions. One is the excellence of the heathen and the other is the imperfection of Christians. I cannot but think that both of these objections disappear, if such an idea of Foreign Missions as I have tried to set before you this morning is thoroughly understood. What shall we say about the first difficulty? You know how common it is. When we talk of going to tell men in heathen lands the story of the revelation of God in Christ, we are reminded that they know very much of God already. "They are not Godless," we are told. Their sacred books are opened, the holy lives of their best men are pictured, and the whole power of their present knowledge of heaven, of the Deity, and of the soul, seems to be set as an objection in the way of their chance of receiving the fuller light which Christianity claims to be ready to bestow. Now, grant, for the moment, the whole force of the objection, just as it is stated, and yet see how powerless it is. If Christianity were set forth as man's only way of knowing anything about God, it might indeed be puzzling to the missionary, when he came to his heathen land, to find a great deal of the knowledge of God there already. But if Christianity be what we have pictured, a redemption, a bringing back and reclaiming for God of an earth which has always belonged to Him, then surely the messenger of that redemption will not be surprised, but only devoutly thankful when he finds some consciousness of that belonging of the earth to God awaiting him wherever he goes. No land so dark that there is not some such light there! No brutal savagedom so savage that, in some breast of nobler sort, or, it may be, kept only in some fantastic rite whose spiritual meaning has long been lost, there is not uttered some sort of craving for the true nobility of servantship to God, of stewardship for earth. There can be no grudging of any such illumination. Christianity has not got to explain it away. She is all ready to lay hold on it and magnify it all she can. If to-day, in some as yet unopened island of the southern seas, there should be found a type of spiritual life far surpassing anything which heathenism ever yet has shown, a fear of God and a sense of duty and desire of holiness which made that island shine in the midst of heathenism like a star —what would be the true feeling of Christianity towards that island? Would there not be a special impulse to send our missionary there? Not the same impulse indeed which makes us want to send him to some horrid land, where men are murdering and torturing each other in their cruelty and lust, but a yet higher impulse; not the impulse which makes you want to put just one ray of light into the utter blackness of the midnight, but the impulse which makes you want to pour the full glory of the noontide into the beautiful but imperfect glory of the morning.

And then the other objection to the work of Foreign Missions lies in the imperfection of Christians. You know the venerable argument which was never very strong, and which halts and stumbles now from age and long dishonorable service: "The heathen in Boston!" we are told. "Look how poor a thing our home religion is. Shall we not make our own religion strong, convert our own masses, conquer our own sins, before we go around the world to preach our yet unappropriated gospel to the heathen?" It is not always those who are most earnest or active to complete our home religion who use such an argument. But that is not the point. It all proceeds upon a wrong idea of Christianity, and of its way of gaining power over man. If we recur a moment to the simple figure which I used awhile ago, and see the one child who stands nearest to the door taking his father's message first, the question comes at once: What right has that one child to keep the message all to himself, until such time as he has perfectly read and learned and inwardly digested it, before he gives it to his brothers, whose it is as much as his? What right has Andrew to wait till he is sure that he has perfectly comprehended Jesus, before he findeth his brother Simon, and pours into his ears the tidings which belong to both, "We have found the Messias"?

Probably it is not an argument with which it is worth while to argue, but we cannot help thinking where, with such an argument in force, would have been the richness of Christian history! If every land must for itself have made the very best and fullest use of the Gospel before it could offer it to any other land, how the great work would have halted and stayed in its first littleness. Still, on the desolate fields of Galilee, or amid the ruins of Jerusalem, a few disconsolate and hopeless Jews would be telling to-day to one another the unbelieved and unused story of the cross. The earnest heart and manly intellect of Paul, full of the spirit of his Master, soon broke the spell of such a sophistry as that, and Europe saw the light through the dim medium of a Judaism which was itself still more than half darkness.

Truth is too eager to wait for any one soul to appropriate it perfectly before it presses on through it to other souls. Truth will crowd like the river through narrow gates of rock, to reach the open valley which waits for her beyond, and will not deny her richness to the open valley until she has worn herself a full broad passage through the slowly yielding rock. A little child finds a strange shell upon the sea shore, and he need not wait until he has himself completely understood it before he carries it to the great naturalist and gives him in it the one golden key to whole regions of knowledge which have been locked up and useless. Indeed there is no nobler sight than to see the weaker thus ministering to the greater of its own half appreciated knowledge of the works of God. Let every man tell what he knows of truth, of nature, and of God; and other men hearing his message, shall send back to him interpretations of it which he could never have discovered for himself. Reflected out of other men's experiences it shall come back to enlighten him. That is the only principle.

This is the simple principle of foreign missions. See what we have to-day. The world is growing more and more open every year. No longer like a ship with watertight compartments, any one of which might be flooded with blessing or with ruin, and the rest remain unconscious of the change, no richer and no poorer than they were before; but now, with all its bulkheads broken down, so that the whole great system is but one, and what belongs to any part belongs to all, so lives the world to-day, so it is evidently going to live more and more in days to come.

No longer are there clearly defined limits of Christendom and heathenism. The Chinese Joss House grins in its fantastic worship on the streets of San

Francisco, and the truths of Christianity are debated on the highways of Japan. For the first time in the history of the world there is a manifest possibility of a universal faith. Distance has ceased to be a hindrance. Language no longer makes men total strangers. A universal commerce is creating common bases and forms of thought. For the first time in the history of the world there is a manifest, almost an immediate, possibility of a universal religion. No wonder that at such a time the missionary spirit which had slumbered for centuries should have sprung upon its feet, and the last fifty years should have been one of the very greatest epochs in missionary labor in the whole history of the world.

I have indicated clearly enough to-day what is the special character of this new missionary spirit of these modern times. It is not arrogant. It is humble. It tries to learn as well as teach. It does not hesitate to feel and to declare its honor for very much of the greatness and spiritual power of the paganism to which it brings the Gospel.

That spirit is a mighty gain. It is the spirit of light, and honesty and truth. It is full of faith in God and man. I have tried to show also that it is the spirit of an intensified and not of a diminished energy in missionary work.

And yet we must not let that spirit run to false extremes; we must not yield to false exaggerations. We must not idealize heathenism while we see all the faults and flaws of an arch-Christianity. The fact remains, beyond the contradiction of the wildest

The Earth of the Redemption. 191

folly, that the best part of the world to-day is Christian, and not heathen. The healthiest life, the truest brotherhood, the noblest thought, the fullest manhood, where is the advocate of heathen virtue, where is the critic or foe of Christian faith, who will deny to-day, as a plain fact, that all these great things are to be found within the sound of the Gospel, within the light of the cross, and not under the shadow of any heathen temple in the most beautiful of pagan lands?

This is our plea for foreign missions. God has given the earth to the children of men. But the children of men are God's children too. Only in His name and fear do they truly possess the earth which He has given them. To claim the earth for Him was the great work of Christ. To claim the earth for Him must be the work of every servant of Christ who in any degree is like his Master. That claim is to be made first by living ourselves brave, pure, faithful, Godlike lives upon the earth, letting men see and proving to ourselves that a man may live upon this wicked earth as the true child of God. It is to be made again by telling to all mankind, in the never outworn, never outgrown story of the Incarnation, that they and the earth on which they live are not their own but God's; are their own only because they are God's; have been made truly and thoroughly their own by being redeemed to God in Jesus Christ.

SERMON XI.

The Man with Two Talents.

" To another he gave two talents."—MATTHEW XXV. 15.

IN the parable of Jesus the master stands with three servants before him. He is just ready to start upon his journey, and he is giving them his last commissions. For reasons of his own, he makes a difference between them. To one he gives five talents, and to another two, and to another one. "To every man according to his several ability," the story adds. Then he goes off and leaves them, and each is faithful or faithless in the use of the money with which he is entrusted.

I want to speak to-day about the man with the two talents. He has his own peculiar interest, as he stands in the little group of three before the master. He is significant, we may almost say, because of his insignificance. As their Lord puts the money in their hands, we can see them look at it, and can guess what they think about it. The man to whom five talents are given, is surprised that he should receive so much. He is exhilarated and inspired; or perhaps, on the other hand, he is paralyzed and overcome. The man to whom one talent is given is startled at the smallness of the trust. He too feels a positive emotion. Either he is stung to energy and determines that he will do something strong and good, even with this little gift. Or else he is crushed into despair. Is this then all of which his Master thinks him worthy? Both of these men are interesting. They represent extremes. But the man of two talents stands and looks at his trust, and it is just about what he might have expected. It is neither very great nor very small. It does not exalt him, and ir does not make him ashamed. He turns away and goes out to use it with a calm, unexcited face. He is the type of common mediocrity. He is the average man.

It is very easy to be interested in the man of five talents, or in the man of one talent. Their interest takes hold of us at once. But I think that, as we look at life longer and study it more deeply, we feel more and more the importance of their less sensational brother, the man of the two talents, and are more and more interested in seeing what he does with his money, have more and more respect for him when we see him going conscientiously to work to turn it to its best result. Let us think of him awhile this morning; the man who is neither very rich nor very poor, not notable because of excess or of defect, the man with gifts like a million others, the average man.

He ought to interest us, for he presents the type

to which we almost all belong. There are none of us probably who are conscious of anything which separates us as notably superior to the great mass of our fellow-men. On the other hand it is not probable that many of us count ourselves distinctly below the average of human life. We do not lay claim to the five talents; we will not confess to the one. It is as men and women of two talents that we ordinarily count ourselves, and ask to be counted by our brethren. Therefore this quiet, common-place, unnoticed man, going his faithful way in his dull dress which makes no mark and draws no eye, doing his duty insignificantly and thoroughly, winning so unobtrusively at last his master's praise, ought to be interesting to us all.

He ought to be interesting also because he represents so much the largest element in universal human life. The average man is by far the most numerous man. The man who goes beyond the average, the man who falls short of the average, both of them, by their very definition, are exceptions. They are the outskirts and fringes, the capes and promontories of humanity. The great continent of human life is made up of the average existences, the mass of two-talented capacity and action.

It is so even in the simplest and most superficial matter of the possession of wealth. The great fortunes, with their splendid opportunities, and their tremendous responsibilities, rise like gigantic mountains which everybody sees out of the general level of comfortable life. On the other hand, excessive poverty, actual suffering for the necessities of life, terrible as it is, is comparatively rare. A part of its terribleness comes from its rarity. The great multitude of men are neither very rich nor very poor. The real character and strength of a community lies neither in its millionaires nor in its paupers, but in the men of middle life, who neither have more money than they know how to spend nor are pressed and embarrassed for the necessities of life.

The same is true in the matter of joy and sorrow. The great mass of men during the greater part of their lives are neither exultant and triumphant with delight, nor are they crushed and broken down with grief. They do not go shouting their rapture to the skies, and they do not go wailing their misery to the sympathetic winds. They are moderately happy. Joy flecked and toned down by troubles; troubles constantly relieved and lighted up by joy; that is their general condition; that seems to be their best capacity. The power of the intensest joy and the intensest pain belongs only to rare, peculiar men.

Or if you think about mental capacity. Most men are neither sages nor fools. Or if you think about learning, few men are either scholars or dunces. Or if you think about popularity and fame, those whom the whole world praises and those whom all men despise are both of them exceptional. You can count them easily. The great multitude whom you cannot begin to count, who fill the vast middle-ground of the great picture of humanity, is made up of men who are simply well enough liked by their fellow-men. They are crowned with no garlands, and they are pelted with no stones. They have their share of kindly interest and esteem. You cannot well think of them as either losing that or as gaining much beyond it.

And when you come to the profounder and the more personal things, when you come to character and to religion, there too it is the average that fills your eye. Where are the heroes? You can find them if you look. Where are the rascals? You can find them too. Where are the saints? They shine where no true man's eyes can fail to see them. And the blasphemers, likewise, no one can shut out of his ears. But the great host of men, do you not know how little reason they give you to expect of them either great goodness or great wickedness? You do not look to see their faces kindle when you talk to them of Christ. You do not either look to see them grow scornful or angry at his name. You do not count upon their going to the stake for principle. But you do count upon their paying their honest debts. You have to shut your thoughts about them in to this world, for when you think of them in eternity heaven seems as much too good for them as hell seems too bad.

Sometimes, when we let it crowd itself upon us, this fact of the predominance of mediocrity, or of the average in life, becomes oppressive. It seems to level life into a great, broad, flat, dreary plain. The men of two talents seem to have the world to themselves. Finding ourselves men of two talents, we sometimes seem to be simply adding by our existence a little more monotony and oppression to the monotonous and oppressive life of the great world.

We cannot get rid of such oppression, and the demoralization which it brings, by simply denying or ignoring the fact of the preponderance of mediocrity. The fact is too unquestionable. Only by redeeming mediocrity, in our own and other men's esteem; only by asserting and believing that the man of two talents has a great place and a great chance in the world, only so can we restore the healthy thought of life which the first sight of his numerousness disturbs. This is what I want to try to do this morning. I want to speak first of the dangers which come to us when we know ourselves to be two-talent men, and then of the escape from those dangers as we come to know the special powers and privileges which belong to our limited and middle life.

We need to remember very clearly that what we are speaking of all along is the possession of powers, not the use of powers. Every man is bound to use the powers he possesses to their fullest. But the limit of the powers which each man possesses is not in his own hands, and there is where the vast majority of men are obliged to make up their minds to mediocrity.

It is not always an easy thing for men to make up their minds to mediocrity. We cannot tell in how many natures there comes deep struggle and sad disappointment before the lot of the average man is cordially accepted. A young man starts untried.

He is a problem to himself and everybody else. Who can say what strange capacity is folded in this yet unopened life? It is a young man's right, almost his duty, to hope, almost to believe, that he has singular capacity, and is not merely another repetition of the constantly repeated average of men. Before he unfolds the bundle which his Lord has given him, he may well see in his imagination the five bright talents shining through its folds. We would not give much for the young man to whom there came no such visions and dreams of extraordinary life. To see those dreams and visions gradually fade away; little by little to discover that one has no such exceptional capacity; to try one and another, of the adventurous ways which lead to the high heights and the great prizes, and find the feet unequal to them; to come back at last to the great trodden highway, and plod on among the undistinguished millions, that is often very hard. The fight is fought, the defeat is met, in silence; but it is no less, it is more terrible. The hour in which it becomes clear to a young man that that is to be his life, that there is nothing else for him to do except to swell the great average of humanity, is often filled with dangers. Let us see what some of those dangers are.

In the first place, the man of two talents has to make up his mind to do without both of the different kinds of inspiration which come to the men who are better off and the men who are worse off than he is. The man of five talents, the man of exceptional gifts and opportunities excites admiration and excites expectation. He is conscious of abilities, and of the demands which other men make of him because of those abilities. He feels men's eyes upon him. Wherever he goes there is a hush to see what he will do. He is surrounded with an atmosphere of responsibility. Men hang upon him for his help. Men's jealousy even, and their readiness to criticise him, and his own fear lest he fall short of his possibilities, are continual safeguards and incentives. This must be more to him than we can begin to estimate. And on the other hand, the man who labors under constant disadvantages, he also has a sting and a spur of quite another kind. To do great things in spite of difficulties, that is a very bugle-call to many men. There comes a desperation which is inspiration. To hear all men saying, "you can do everything," there is great strength in that. To hear men saying, "you can do nothing," in that too there is strength. Have you read the delightful biography of Henry Fawcett the English statesman, who, in total blindness, fought his way to the House of Commons and became a power in the realm? It has been the hopelessness of their lot that has made the noble lives of many of the noblest men the world has seen.

But now to the middle man, the man who is neither very much nor very little—the man who has two talents, but only two—both of these forms of impulse are denied. He is neither high enough to hear the calling of the stars, nor low enough to feel the tumult of the earthquake. What wonder if he often falls asleep for sheer lack of sting and spur. What wonder if he does the moderate things that seem to be within his power unenthusiastically, and then stops, making no demand upon himself, since other men make no demand upon him.

And then again the work which the five-talent men and the work which the one-talent men undertake is apt to have a definiteness and distinctness which the work of the average man is very liable to lose. Genius, by its very intensity, decrees a special path of fire for its vivid power. Conscious limitation, on the other hand, knows there is no hope for it except in one direction. Both have the strength which comes by narrowness. But the man who knows himself to be only moderately strong, is apt to think that his strength has no peculiar mission. He wastes himself on this and that in general, and aims at nothing in particular. The commonplace man is the discursive man. He has neither the impetuosity of the torrent nor the direct gravitation of the single drop of water. He lies a loose and sluggish pool, and flows nowhither and grows stagnant by-and-by.

And yet again, there is the constant danger of being made light of by other men. The man of whom we speak becomes uninteresting to other people, and so loses interest in himself. He attracts no reverence and he enlists no pity. Men do not say of him, "How great he is!" nor do they say, "Poor fellow!" He finds himself unnoticed. He must originate out of himself all that he comes to. He hangs between the heaven and the earth, and is fed out of neither. What he does seems to be of no consequence, because it wakens no emotion in his brethren. He has no influence on other men, and so there is no effluence, no putting forth of life from him.

Am I not telling a familiar story? Suppose yourself an apostle of the Lord, a gospel exhorter, trying to stir men's souls to repentance and to faith. Do you not know what you would say to the man of brilliant genius, how you would adjure him to consecrate his splendid powers to God? Do you not know what you would say to the poor human creature who seemed hardly more than a brute, begging him to claim his place in spite of everything among God's children? But to the man of ordinary faculties and decent life and sluggish will, what can you say? I think of Jesus looking in the face of John, and John's whole soul is stirred. I think of Jesus gazing mournfully at Judas, and I cannot estimate the power of that sorrowful reproach. There must have been a middle class; a temperate zone of the apostolic life— James the son of Alphæus, and Lebbæus whose surname was Thaddæus—between whom and the Master, life and the giving and receiving of emotion was more tame and less intense. However that may have been, the dangers of the temperate zone in life, less immediately under the Lord's eye, are manifest. Routine respectability in conduct, unenterprising orthodoxy in opinion, an absence of high self-respect, which easily makes way for petty self-conceit, humbleness which is not true humility, and calmness which is not energetic peace, these are the dangers of the men who have counted the talents which their Lord has given them and found them only two.

Of course the other men, the richer and the poorer men, have both of them their dangers, of which one easily might speak in other sermons. Whether they are greater or less than this man's dangers, is but an idle and unanswerable question. This man's are very real and very great.

And yet in spite of all of them (to come to the second of my two divisions), the man with two talents has a great chance in the world. Alas, for the world, if he had not! For, as I said, it is of him that the world mainly is composed. Let us turn now and try to see what his chances are. I would fain seem to myself to be looking, as I speak, into his oppressed and discouraged face, and would try to stir him to a more vigorous and hopeful and enthusiastic spirit.

And I would say first, ought you not to remember that it is the quality, more than in the quantity of talents that their true value lies? Your talents may be two, another's five, another's one; the real point of importance is that yours, whether they be few or many, that yours, as much as anybody's, were given you by God and constitute a true, direct, and sacred connection and channel of intercourse between your soul and His. That belongs to the very fact of gift. What matters it that hundreds of millions of other men have received about the same amount of gift from God as you? What would it matter if hundreds of millions of other men's gifts had been exactly and absolutely identical with yours? That is not true. Your gifts, whatever they may be in bulk, are different in kind from any other man's that ever lived. But what if that were true? Would not your gift be still as truly yours, and open to your soul as true a possible communion with God as if you had been chosen to be the one only two-talented man in all his kingdom of humanity? You must forget your brethren, and think of Him. You must get beyond the relative and get into the absolute.

And if your place in the great crowd of mediocrity makes it the harder for you to attain to this, it ought to make the attainment all the more clear and sure when it is won. It is easy for the mountain to trace the sun's ray direct from the sun to its illuminated peak. It is harder for one wave on the tossing sea to believe that it too has its bridge of sunlight to the sun; but when it once has found it, the undiscriminated wave must cling to that radiant bridge even more eagerly and strongly than the single separate mountain summit.

But then, when you have once separated yourself from the great mass, and realized your direct relationship to God, then you may come back into the mass again and see what are the special advantages which belong to a faithful life lived in the average condition, lived with the average capacities of man.

Such a life brings out and makes manifest the solid strength which belongs to the simple qualities of manhood. We are so apt to grow frantic and fantastic in our struggles. We paint our heroes fighting their battles in the clouds or in the depths. Types of power which can only be developed in supreme joy or supreme sorrow enthrall our imagination; and then some plain man comes who knows not either rapture or despair, who simply has his daily work to do, his friends to help, his enemies to forgive, his children to love and train, his trials to bear, his temptations to conquer, his soul to save; and what a healthiness he brings into our standards, with what a genuine refreshment he fills our hearts. Behold how great are these primary eternal qualities—patience, hope, kindness, intelligence, trust self-sacrifice. We do not accept them because we cannot have something finer. They show us their intrinsic fineness and we do them reverence. The arctic frost! The torrid heat! behold the true strength, the real life of the planet is not in these. It is in the temperate lands that the grape ripens and the wheat turns calmly yellow in the constant sun. Blessed is the life which grows itself into the consciousness of how strong a man is who with the average powers of a man keeps his integrity and purity, becomes ever more upright and pure, and also encourages the lives of other men. Blessed is the life which becomes always more aware of this, and makes it more evident to its brethren.

It is perhaps only saying the same thing in another way to claim that the man conscious of mediocrity has the advantage of displaying in his life and character the intrinsic and essential life of human nature. I have already said that he need not be lacking in the sense of personal distinctness. He gets that from his immediate connection with God. But the other sense, the sense of being thoroughly one with fellow-men, that too is very necessary for the fullest life. Let it exist alone, and it may only amount to being lost in the great mass. Let it exist along with a clear consciousness of personal commission from the hand of God, and it is full of value. It backs the single career with all the history of man. It surrounds it with the warm domestic atmosphere of human society. Anything which breaks in upon that sense of living the intrinsic life of humanity and makes the personal life seem to be exceptional and original and solitary, whatever compensations it may bring, brings surely harm. It cannot be good for any man to live constantly in a condition which makes him count himself exceptional, or rather in a condition which makes him think more of the exceptional than of the universal element in his life. Sometimes, as a separate and temporary experience, it may be good. Sometimes to count oneself happy beyond any other man's experience of happiness, sometimes to be compelled to cry "Behold and see, was there ever sorrow like to my sorrow!" that may be very good. It is very good for the single drop of water here and there to be cast up out of the stream and flash an instant in the sun alone, or be whirled alone a moment by the furious wind; but its great normal strength is for it to be part of the great current, to feel the universal purpose round and in itself. So only does it flow on in power and peace, and at last come to the sea.

And if the man of two talents is able thus peculiarly to feel his oneness with his race, that does not only make him calm and happy. It also makes him strong. It is a source of power. It gives him the ability to help his fellow-men in ways which, whether they be greater or less than other men's ways, are peculiarly his own. We naturally exaggerate the influence of notable people. I would not underestimate it. When God sends forth some shining herald of Himself, whose supreme felicity makes all men gaze in wonder; or when he opens and displays in some one of his children's lives the depths of man's capacity of pain, so that all other men stand overwhelmed with brother-pain and pity; in either case he dowers those exceptional careers with special capacity of helpfulness. But the world does not, cannot rest for its perpetual needs on lives like those. It is not the wind which breathes upon the planet from without. It is the instinct which resides in each particle bedded deep in the mass of the planet, and which draws it always to the centre of its gravitation, that keeps the planet in its place. The man in whom men recognize simply an average human nature like their own, no greater and no less, who they know has all their passions and infirmities and no more than their strength to meet them with, he is the man who, being faithful, pure, serene, brave, hopeful, has power to make his brethren all that he tries to be, of a kind which no brilliant leader of his race can show.

For he can at once show men what is good and make it seem possible. These two together make the moral need of humankind. Men have perverted and false standards; and when they see what the true standard is, the life to which it seems to call them seems impossible. But here, lo! is a man whom they cannot call exceptional. And see, with just their tools he does this finer work. The thing they call impossible for men like them, he, being a man like them, does. Is there not here a power, and is it not a power which belongs distinctly to the man's mediocrity, to the fact that he is an average man, and no exception?

Can you not conceive of a man's feeling that inspiration, and is it not a noble inspiration for a man to feel? You answer me, perhaps, "Yes, but for the average man to feel that inspiration would prove that he was *not* an average man. The power to feel an inspiration such as that, constitutes him immediately an exception." But I remind you that I am not talking of any mediocrity except that of powers or of circumstances. Not of a mediocrity in will or purpose. I am supposing a man of thoroughly commonplace and ordinary powers, and of perfectly monotonous life, who at the same time wants to serve his fellow-men. There is nothing violent, nothing incongruous in such a supposition; and what I claim is that such a man has, in the very things which make his chance seem most hopeless, a chance of influence and usefulness and power which is peculiarly his own.

Two other possible advantages of average life I can do no more than just suggest to you. May it not find a self-surrender to the help of other lives more easy, and make that self-surrender more complete just in proportion as it is released from that desire for self-assertion, that consciousness of being something which is worthy of men's observation, that self-value which must haunt the lives of those who, in any way, on either side, find themselves separated from the great bulk of their fellow-creatures?

And is it not true that all that assertion of the intrinsic value of every life, which is the very essence of our Christian faith, all that redemption of the soul, in the profoundest and the truest sense, which was the work of Christ, must come with special welcome and appreciation and delight to any man who feels his insignificance, and is in danger of losing himself in the vague mass of his fellows? Christ redeems him. Christ says, "Behold yourself in me, and see that you are not insignificant." Christ says, "I died for you." Set thus upon his feet, made a new man, or made to be the man he is, with what gratitude and faith and obedience must that man follow the Christ who is his Saviour!

Here let us pause. Shall we not seem to see this man of the two talents standing with what seem to be the respectable and comfortable, but uninspiring and uninteresting conditions of his life, this man for whom the prophecy of Agur, the son of Jakeh, has been fulfilled, and who has been given "neither poverty nor riches." What shall he do? If he were strong and abundant, he would stand up joyously and sweep away evil, and set wrong right, and build some corner of the kingdom of God, to the sound of psalms and trumpets. If he were wretched and destitute, he would defy his circumstances, and make their very desperation sting him into strength. But now what shall he do? Just settle down into a life of uselessness and thoughtlessness and harmlessness and base animal comfort? That is what the temptation is so strong to do. Oh, that we might see to-day that something else is possible! Oh that we might know that no child of God is lost into indiscriminateness from his Father's sight! Oh, that we might see how out of the very fact of our mediocrity come opportunities of special faithfulness and of peculiar service to God and to our fellow-men!

"He that had received two talents, he also gained other two." Those words, two verses on, complete the story of the average man, faithful in mediocrity. What an epitaph those words would make to write upon the tombstone of a man who, neither very rich nor very poor, neither very joyous nor very sad, neither very wise nor very ignorant, neither very strong nor very weak, had done his duty bravely and unselfishly, and then passed on, to be lost again among the hundred and forty and four thousand who follow the Lamb, but to do his portion of God's work in heaven as he has done it on the earth. What soul could ask for better destiny or praise than that?

SERMON XII.

Destruction and Fulfilment.

"*I am not come to destroy, but to fulfil.*"—MATTHEW v. 17.

IT was necessary that Christ the Son of God, manifesting His Father to mankind, should live at one special point in human history and at one special spot in the world's geography. There had to be some one age whose peculiar circumstances should give shape to the events of his life. There had to be some one land which should become forever memorable and sacred as that on which his feet had walked. But yet, while this is true, everybody who understands Christ, knows that what took place visibly in Palestine is taking place spiritually everywhere and always. Christ is always coming. And that coming of the gracious presence which men saw and touched, and whose words fell with warning or exalting power on their ears, while it had its own separate and unshared value, was also representative of what is continually going on. What Christ was then, he always is; what Christ did then, he is always doing. And so if we want to know how

Destruction and Fulfilment. 211

Christ works to-day, we have the Gospel for a perpetual guide. The phenomena of that first coming must be the phenomena of all Christianity. Take out of them that in their tone which is manifestly local and temporary, and the words which Jesus spoke of and to the Judaism of his time are the same words which he is always speaking to the Judaisms of all times. So long as His salvation is not yet complete, He walks unseen in the world, as once he walked seen in Jerusalem, and speaks to men's attentive souls as once He spoke to their listening ears.

The words which I have chosen for my text this morning illustrate this. When Jesus came into the world to establish the perfect religion, he found here an imperfect faith. The old faith of the Jews, into the very heart of which the Lord was born, and where his life was lived, knew much of God; indeed knew more of God than any other religion which the world possessed. Jesus knew still more. He brought a higher and diviner presence. He came with a complete salvation. How should he treat this partial, this imperfect faith which was already on the ground? He might do either of two things. He might sweep it away and begin entirely anew, or he might take this imperfect faith and fill it out to completeness. He might destroy or he might fulfil. With the most deliberate wisdom he chose one method and rejected the other. " I am not come to destroy, out to fulfil," he said. Those are most critical, decisive words. They declare the whole fundamental method of the Master's ministry. They have their root and necessity, as I think we shall see, in the Master's nature. It is right that we who live in a world where Christ is still at work, should understand his method and see what it means, both for the world and us; that he who comes to save the world and to save men declares that it is as a fulfiller and not as a destroyer that he comes.

A fulfiller and a destroyer. Let us first clearly understand the difference; and that we may understand it best, it will be well to look at it in regions with which we are familiar.

Look at it in nature. What is the truly majestic power of the earth? Surely not destruction! Surely not the forces which sweep out of being the things which are harmful and mischievous! There are such forces, but the thought about the world which made those forces seem the venerable and admirable forces, the forces to which men's worship and admiration ought to be given, would be horrible! It is the forces of fulfilment, the forces which are always crowding every process forward to its full activity, crowding every being and structure out to its completest realization of itself, the forces of construction and growth; these are the real vital forces of the world. Nature takes hold of every capacity of living which she finds anywhere, and turns it into life. Her rain and dew find out the least vitality and feed it. To make each imperfection a little less imperfect, to bring each partial being a little nearer to completeness, to minister growth and not decay, to minister decay only as an incident and a means to growth, not to destroy but to fulfil, that is what nature comes for with her orderly seasons and recurring years.

Let this serve us for an illustration. Go further on and think of what man does to his fellow-man. We are so often set to be, as it were, natures to each other. Lives bend over other lives as the sky bends over the earth. Influences come from man to man as the dew and sunshine come from the bounteous heavens to the ready ground. There is no one of you who has not some other nature which lies under your nature, as the field lies under the rain-cloud to receive its richness. When you think of that other nature waiting for your ministry, are you not aware of two different treatments, either of which you may give it? Your child, your scholar, your servant— you may fulfil him or you may destroy him. You destroy him if you fasten on everything that is bad and crude and ridiculous about him, and pour out upon it rebuke and contempt. You destroy him if you make him feel himself weak and insignificant, and drive him to despair. You destroy him if you make his great feeling about his own life to be shame. On the other hand you fulfil him, you fill him out to his full, to his fullest, if you catch everything that is good about him and water it with judicious encouragement and praise. You fulfil him if you recognize every feeblest and clumsiest effort to do right, if you inspire him with hope, if you make him seem to himself worth cultivating and watching and developing.

A friend told me the other day of walking along the crowded street close by two young people who were evidently coming home from work, and how he necessarily overheard their talk with one another. And one of them said, evidently referring to some act of an employer, "It was only a little thing, but I was so tired and discouraged that nothing ever did me so much good." Some word had been spoken, some deed had been done which had fulfilled that tired and discouraged life a little. How easy and simple it appears, and yet how rare it sometimes seems. To say "well-done" to any bit of work that has embodied good effort, is to take hold of the powers which have made the effort and confirm and strengthen them. But if you have nothing to say to your child or to your scholar except (what may be perfectly true) that much of his work is badly done, that he is wasting opportunities and losing the value of his life, then you are coming to him not to fulfil but to destroy.

I beg you to think of this, you who are set in positions of superintendence and authority. Make a great deal more of your right to praise the good than of your right to blame the bad. Never let a brave and serious struggle after truth and goodness, however weak it may be, pass unrecognized. Do not be chary of appreciation. Hearts are unconsciously hungry for it. There is little danger, especially with us in this cold New England region, that appreciation shall be given too abundantly. Here and there, perhaps, in your shops and schools and house-

holds, there is some one who has too lazily sunk
down upon the praise he has received for some good
work, and rested in sluggish satisfaction on it; but
such disasters hardly count among the unfulfilled
lives which have lived meagrely and stuntedly for
the lack of some simple cordial human approval of
what they have honestly, however blunderingly,
tried to do.

Upon a larger scale do we not know how in the
world at large there are the two kinds of men, the
fulfilling and the destroying men? There are some
men who call out the best of their brethren everywhere. There are men in history whose whole work
has been of this sort. They made the better parts of
human life seem possible and seem worth while. They
were like sunshine; and the plants under their influence lifted themselves up and hoped to live. When
such men died, they left the world more vital and
complete because they had lived in it. There are
other men whose whole mission is to destroy. The
things which they destroy are bad and ought to be
destroyed, but none the less the issue of the work
of such men is for disheartening and not for encouragement. We are rich in such men now-a-days, perhaps never more rich. They count the tares so loud
that the field grows ashamed of itself, and forgets to
tell itself that there is wheat. Alas, for the city, the
state, the nation or the church where mere de-
structive criticism has possession of men's tongues
and ears.

If any of you who are trying to do right are overcome sometimes by the abundance of criticism on your failures and the absence of recognition of your struggles, what shall you do? Rejoice that behind all your fellow-men is God! Rejoice that there is one soul so sensitive to good that no poor struggler, no weak child in any corner of this universe can make the slightest struggle after goodness without that great good soul's feeling it instantly and recognizing it with eagerness and joy. If I can know that I am strong, let all my brethren, if they will, see only the bad in me and not the good. I will not be indifferent to what they see. I will regret it and deplore it; but every effort which I make for righteousness shall fly past their indifference, and find God, and report itself to Him. Fixed in His sympathetic recognition, every such effort becomes a mark of attainment from which I cannot afterwards recede, and so with each such effort the gradual fulfilment of my life grows more complete.

The nobility and dignity of any work is measured by the powers which it demands and uses. And so, I think, that the greatness of the work of the fulfiller, as compared with the work of the destroyer, is indicated by the faculties and qualities which it requires. Destruction calls for nothing but hatred and vigor. Fulfilment calls for sympathy, intelligence, patience and hope. It is so easy to give the bruised reed one blow and break it, to put a summary hand upon the smoking flax and quench it. Just to stand up in the community, and abuse its meanness, or its irreligion, just to arraign some sinner and upbraid his drunkenness or his licentiousness, that is so easy. But to take the latent generosity, or the half-conscious religion of a community and educate it and encourage it, to take the remnants and the seeds of good which are in the poor, broken, besotted life of the wretched libertine, or drunkard, and rebuild them into a new career, that is so hard. The one needs only hatred and vehemence; the other needs love and intelligence and patience and hope. I know that the second is the nobler work, because of the nobler powers it demands. I know that it is better not merely for the soul which I try to fulfil, but also for my soul, that I should be the fulfiller and not the destroyer of my brother.

But there is one more truth, which we must remember, to make our statement with regard to fulfilment and destruction entirely complete. And that is, that fulfilment of itself involves destruction. The fulfilment of the good involves the destruction of the bad. Make anything in the world complete and perfect after its true nature, and you must thereby drive out whatever there is of falsehood and positive corruption in it. That statement does not deny the fact, nor change the character of sin. God forbid! I have no patience with the foolish talk which would make sin nothing but imperfection, and would preach that man needs nothing but to have his deficiencies supplied, to have his native goodness educated and brought out, in order to be all that God would have him be. The horrible incompetency of that doctrine must be manifest enough to any man who knows his own heart, or who listens to the tumult of wickedness which rises up from all the dark places of the earth. Sin is a dreadful, positive, malignant thing. What the world in its worse part needs is not be developed, but to be destroyed. Any other talk about it is shallow and mischievous folly. The only question is about the best method and means of destruction. Let the sharp surgeon's knife do its terrible work. Let it cut deep and separate as well and thoroughly as it can, the false from the true, the corrupt from the uncorrupt: it never can dissect away the very principle of corruption which is in the substance of the blood itself. Nothing but a new reinforcement of health can accomplish that. There is the whole story. Tear your sins away. Starve your tumultuous passions. Resist temptations. Aye, if you will, punish yourself with stripes for your iniquities. Cry out to yourself and to your brethren, with every voice that you can raise, "Cease to do evil;" but all the time, down below, as the deepest cry of your life, let there be this other, "Learn to do well." If you can indeed grow vigorously brave and true and pure; then cowardice and falsehood and licentiousness must perish in you. O wondrous silent slaughter of our enemies! O wondrous casting out of fear as love grows perfect! O death to sin, which comes by the new birth to righteousness! O destruction, which is but the utterance of fulfilment on the other side! O everlasting assurance, that evil has of right no place in the world: and that if good would only lift itself up to its completeness, it might claim the whole world and all of manhood for itself!

Therefore with all the strength which God has given us, let us be fulfillers. Let us try to make the life of the world more complete. What can we do? First, each of us can put one more healthy and holy life into the world, and so directly increase the aggregation of righteousness. That is much. To fasten one more link, however small, in the growing chain that is ultimately to bind humanity to God beyond all fear of separation, is very much indeed. And besides that, we can, with sympathy and intelligence, patience and hope, bring up the lagging side in all the vitality around us, and assert for man, the worth, the meaning and the possibility of this his human life. If all the men and women here were doing these two things, what a bright corner of the world this town, this church would be!

I have dwelt long on this most general statement of our truth, and my sermon is more than half done before I come to trace in several particulars how the method of fulfilment as distinct from the method of destruction, is, and always has been distinctively the method of the Christian faith. Let me do this as briefly as I can.

Christianity from the beginning adopted the method of fulfillment for its own propagation. It has wandered from it sometimes, but the inherent genius of its character has always brought it back to the idea that it was not directly to fight with and destroy the other religions of the world, but to satisfy the longings which these other faiths expressed, and to lead on the powers which those faiths were using, to their fuller development and loftier employment. Christ, in the eyes of the first preachers of Christianity, Christ in his own eyes, was so completely the Master of this world, so thoroughly the sum and culmination of all good in the world, that every good work was capable of being taken up into him and made to open in his light into before unconscious and unsuspected power. St. Paul, preaching at Athens, is the representative speaker of that truth; but it is everywhere in the New Testament. In its more vivid re-appearance, in its more unhesitating re-assertion, lies the hope and prospect of the future triumphs of the Gospel.

And as with regard to other religions, so with regard to that which does not call itself religion at all, so with that which, rejecting the very name of religion, calls itself simply morality. Here is a man who is trying to do right. He does not talk of God, he does not think of God. He simply tries to do right. That man is somewhere here this morning. What does Christ say to him? We need not be in doubt, for something very like his story is written in the Gospels. John said one day to Jesus, " Master, we saw one casting out devils in thy name, and we forbade him, because he followeth not with us." And Jesus said, Forbid him not; for he that is not against us is on our part." " He that is not against us is on our part." There are only two parties in this world, the party of the right and the party of the wrong.

He who is not for the wrong is for the right. The crudest, the least educated, the least developed, the most mistaken of the pleaders for the right, of the men who want to do right, is on the same side with the deepest soul, the most spiritually minded child of God, with Christ himself.

We can well imagine that Jesus afterwards found out this half-instructed caster-out of devils, and displayed Himself to him, and fulfilled his partial power, and made him one of his disciples. Certainly to the secular moralist He is forever going. That perpetual tendency of morality to become religion, to which all history bears witness, is but the continual effort of Christ to fulfil the imperfect. It fails again and again, but somewhere, sometime, it must succeed. If not here, then in some world of larger freedom and more light, the soul which has here earnestly struggled to do right simply because it is right, must see God and recognize face to face the power which it has always been dimly feeling, in blind obedience to which it has heroically lived. Surely there shall be no more touching or impressive sight upon the borders of the eternal life, than this, the unreligious doer of duty seeing God, understanding, perhaps in a lightning flash, whose is the authority which he has been obeying, whose is the strength on which he has been really resting all these years: and in one instant made religious, finding his imperfectness fulfilled with God, and casting himself in adoration and in love before the throne.

God sees our wickedness and pities it, through all his anger. God also sees our emptiness, and who can tell what is the feeling with which he looks at that. Our emptiness is our falling short of that which it is possible for us to be. It is not emptiness for us to be without that which it does not belong to our nature to possess. The pint measure is not empty that it does not hold a quart. The eagle is not empty of the power of running, nor the horse of the power of flying. Emptiness is defect. There is no defect where there is not a falling short of some original design. If you were not made to serve God out of love, the implanting in your life of loving service would not be the fulfilment of your life. It would be an addition to it. It would be as if you tied wings to the horse's shoulders, not as if you bade them spring out of the eagle's sides.

Do you not see the value which this gives to the declaration of Christ that he comes to be the fulfiller of the life of man? He comes to give us divine enthusiasms, celestial loves. But it is not as strange, unnatural things that he would give them. It is as the legitimate possessions of our human nature, as the possessions which, unconscious, undeveloped, are ours already. The kingliness of nature which the human side of the Incarnation declared to be man's possible life, the divine side of the Incarnation makes to be the actual life of every man who really enters into its power.

The same is true about that experience often so perplexing and distressing, in which one passes from a lower and a narrower to a higher and a broader form of faith or belief. These too Christ fulfils and does not destroy. Evidently such progress is possible. Many of us humbly rejoice in the belief that we have made such progress. And we believe in no portion of our lives have we more truly been under Christ's immediate guidance than in the making of that progress. But what became of the old faith? Did Christ destroy it as a useless thing, a poor delusion, too false for any soul to live in? Alas, for any one of us who sees no more in what he did for us than that! He who thinks so must look back on the years in which he lived in his old faith, and call them years of waste. How could it be that God let the soul of his child live so long in prison? But what if it were not a prison? What if I can think of the advance which God has made possible for me into a larger faith, not as the setting free out of a dungeon, but as the movement forward from the imperfectness of youth into the riper life of manhood? Call youth a prison, if you will. It is a prison whose walls are transparent hopes, and whose window-bars are sunbeams. There was no waste in those years of immaturity. It is easy to see that the years in which we believed narrowly and waited for the fulfilment which in part has come, were not wasted years, and it is not strange that God let his children remain in them so long!

I hate to hear a man who has passed out of a narrower into a larger faith, upbraid and revile the faith in which he used to live. It is making the Christ who has led him, to be not the fulfiller, but the destroyer. It is shutting the flood-gates between the past and the present, so that what the man is gets no help from what he used to be. What shall the man who thinks so about the past make of the future? Does he think there are no changes still awaiting him? Does he think he has attained all truth? If not, if there are new advances for him still to make, will the time come when on this which he is now, he will look back with the same hatred and scorn with which he looks back at this moment on his childhood's creed? The man who talks so is at heart a dogmatist. He has not learned the great truth of our Christianity, the truth of Christ, that that to which we belong is not an idea, however true, not a creed, however broad or narrow, but a friend, a father, God. Wherever God has given himself to us, that must be to us forever sacred ground. Whenever he has led us out from more imperfect into less imperfect truth, it has been fulfilment, not destruction of that in which he kept us living for awhile before we made the progress and saw the fuller light. God never destroys any real belief. When the Hindoo becomes a Christian, when the moralist becomes a Christian, when the narrow Christian becomes a broader Christian, it is a deeper heart in the old life that opens. The old creed, the old experience lives more truly, and does not die, as it gives place to the new.

How often, as you grow more earnest in your new faith, your old faith, which you seemed to have quite done with, re-appears and grows more sacred to you, and you are sure that it has not perished, but is living in the heart of what you now believe. You become sure that in the perfect earnestness of heaven, all that you ever thoroughly believed on earth will come back to you, and you will see that, however in your after life you rejected it, it was not in vain that you had once believed it. It will make part of your eternal faith. As I grow more and more earnest, I expect that my dead faiths will rise and show they are not dead. Let true faithfulness walk over the graves of a buried belief, and the dust of the long silent faith

> "Would hear her and beat,
>   Had it lain for a century dead—
> Would start and tremble under her feet."

They are not dead but sleeping, all that our hearts have ever truly, thoroughly believed.

Let us fill ourselves with Christ's conception of himself, and how full of richness and peace life becomes. Christ is always fulfilling us, while we wake and while we sleep, in work and rest, in joy and sorrow. He is always leading us forth into new and richer rooms of character and life and truth. Obedience, docility, perfect readiness to be led, that, that alone is what we want. May He give us that, and then fulfil us with Himself more and more, as our emptiness opens wider and His grace abounds more and more richly through all eternity.

SERMON XIII.

Make the Men Sit Down.

"And Jesus said, Make the men sit down."—JOHN vi. 10.

IT was on the farther side of the sea of Tiberias, a region which Christ seldom visited, a region which is to-day a wilderness. A multitude had followed the Lord across the water and were filling the empty place with crowd and clamor and confusion. Curiosity was all alive. What he had done last, what he would do next, was flying about in question and answer from mouth to mouth. The scene was full of movement. Every man was on his feet. Old friends were meeting. Christ's adherents were eagerly pleading for him. The enemies of Christ were violently claiming that he was an impostor. Gestures were furious; words came fast; faces glowed; eyes sparkled; feet hurried back and forth. Such is the picture which seems to paint itself before us in the first verses of this sixth chapter of St. John.

And then there comes a change. The midday sun grows hot. Hunger and exhaustion take possession of these excited frames. The need of rest overcomes the eagerness of action. And out of the midst of the flagging tumult comes the calm voice of Jesus, saying to his disciples who are closest to him, "Make the men sit down." And the disciples pass here and there through the crowd, doing their Master's will, until five thousand men are seated on the grass.

Then a new scene appears. Quiet has come in place of the noise; repose instead of action. Faces which just now were flushed and excited have grown calm. And, what is really at the heart of all, there is a change in the whole crowd's activity. It has become receptive. It is waiting to be fed. Not only with the barley loaves and fishes. The presence of Christ is before it and it receives that. By-and-by the words of Christ fall on it and it receives them, until at last there begins to break forth from the seated ranks the declaration that they have indeed received him, and they whisper to one another, "This is indeed the prophet that should come into the world."

This is the meaning which I find in the words of Jesus when he said to his disciples, "Make the men sit down." It is the change from the active and restless to the receptive and quiet state, from the condition in which all the life was flowing outward in eager self-assertion, to the other condition in which the life was being influenced, that is, being flowed upon by the richer power which came forth from him.

If we let our thought separate one individual out

of the multitude and dwell on him, we can feel what
I am speaking of more clearly. Here is a man who
has come down out of Capernaum and crossed the
lake and gone up after Jesus either as friend or foe.
He has wanted to say something, to do something,
to utter himself. He has been eager, active, confident, vehement. By-and-by one of the disciples, John
or Andrew or Bartholomew, has come to him as he
was standing vehemently arguing, or as he was
rushing hither and thither, shouting out his oracular
judgments, and has said to him, "The Master bids
you sit down and wait quietly until he feeds you."
Can you not see the change which comes over the
man's face? In a moment he finds himself silent in
the presence of a great divine graciousness, a wisdom and power which is active for him. The sense
of being fed, of having another's richness poured
forth on him, takes possession of his soul. With the
supply, the consciousness of needing to be fed grows
deeper. Self-sufficiency, self-assertion fades away
and is lost. Humility, docility, faith fills his whole
nature. It is a new man that hardly knows the
old. All this deepening and richening has come
since the word of Jesus bade him sit down and be
fed.

If I have made the suggestion of the story clear,
then we may almost entirely leave the story and pass
on to the subject of which I wish to speak to you this
morning. It is the need which comes to men of
simply being fed by God, of ceasing from forth-puttingness and self-assertion, and simply being recep-

tive to the influences which come to them from divinity.

Before I really begin to speak about that subject, I am moved to take my congregation into my confidence. I am moved to tell them of how a minister feels very often, and of how I feel to-day, what a great danger there is of the wrong people taking the wrong sermons to themselves. A minister preaches a sermon on the need of visible activity and utterance, and very often the man whose life needs meditation and quiet self-study takes the sermon to himself, and rushes forth to even more of wild and superficial action. Again the preacher preaches on the necessity and duty of quietude, and just the soul which needs to put forth in action the impulse which it has already quietly accumulated, plunges itself more profoundly into quiescent calm. We take each other's medicines and often increase instead of healing our diseases. Many a time one wants not to take back a sermon he has preached, but to send quickly after it another which shall preach the other truth, and find the souls for which this, and not the first, was meant. I can only beg each of you to listen conscientiously to-day, and see whether what I shall say is meant for you.

There is a danger then for many men, if not for all, in the perpetual outgo of energy which so much of our life involves. Life is made up of tasks and problems. How soon they meet us. How constantly they are with us all our days. "Come and do this," the world says to the little child, hardly more than a baby, holding out to him some of its crude material which needs to be transformed into some other shape. "Come and see what you think of this," she says again, holding up some hard and knotty problem, and bidding him exercise his ingenious intellect upon it. It is one process of education, the calling out of powers by their use. It is the tendency of all the practical necessities of life, the constant outward movement of activity. "All is going out, nothing is coming in;" is not that the dismay and the despair which settles down upon many an experience as it attains to middle life? Existence comes to feel to many of us like a great river, which is always flowing with unbroken force downward to the sea. It never stops. It is always pushing its waters outward. It gives the sea no chance to flow up into it. So is the ever energetic life of one whose sole idea is to exert influence, to make himself felt in some result. How often the river must long to pause. How often it must become aware that its impetuous rush is losing for it the richness of the great deep salt sea. How often the busy life of man becomes aware that somewhere round it there is richness which it does not get because it opens outward only, and not inward. How often it desires to pause and grow receptive, and take into itself the richness which it now is keeping out.

All this perhaps sounds very strange to some of us, this statement of the need of rest and receptivity. It will be good for us to stop a moment and remember that there are races, and there have been times to which it has been anything but strange, to which it has been the most familiar truth of life. You open the record of the Fourth Century and it is full of the pictures of hermits sitting on rough mountain sides, or beside the great silent river of Egypt, just listening for the voice of God. You let your boat drop quietly down the Ganges to-day, and along its banks the silent figures sit like carved brown statues, hour after hour, day after day, with eyes open and fixed on vacancy, clearing themselves of all thought, emotion and desire, that being emptied of self, they may see God. The most populous religion of the world to-day is that which flows out from the sacred seat, under the sacred tree at Gaya, where Buddha sat for six years silent, receptive, until the great illumination came. The East believes only too readily what the West finds it so very hard to realize and accept, that no life is complete which does not sometimes sit trustfully waiting to be fed by God.

Are there not times enough in all our western lives, in all our lives, simply because and so far as they are human lives, when this same necessity bears witness of itself to us all? The days of childhood, before action has begun; the days of old age, when action is over; in both of those times the soul is sitting before God. Childhood is full of wonder and expectancy. Sitting at the father's knee. looking up into his face, that is its truest picture. Old age is not at its best if it is simply retrospective. It has travelled across the continent and stands upon the border of the great Pacific Sea. It feels the leagues of weary delightful journeying behind it, but its face, as it waits upon the seashore, is towards the west, and not towards the east. God is speaking to it out of the awful emptiness of the ocean and the unknown richness of the lands beyond. The same is true of a great dismay, a great discovery, a great sorrow or a great joy. Can we find a truer description of that which has taken place some day, in the homes of all of you into whose faces I am looking now, than is included in the figure which I used a while ago? Some day the headlong current of your life was stopped. The river ceased to flow. The waves stood still, and then the ocean which the flowing of the river had kept out, poured up and in, and there were sacreder emotions in the old channels, and deeper hopes and fears beating upon the well-worn banks. The day when your great bereavement came—the day when the neighbors knew that death was in your house—the day when joy, with that subtle look of the possibility of deep pain which is always in her eyes, came to your door and knocked, in the first splendor of the rising sun—the day when being weak and ill you did not go to your business, and the streets which you knew so well seemed strange to you as you looked out of the window: those were the days when God was feeding you. You lost the sense of being one who was to act, and you were one to whom God was to do something. You were for the time all oriental then.

How sacred and rich afterwards become the rooms where such experiences have taken place. The stream may start again and push the intrusive ocean once more back into its bed, but the river-channel can never quite forget its overflow. The house may go back to its common uses, and its doors open and shut upon the comers and goers of ordinary life, but it will never be quite the same that it was before the day on which the unseen presence filled it. It can never be perfectly secular again. This is the way in which the new houses which are so crude and raw when we move into them mellow and ripen as the years go on; as the earth which is so harsh and earthly in the glare of noontide, is softened and richened by the ever-returning dusk of morning and evening, in which it seems as if it once had been, and might again be, heaven.

I want you to notice, with regard to this blessedness of a pause in the outflowing energy of life, that it applies not merely to what we call our secular occupations, but to our sacred and religious ones as well. Indeed it often seems as if there were a sense in which it might be said that nothing so tended to keep God out of our lives as work for God done in a wrong and superficial spirit. This is one of the places where I am most anxious that the right people should take my sermon to themselves, and not the wrong ones. The Scripture reader, the Sunday School teacher, the Evangelist, the minister, the working layman, all of them I am sure have felt how religious work tries to push out religious thought and to kill the soul's receptivity. Thought made practical, turned into duty, tends to become like air turned into wind. That which was the most yielding and penetrable of all substances, becomes the most impenetrable. There is no man whom I should less hope to teach the deeper spiritual truth, or to lead into the tenderest communion with God, than the man who with a hard set doctrine of salvation is most intensely devoted to the salvation of his fellow-men. The disciples as well as the stragglers from Capernaum—perhaps the busy disciples more than anybody else in all the crowd—must have needed Christ's call to sit down and be fed. The more earnestly you are at work for Jesus, the more you need times when what you are doing for him passes totally out of your mind, and the only thing worth thinking of seems to be what He is doing for you. That is the real meaning of the days of discouragement and self-contempt which come to all of us, O fellow laborers for the Lord.

More precious then perhaps to one kind of worker than to another, but yet precious always and to all, are the days or moments when the flow of the river slackens, and the ocean pours itself up into the stream. I wish that I could speak effectively to all the busy young men here, and make them value those moments in their lives. None of you young men are so busy that you are always the slaves of your trades or business. You have your evenings. You have your Sundays. You have stray moments and half-hours here and there. You have your sickness now and then. Make them times for the real feeding of your minds and souls. Have associates and friends outside of the limits of your own profession, as able and intelligent young men as you can find, to whom life means other things from what it means to you, and who can help you to enlarge its meaning for yourself. Be interested in some pursuit which will take you into quite unfamiliar fields. Make yourself at home in the Public Library, that great organ-forest of sweet and solemn and inspiring sounds, which will speak to us if we come and sit and are hungry for its music. Let the country, when you can, scatter the cobwebs of the city out of your brain and send you back to its richer life refreshed and simplified. Above all, let the peace of God, the peace of trust and love, the peace of religion, flow in upon your consciousness the moment that business care gives it a moment's freedom. Whenever necessary thought of self gives way for an hour, O how good it is if the thought of the Father instantly, without waiting to be summoned, takes possession of the child.

And now it is time for us to see whether we cannot go a little deeper into our subject than we have gone thus far. I should do little credit to your thoughtfulness if I did not believe that you had felt the difficulty in what I have been saying. I have pointed out how the active life needs oftentimes to stop and sit down and become receptive. That is all true enough; but if we state it as the sum of the whole matter, we feel its imperfection. It makes a spotted and spasmodic life, a life which is forever expecting alternations of exhaustion and repair. " Go on," it seems to say, " live for awhile your outgoing life, and then, when that has gone on long enough, stop and accumulate new strength, and then start out and use it," and so go on, "getting and spending;" and so you will surely in the end, "lay waste your powers." It makes spiritual supply almost like the dinner for which you leave your workshop, only to hasten back to the place of toil again when the hurried meal is done.

There must be something better than that. The question inevitably rises in the mind of any active thinking man, Is it not possible instead of working and resting, to rest in working, so that in the very act which exhausts, I shall get my renewal and supply? How good that would be! That would make the feeding of life by God, the divine supply of life, to be not like the eating of a dinner, which is exceptional and an interruption of the life, but like the breathing of the vital air which is going on all the time, and is not done deliberately, or as a special act, but does itself, as it were, by the movement of those same lungs which the exercise of labor sets in motion.

Let us see whether we can make this plain. Here is a man who, we may say, is engaged in a wholly secular employment. He is a merchant selling goods. At the same time he is a distinctly and devoutly Christian man. He loves Christ, and knows that he must have Christ for his helper and his friend. But all the day he is completely busy at his store. He knows how his life always is outgoing. He longs for something to come in, something diviner and more spiritual. What can he do? Once in awhile he turns aside. He shuts the door. He leaves the business to take care of itself. As truly as if he went into a desert cave, he goes apart. He makes his Sunday genuinely sacred. He consecrates his hour of prayer. What happens then? The blessing surely comes. The ocean hears the stopping of the stream, and knows its opportunity. God comes and feeds the docile and expectant life, and it goes back to counting-house and counter, stronger, purer, greater. That is very good. The man will sell goods more nobly for the peace of God which he has gained in the desert. But just suppose that he did not have to go to the desert for the peace. Suppose that he could have not merely used devoutness, and faith, and piety in the store, but actually gained them there. Suppose that in the compass of one single specific mercantile transaction, there could actually have been present the two sides of this man, one alert, watchful, active, standing on its feet; the other humble, hungry, receptive, sitting down in the very compass of that action before God: would not that surely have been better? Would it not have brought the food nearer to the hunger? Would it not have kept the man's unity, which it is one of the worst tendencies of life to divide and lose? Would it not have made his business sacred and his devotion intensely practical at once?

And then is an ordinary business action possibly large enough to be thus at the same time the exercise of the merchant's activity and also the medium through which God feeds the merchant's soul? Before we give an answer to that question, we must stop and force ourselves to remember that a whole act includes its motive. An act of yours is not simply the thing you do. It is also the reason why you do it. Make the conception of the act as large as that, and then I think it certainly may include all that I said. Why are you selling your goods? If without falsehood you can say, " Because it is my duty, in order that I may maintain my family and serve my generation and honor God by usefulness," then certainly the act opens itself and becomes a Church. It is the house of God. It is the gate of heaven. God is there in that act; and your soul doing its work for Him, is humbly in His presence; and the soul cannot be humbly in the presence of God without being receptive of Him. In every act consciously and devoutly done for God's sake, God gives himself to the soul and feeds it, in the act; not after it and in reward of it, but *in* it.

What is the reason then that our ordinary actions are not able to do this, at the same time to exercise the actor's power and to be the medium through which God can feed the actor's soul? Is it not simply that our ordinary act is not complete? It is not the whole act. It is only the body of act, and not the soul. It is the form of the act, without the motive. That is the reason why it is too small to hold this inflowing force as well as the outgoing influence. Make your most simple act complete; do your most common daily duty from its divinest motive, and what a change

will come! Still your life will need days of retirement,
when it will shut the gates upon the noisy whirl of
action and be alone with God. But it will not be
upon them that it will mostly depend for spiritual
nourishment. They will be like great exceptional
banquets and extraordinary feasts of grace. The
daily bread of spiritual life, the ordinary feeding of
the soul on God, which really makes its sustenance,
will be in the perpetual doing of the works of life
for Him. The real sitting down to be fed will be
mysteriously identical with the most eager and
energetic standing on the feet to do His will!

Behold the meeting of the effective and the receptive life. I told about the East all given to contemplation and the waiting for the coming God, and
of the West, all full of self-reliance and the stir of
action. The Ganges and the Mississippi, what different scenes of human life they see! We might
have seen in the same way how between two centuries of the same race's history, or between two men in
the same century, or between two moods of the same
man, there lies this picturesque and striking difference. One is energetic, forever sending out force
upon the world. The other is receptive, always
drinking in influence from God. Such differences
there will always be. But behind and beneath all
such differences, there will always be this other
truth, that in each single race, or age, or man, or act,
if the fullest life were there, the effective and the
receptive capacities would each be present, and the
two would minister to one another. The Ganges and

the Mississippi, in the complete world, will have subterranean communication with each other, and the two together will unite to make glad the city of God. Rest and action in the experience of the completest soul are not antagonistic; they are hardly distinct from one another. Action is the most refreshing rest, and rest is in some sense the most effective action to the soul that lives on complete dependence and obedience to God.

There are few features in the life of Jesus which impress me more than this: the way in which his work and his growth, his effective and receptive life went on together. What he did for man and what his Father did for him, were not separate parts of his life. They were enfolded in the same experiences. True, there were times when he withdrew himself, and, leaving all activity behind, lay on the mountain days and nights, passive before his Father, waiting to be more completely filled with him. But those were rare, exceptional occasions. The ordinary dependence upon God was perfectly expressed by those words to his disciples, "My meat is to do the will of him that sent me!" When he gave the Sermon on the Mount, when he calmed the tempest on the lake, when he raised Lazarus from the dead, we do not doubt that both processes were going on, enfolded in the completeness of each of those actions. He was saving the world, and he was becoming more perfectly his Father's Son at once. And at the last, what is it that makes the perfect wonder of the cross? Is it not the double assurance that in those agonies, under that darkness, the world is being redeemed and the Son of Man is being glorified, both at once. The "It is finished" told of the completion of his nature and the completion of his work together. Nay, it is even more intimate than that. The completion of His nature was the completion of his work, and the completion of his work was the completion of his nature. He could not have completely been the Son of God without saving the world, and he could not have completely saved the world without being completely the Son of God.

So labor and patience, activity and the growth which comes by passive suffering, ought always to make one single total life. Some of you will remember how in the old church at Innsbruck, among the magnificent bronze people who stand about the tomb of the Emperor Maximilian, is the great Godfrey of Boulogne, the illustrious crusader. Upon his head he wears his helmet, and on the helmet rests a crown of thorns. The strange conjunction may mean many things. No doubt the crown of thorns is meant to represent the sacred cause, the rescue of the place of the Lord's crucifixion and burial, for which the soldier fought. But is not such a union of symbols a perpetual picture? The helmet and the crown of thorns! Activity and suffering, fighting and growing, the putting forth of energy and the drinking in of strength; these two were represented not as coming in by turns, not as chasing one another into and out of the life, but as abiding together, making one temper, filling one character. The helmet and the crown of thorns worn together on the consecrated head, that makes the noble, useful, growing life.

Is not this essentially the great promise which is given us about the eternal blessedness? We are told of heaven, that there is no temple there to which the worshippers go up. There will be no turning aside to refresh the exhausted reverence and faith and love; no special feast times in the everlasting festival, but in the very acts of service the souls, all afire with love for Him they serve, shall drink His love and wisdom into their open natures. "His servants shall serve him, and his name shall be in their foreheads." The effective life and the receptive life are one. No sweep of arm that does some work for God but harvests also some more of the truth of God, and sweeps it into the treasury of the life.

We must anticipate heaven, and make earth as like to it as possible.

May not two lessons come to us out of what I have said to-day?

The first is this. Seek your life's nourishment in your life's work. Do not think that after you have bought or sold or studied or taught, you will go into your closet and open your Bible and repair the damage and the loss which your day's life has left you. Do those things certainly, but also insist that your buying or selling or studying or teaching shall itself make you brave, patient, pure and holy! Do not let your occupation pass you by, and only leave you the basest and poorest of its benefits, the money with which it fills your purse. Compel it to give up to you the charity and faith and character and godliness which it has at its heart, which it hides charily, but which it must give to you if you insist upon it and are able to receive it.

The other lesson is: Make your most restful contemplation and your most receptive listening at the lips of God, not to be mere spiritual luxuries, but to be forms and modes of action. Make them acts. Let them call your powers into play. Let them be not listless, but full of vigor. Let them anticipate work for God and service of his children so earnestly and eagerly, that they themselves shall be work and service.

He who learns these lessons lives a life as deep as the ocean and as powerful. There is no tedium or fretfulness for him. His life catches the quality of the life of God. He works while it is called to-day, and yet he has already reached the rest which remaineth for God's people. Such lives may God help us to live.

SERMON XIV.

Timeliness.

"He hath made everything beautiful in his time."
ECCLESIASTES iii. 11.

FITNESS or timeliness is one strong element in every idea of beauty. A place for everything and everything in its place, a time for everything and everything in its time, these are the principles that lie at the bottom of that enjoyment of things which we call a sense of beauty. There is nothing which has such absolute self-contained loveliness that we can say of it that it would be lovely everywhere and always. Put it into certain surroundings, throw certain lights upon it and it would seem ugly. The writer of the Book of Ecclesiastes reverses this truth, gives us the other side of it. He says that there is nothing so essentially unbeautiful that, put into its true place and time, it would not become beautiful. The disorder of the universe, the things that shock us and distress us and disgust us in it, come not from the essential badness of the material of the universe, but from its dislocations. It is in the disarrangement of what needs arrangement. It is the stoppage of the machine by some part of its own machinery which has wrenched itself out of position and got between the wheels. It is the spoiling of the picture by the casting of the strong color here which was needed there. These are what make the mischief in the world and what destroy its beauty. Our own instincts of beauty recognize the law. They demand harmony and timeliness and fitness. They are not chained to any conventional standards. They are willing to see things in new arrangements, provided they are recognized when they are seen as natural and fit arrangements. But the shock and startle which comes from the sight of unnatural arrangements, from seeing things out of place, this the pure taste discriminates at once, and knows that what creates it is not beautiful but grotesque, and that the pleasure, if it gives any, is not healthy.

The necessity of timeliness or fitness to the truest beauty, and the beauty of everything in its true time and place, these then are the two sides of the truth of which I wish to speak to-day. I will not speak abstractly. I will come closely enough to practical matters of our daily life. It is a truth which has its applications everywhere. It touches what we may almost dare to call the responsibility of God. If the good and evil, the benefit and harm of things is not in things themselves, but in the places where they are put, then not on God who made the things of which the world is full, but upon man, who with his free will is always shifting things to suit himself, must lie the blame of the injury things do him. You lay your own stumbling block in your own way. God made the block indeed, but He made it for a part of the strength and beauty of the walls. It was you who dragged it down to the floor and insisted upon laying where you could stumble over it.

And again it touches the old question of failure or success in life. It lets us see why it is very often not the best furnished but the best arranged life that succeeds, not the richest but the most timely life; which is something that so often puzzles us.

And again it knits things into an interdependence with one another which is pleasing to the human mind. It rescues the universe from fragmentariness and shows us how "all is needed by every one, nothing is good or fair alone." In all these ways this truth, that everything is beautiful in its time, and nothing is beautiful out of its time, comes close home to our lives.

And one thing is very striking about this truth, which indeed is characteristic always of the highest truths, that it becomes more manifestly true in things in proportion as their nature rises. It is less manifest in the lower, and more manifest in the higher natures. See what I mean. Everything in the world must be in its true place and time, or it is not beautiful. That is true from the lowest to the highest; only with the lowest it is not easy to discover it. It does not seem to matter where the pebble lies, on this side of the road or on the other. It may indeed do sad mischief out of its place; but its place is a wide one. It may lie in many spots and do no harm, and seem to show all the beauty and render all the use of which it is capable. But the things of higher nature are more fastidious in their demands. The plant must have its proper soil to feed its roots upon, or its bright flowers lose their beauty, and even there, only in one short happy season of the year is it in its glory, while the pebble keeps its lustre always. Higher still, comes the animal, and he has more needs which must be met, more arrangements that must be made, a more definite place in which he must be set, before he can do his best. Some sort of a home to live in, some faint beginning of society, some growth and education, bring him to his best beasthood. And then highest of all comes man, and with his highest life comes the completest dependence upon circumstances. He is the least independent creature on the earth. The most beautiful in his right time and place, he is the most wretched and miserable out of it. He is the most liable to be thrown out of place of all the creatures. He must have all the furnishings of life, friendships, family, ambitions, cultures of every kind, or his best is not attained.

And this same law holds between different kinds of men. The highest natures are most dependent upon timeliness and fitness. They must act at the right moment. There are such things as right moments for them. Have you not been often struck by seeing how a commonplace and ordinary man will fall in with the world anywhere, and make himself at home and be at ease and use his powers very satisfactorily, while a man far his superior will stand waiting and awkward, apparently quite unable to get to work, until, by-and-by, all of a sudden, his opportunity arrives, and instinctively he knows it and falls to work, and in an hour has done more than the other did in days. It is not mere fastidiousness. It is not conceit. Fastidiousness and conceit are the shams and imitations of which this is the genuine. Fastidiousness betrays itself by its self-consciousness and by its unwillingness to step in, even when the true time has come. We all know this difference of men. There are men about us who we feel might have lived at any age from Abraham's time down to ours, and they would have been just as much at home in any of the strange old centuries as they are here. A little change of dress, a little different manners, a different language, and that would be all the alteration. But there are other men whom you cannot transfer. They belong here and now. You are sure that in any other time their lives must have been hampered and dumb. Now they find voice and power, because their time is come.

When the great feast was ready at Jerusalem, and the brethren of Jesus were going up from Nazareth, as they went every year, they urged Jesus to go with them. And his answer was, "My time is not yet come, but your time is always ready." There was something so sad and so noble in his words. They, with no recognized mission, might go when and where they would. They, with no burden on their shoulders, might walk freely over the whole earth. But he, with his task, his duty, his Father's name to glorify, his brethren's souls to save, the kingdom of heaven to set up, he must wait till the door opened. He could walk only where the way was wide enough for him to pass with his burden. Nothing can be farther from the coveted ideal which hangs before the eyes of multitudes of our young men, the easy, ready man of the world, who is at home anywhere, with a conscience that can pass through any crack, with convictions that can turn to any color, with the self-possession that succeeds everywhere; nothing can be farther from him than Jesus was, with his clear purposes and strong truth and mission of God. O that you all could learn that! Such universal popularity, such universal adaptability is not the highest character or life. As you emphasize your life, you must localize and define it. The more truly and earnestly you come to do anything, the more clearly you will see that you cannot do everything. He who is truly good must be good for something. To be good for everything is to be good for nothing. The strength of a life makes up for and glorifies its specialness. The dog with his kennel full mocks at the lion with his solitary whelp. "Yes, only one, but a lion," answers the proud beast. Always the higher a life is, the more it is beautiful in its place, and can be beautiful nowhere else.

It belongs then to the highest and most gifted lives, to seek their places in the world. It is the prerogative of their superiority. Surely it would be good for men if they could learn this early. It would scatter many delusions. It would dissipate the folly of universal genius. The tendency of our time is to special education, to find what every man is fit for and to train him specially for that. It may be carried to excess. It may be made too narrow. In their desire for special culture men may cut off those streams of education which, flowing in from distant regions upon every side, supply and feed the current of the special life. The special life may be too narrowly conceived. That is of course the danger. But still we cannot help rejoicing in the increasing prominence of the idea that every being whom the world contains has his true place, written in the very make of his nature, and that to find that place and fill it is success for him. To help him find that place and make him fit to fill it, is the duty of his educators in all their various degrees.

Such an idea is always tending to become religious, is always on the brink of faith. It does not seem possible for men to permanently hold it and yet be satisfied with a chance-governed world. Who made the nature and the work for one another? Who touched the unborn soul and the undone task with such harmonious colors that, when by-and-by they met, their colors recognized each other, and blended into a beauty of active life, which all the world could see? The whole idea is full of God. Men may state it as atheistically as they will, they cannot get God out of it. Like every assertion of order in the universe, it must ultimately be an assertion of Him.

And then again, the constant holding of such an idea about a man's own life is always tending to make a man personally religious. The man who thinks he is an accident, and has no place, grows flippant with his life. But all that made the lives of Moses and David, John and Paul and Luther, serious, responsible, devout, comes to the humblest man who is able to believe in a true place, a true calling for himself. It must come to the whole world, making it lofty, earnest, tuning its whole music to a higher key, when this truth of the beauty, the necessity of timeliness shall grow everywhere clear.

So seek your place and fill it. You know the satisfactory feeling that we all have when one of the universal men who has been good at everything and so good for nothing, who has been slipping about loosely over the surface of life, in everybody's way, for years, at last suddenly finds the hollow he was made for and drops into it and fits it. It is an immense satisfaction and relief. Perhaps it seems at first as if he had disappeared; but by-and-by we find that he has been taken up by the great system of life and made a portion of it. His movement becomes orderly, makes part of the universal rhythm. He has found his time and place, and become beautiful. There are children in your households, boys in your schools, the very best boys there, who make the most trouble because, being the best boys, the largest, strongest characters, they most need to find their place. They most truly have a place to find. The average commonplace boy fits in almost anywhere, and makes no trouble. But in that graceless, awkward, interfering character there is the real pivot, which if you can help into its right place, will help to hold the structure of the world together and let many other characters revolve upon it.

So much we say of men, of human beings in or out of their true place and time. But let us now pass on to something else. Let us go on to see how everything, all the events of life, all of God's dispensations, get their real beauty or ugliness from the times in which they come to us or in which we come to them. We are always giving things absolute arbitrary characters. This thing is good, that thing is bad, we say; but really badness or goodness, beauty or ugliness are not in things themselves, but in the ways those things relate themselves to us. Look at trouble, look at temptation. They are not beautiful, surely, we say. The calm soul, living its peaceful life upon the sunny plain, gathering its flowers, singing its gentle songs, sees stalking up towards it, hiding the sunlight from it, casting its shadow far before itself, the great figure of a coming woe. Does it seem beautiful? Can the arms open to welcome it? See how the form withers and seems to shrink, drops in upon itself with terror as the trouble comes on pitilessly. But by-and-by when it has come, when the soul smitten by it has had to lay hold with new strength on Christ, when the superficial things of life have all been blown away and the real precious things of life have been displayed anew under the tempest—what then? Is there no beauty in the trouble then? Ask many a heart who never knew what spiritual beauty was until it saw it under the form of timely sorrow.

Even punitive sorrow, punishment, has a beauty about it which men are not slow to feel. When a man has been sinning and sinning on, and when at last an exposure and pain comes, and then by the shame and purification of that suffering another life begins, is there anything more beautiful than that pain standing there "in his place" between the old life and the new, between the sin and the restoral? It is beautiful with reference to the past. It satisfies man's feeling about the necessary consequence of sin, and it is beautiful with reference to the future. It clears the field for the new things that are to come.

If there is one thing especially of which many people cannot possibly believe that under any circumstances it should seem beautiful, I suppose it must be death. That must be always dreadful. Men seldom see any misery in life so great as to outweigh the misery of leaving it. But yet it comes to all of us that He who made death made it like all things else to be beautiful in his place and time. When a life has lived its days out in happiness, grown old with constantly accumulating joys, and then at last, before decay has touched it or the ground grows soft under its feet, the door opens and it enters into the new youth of eternity: when a young man has tried his powers here and dedicated them to God, and then is called to the full use of their perfected strength in the very presence of the God whom he has loved: when a man has lived for his brethren, and the time comes that his life cannot help them any longer, but his death can put life into dead truths and send enthusiasm into fainting hearts: when death comes as rest to a man who is tired with a long fight, or as victory to a man who leaves his enemies baffled behind him on the shore of time, in all these times is not death beautiful? "Nothing in all his life became this man like his leaving it," they said of one who died.

Look at the death of Christ. Men said, "It is terrible. It is disgraceful." Christ himself shrank and trembled at it. It was what we call a violent, an untimely death, but it was really in its true time, and all the world has felt its beauty. For Jesus it was victory and peace. For the world it was salvation and new life. On the evening of Good Friday, in spite of all their pain and disappointment, His mother and disciples must have begun to feel already how beautiful it was.

We transport ourselves to God's standpoint and imagine how He must think about it all. To Him, seeing the whole, seeing both worlds, the passage from one to the other must be as natural as is the passage from one period of this life to another. A man may be unprepared for it, and so the passage from boyhood into manhood may be a dreadful, ruinous thing. A man may be unprepared for it, and so the passage from time into eternity may be dreadful and ruinous, like any other passage, but in itself not one more than the other. One, like the other, is the summons of God, to come on, to come up, to something richer, larger, more complete.

One law applies in full to the coming of different stages in the life of man. Each period of life is beautiful in its time. Old age is beautiful when men are really old, and youth when men are really young; but everybody feels the lack of beauty when the character of either period is transferred into the years of the other. A precocious boy and a young old man alike repel us with an incongruity. This is why boys shun their companion who is solemn and wise beyond his years, and men laugh at a man who does not know how to grow old, but keeps the ways of youthfulness long after the freshness of youth which gave them all their charm is past. It seems as if life might all be so simple and so beautiful, so good to live, so good to look at, if we could only think of it as one long journey, where every day's march had its own separate sort of beauty to travel through; and so if we could go on clinging to no past, accepting every new present as it comes, finding everything beautiful in its time, and suiting ourselves to each new beauty with continual growth. And that can come to pass in the soul that really loves and lives in a living, loving God.

There are continual applications of our truth—the necessity of timeliness to beauty—in the religious life. "Everything beautiful in his time," says God. Then each experience of Christian life is good and comely in its true place, when it comes in the orderly sequences of Christian growth, and only there; not beautiful when it comes artificially, forced in where it does not belong. It would do many Christians great good to learn that truth. A young Christian, just beginning the new life, earnest and glowing and immature, loving Christ deeply, but not having yet fathomed his helpfulness, hears some old saint telling of the calm trust in the Saviour which has grown strong in long experience of guidance and mercy. The ardent boy, full of his hopes and fears, gazes upon that tranquil peace, and is fascinated by it. He wonders why it is not his. Perhaps he tries to make believe that it is his, to drill himself into an imitation of it. But no! Everything in its time! That is the grace of ripened life. It will not come to the young experience. The efforts to make it come, the imitations of it, are unreal and bad.

And so again the other way. The aged Christian, full of the peace of eventide, with the long shadows lying back upon the life that he has lived, will often grow anxious and discouraged because the glow and thrill and eagerness of his first faith has passed away. This simply trusting Christ and resting in his love, seems dull and spiritless, beside the excited fervor of his first conversion. And so with some galvanic movement, he tries to reproduce the quick excited activity which he remembers.

So the soul that God has been training into happy confidence sees another soul which God has been shaking with alarms, and reproaches itself because it is so tranquil, fears because it cannot fear.

So the soul which God is training in solitude thinks its life wasted because it is cut off from society, and the soul that God keeps in the very midst of its fellows sighs for the joy and culture of being alone.

If we could only know that in its time only is any Christian mood or condition beautiful, and that God only knows its time! When the day is over the stars will come, and then it is good to see them; but to see them before that, in the sunlight, you must go, men say, down to the bottom of a well, where you do not belong, which is unnatural and unhealthy. When we have done with earth the heaven will come; and, till that, only such heaven—and it is not a little—as is possible upon the dear old earth.

We ought to learn everywhere not to value moods for their own sakes, and so not to try to produce them. They are mere symptoms. Not symptoms, but disease and health, are the important things. People are always setting their hearts on one particular grace or quality, and thinking that it is the perfect character, and so cultivating it and practicing it in the same form under all circumstances indiscriminately. That is what makes the one-sided and misshapen men that we see everywhere. One man says, "Self-reliance is a noble, manly thing," and so his whole notion of strong life is to be self-reliant everywhere, and he becomes totally undocile and arrogant. He is as self-reliant in forming his ideas about the truths of God and eternity, as he is in deciding about a turn of the market or the chances of a bargain. His self-reliance ceases to be respectable, and grows distressing when it stands up unabashed in the presence of the most sacred mysteries.

Or, it may be, doubt and hesitation seem beautiful to you—as sometimes indeed they are—but you take it for granted that they are always good, and by-and-by, you are weak where you ought to be strong; you are hesitating where you ought to be acting. And all the world is sneering at you, and you deserve its sneers.

Or levity, which has its graceful places among pleasant trifling things, is brought in among sacred and awful truths, and how ugly its jesting face and tinsel dress and tinkling bells appear!

Or subtlety, which has its province in curious questions of the intellect, begins to meddle with the clear questions of the conscience, with principle, with right and wrong, and it is disagreeable and repulsive.

No! no one mood is the whole character. Truth, courage, these are universal; but the moods that these create are always changing. The same truthfulness which makes a man bold at one time, will make him fearful at another. What we need is to be simply courageous and truthful men, and let the forms in which our manhood shows itself freely vary with the varying circumstances, each beautiful in its own time. We may lose what men call consistency, but we shall keep what is better—truth and freedom, without which there can be no growth.

Again, it seems as if this truth of ours lay at the

bottom of any clear notion about the character of sin. We say that we are sinful, but really we are always passing over the essential sinfulness into the things around us. It is these wicked things that make us wicked. But here comes up our truth, that there are no wicked things; that wickedness is not in things, but in the displacement and misuse of things; that there is nothing which, kept in its true place and put to its true use, is not beautiful and good. Here is a man who says his business makes him selfish. Coward that he is, he meanly lays the blame of his mean life upon his merchandise and ledgers. But no such pretense will pass. In the next store to him there is a brother merchant, who out of just the same business, has been growing charitable and generous and larger-hearted every year. Here is a woman who says that society is responsible for her frivolousness; that no one can be purely earnest who lives in the midst of this fashionable world. But some other woman by her side confutes her, for she has shown how full social life may fill the character of what is best and sacredest. Here is a man who tells me that no student of physical science can be cognizant of spiritual life or reverent of spiritual forces. On his rocks and bones he lays the blame of his godlessness. But some reverent disciple of a spiritual master convicts him, as he shows how from the deepest study of the laws of God, the soul may come to an ever profounder faith in the God of law. In every case we wretchedly impute sin to things. But when we once are taught that things cannot be sinful—that

sin is a quality which can only belong to wills—
then back upon our wills falls the stigma which we
have tried to cast off on the inanimate material with
which we have to do. The much abused things seem
to lift up their heads and fling back the disgrace
which we have tried so ignominiously to shift from
ourselves to them. The shops cry out indignantly,
"We do not make the misers." Society declares, "I
do not make the triflers." The rocks and bones protest, " We do not make the atheists." They all hold
up the noble uses to which they might have been
put, and say, "Who was it that chose to prostitute
us and degrade us?" Back on the wills of men,
where it belongs, falls the responsibility of sin, and
the convicted soul, instead of going about any longer
complaining that God has put it into such a wicked
world, and abusing the sinfulness of things, owns
its own wickedness, and in clear-sighted, manly penitence cries out, "God be merciful to me a sinner."

This last idea has its encouraging and hopeful side.
The soul, wanting to get away from sin, has not to
make its escape out of a wilderness of sinful things,
in whose midst it is impossible to be good. The
sin is in the man himself. He must be changed, and
then these things about him, just the same things
still, change also with his altered life. He finds
them capable of unguessed uses. The hammer with
which he once destroyed, and in which it seemed to him
as if the spirit of destruction lay, he finds now yielding easily to his new desire to build. How deep the
old story of Genesis goes! The earth which sin

Timeliness. 261

turned to a wilderness, holiness turns back again into a garden! For sin and holiness are not in things, but in souls; and all things are beautiful in the time when a soul uses them for holy uses with a loving, humble, and obedient life.

Let this be then the word with which we close. The human soul sits at the centre of everything, and Christ sits at the centre of the human soul. If he changes us, then everything will be changed to us. "He that sitteth upon the throne saith, Behold I make all things new!" If the world is ugly and bitter and cruel to you: if circumstances taunt and persecute you: if everything you touch is a strain and a temptation, do not stand idly wishing that the world were changed. The change must be in you. To the new heart all things shall be new. The new man shall see already the new heaven and the new earth. If any man be in Christ, he is a new creature; and the new creature is immediately in the new creation. Some of you know already by daily experience what that means. And for all of you, it waits to be revealed, if you will let Christ do His work in you.

SERMON XV.

The Sword bathed in Heaven.

"For my sword shall be bathed in heaven."—ISAIAH xxxiv. 5.

IN a magnificent passage of his prophecy, Isaiah is denouncing the anger of God against the enemies of His people and His purposes. Jehovah Himself speaks in the glowing verse. The imagery is tremendous. "Their slain shall be cast out and their stink shall come up out of their carcasses, and the mountains shall be melted with their blood." How sharp and clear and definite is the Bible picture of the wrath of God! We, in these modern days, dwell most upon the inevitable issues which are involved in the very nature of things. The good moves against the evil and must in the end destroy it. It is a vehement, impetuous and fiery movement, but it is abstract. It is the fight of principle with principle. The Bible is all different from that. "God is angry with the wicked every day." It is a great and passionate Person, whose feeling fills the earth with tumult, who in rage and indignation sets right the evils of the earth and punishes the sons of men for their wrong-doing.

We must be fully in the power of this intense personal conception of God before we can enter into the force of the words which I have chosen for my text this morning. God is about to smite the wickedness of the earth. His sword is in His hand. And then, as a part of the terrible announcement, there comes these words: "My sword shall be bathed in heaven." What does that mean? It draws back the curtain which separates the visible world from the invisible. It reveals celestial regions in which there are also great struggles going on. It lifts up our eyes to the grander movements of the vast world of spirits. And then it declares that the sword which is to be used in fighting what seems to be the petty wars of the Hebrews and the Edomites, is the same sword which has been used in these celestial conflicts; that the means and instruments of righteousness upon the earth must be the same with the means and instruments of righteousness in the heavens.

This is the meaning, I think, of the great words, "my sword shall be bathed in heaven." Another glowing translation of the same words makes them read, "my sword has become intoxicated in heaven." It is not an uncommon figure, this strong picture of the intoxicated instruments of war. You remember the song of Moses in Deuteronomy, where Jehovah is heard declaring, "I will make my arrows drunk with blood." You remember how God in the prophecy of Jeremiah declares, "This is the day of the Lord God of Hosts, a day of vengeance, that he may avenge him of his adversaries, and the sword shall devour, and it shall be satiate and made drunk with their blood."

Here then is God pictured as the mighty conqueror who on other fields has already subdued his enemies with the only weapons which it is possible for him to use, with the absolute righteousness and truth. With those same weapons, all ablaze and living and eager from the fight in which they had been engaged, he declares that he will fight his battles on earth. It shall be a sword bathed in heaven which shall "come down upon Idumea."

We pause a moment and let ourselves think of this suggested vision of the universe all full of moral struggle. We can know nothing of what that struggle is in other worlds than ours. The fields of life are larger than we see, larger than all the history of man has told. Wherever there are beings of free will, there, whether it be in far-off stars or in the depths of space beyond the farthest star itself, there must be struggle, the possibilities of evil, the choice between the evil and the good. And in no part of His universe can God be passive. Everywhere He must be the foe of the evil and the friend of the good. Everywhere therefore throughout the great perplexed tumultuous universe, we can see the flashing of His sword. " His sword!" we say, and that must mean His nature uttering itself in His own form of force. Nothing can be in His sword which is not in His nature. And so the sword of God in heavenly regions must mean perfect thoroughness and perfect justice contending against evil and self-will, and bringing about everywhere the ultimate victory of righteousness and truth.

Out of this celestial, this universal struggle the sword of God, yet hot and fresh from the blows which it had struck, came down among the Jews to fight for them with Edom. That was the message which Isaiah brought. It was good both for Edom and for Israel that it should be clearly known to be the sword bathed in the heavens, the same force which was engaged in the eternal battles, which was to fight for the chosen people and against their enemy. The enemy needed to know it in order that they might be sure that the sword's work would be thorough, that there would be no sparing as long as there was any wickedness to be destroyed. The chosen people needed to know it, that they might understand that even for them God could not and would not fight otherwise than as God; that there would be no mere favoritism, nor any tolerance of means or methods which were undivine. That every struggle of the people of God against evil in this world must be fired with eternal principles, must be instinct with thoroughness and with justice; that is the plain prosaic meaning of the word of God to Isaiah which declared, "My sword shall be bathed in heaven."

You see then, I think, what it is of which I wish to preach to you this morning. It is the truth that all the true battles of the earth really are God's battles, and are to be fought only in God's spirit and

God's way. The old history of Israel and Edom sinks back into a parable. All that history was a crude and elementary utterance of the great truth that there must ever be, so long as the world remains imperfect and is struggling towards perfection, two parts of the world, one of which is God's and one of which is not. The chosen people, the people of the covenant, have passed away. They have fallen from their high estate. They no longer stand above their fellow-men, throned in the favoritism of God. But what that chosen people represented is perpetual. There always is in the world some part of the world consecrated to the struggle to make the world divine. It is not limited by the geography of a nation. It is not handed down to son from father. It is that part of the general humanity, that part of any race, nay, that part of any man—for even the individual life may be divided between God and the enemy of God—it is that part of human nature which is consecrated to God, and trying to do his will. That is the everlasting Israel. That in the Christian constitution is the correspondent of what Judaism, the idea of the chosen people, was under the system which the New Testament describes. In more spiritual ways therefore, with less formality, more flexibly and freely, all that is said of God's relation to the Judaism of the Old Testament, must be the picture and the parable of the relation which God holds to all struggle after goodness, all effort of noble and devoted life everywhere and always. It is in the light of this idea that such texts as this out of Isaiah really become ours.

The first point, then, is that all good struggle in the world is really God's battle, and ought to recognize itself as such. A young man sets out from college determined to do what he can to help set right the evils which are in the world. The ordinary careers which attract men have no attraction for him. He does not care to be rich, or perhaps he is rich already. At any rate, he takes his life in his hand and freely, genuinely, gives it to his fellow-men. What a tumult it is into which he casts himself, what a disorder, what a crossing and recrossing of interests, what a snarl of difficult problems! It is like trying to push back the sea, which eludes you at every instant and with its fluid mass is as solid as the rock itself. But can we not see at once what a difference it will make to this young worker against evil if he is really able to think of the great fight in which he is engaged not merely as his fight but as God's fight; as his fight because it is God's fight and he is God's? Suppose that he is large enough, religious enough, to look abroad and see God gradually occupying the earth with the eternal principles of his righteousness. Every special victory of human progress, the victory over slavery, the victory over superstition, the victory over social wrong, nay even the victory over tough matter, the subduing of the hard stuff of nature to spiritual uses, each of these is but a footstep in the great onward march of God taking possession of

His own. Must it not make a difference to the young reformer whether he is able to think of his struggle thus, or whether he is able merely to think of himself as the empirical student of political economy or social science, or as the expression of an instinctive human sympathy? The poor are God's poor. The slave is God's freeman. This oppressive institution is a blot on God's earth. Surely if he catches that meaning in it all, his whole struggle must be intensified and purified. His struggle may still keep the other truths and motives, but it surrounds them all with this larger and loftier one. Especially two things must come as the result of such a consciousness—the spirit of thoroughness and the spirit of justice. The young man really counting his struggle God's, must determine never to be satisfied until the victory is complete, and he must shrink from and refuse every temptation to use any weapons except the weapons of righteousness in a battle which belongs not merely to himself but to the Lord of all righteousness and truth.

Certain it is that in all ages this conviction has been at the heart of all the most earnest work that the world has seen. The reformers who have really done the work have been those who have dared to call their work a work of God. It has been the voice of God in their ears, it has been the sword of God flashing at their side which has made them courageous as fire and persistent as iron.

May not one plead with any generous young heart which thus is set upon the fight with sin and error.

that it should lift itself up at the very outset, and dare to count its fight a fight of God. Do not satisfy yourself with mere considerations of economy or mere impulses of humanity. Both are good. But greater than both is the enthusiastic sense of confederacy with God. Fight your battle for Him, with Him. So you shall fight it most persistently, most purely. Fight it with the sword bathed in heaven, and so you shall make it victorious, and grow strong and great yourself in fighting it.

I like to trace how a great truth like this applies even to what we call the most common and least spiritual things. I have already suggested that it seems to me to apply even to man's conflict with the obstinate world of matter, his battle with the stubborn stone and wood on which he has to exercise his skill. That is a never-ending conflict. The human mind is meeting the obtuse substance of the earth at every mechanic's bench, in every artist's studio, wherever the railroad is piercing the mountain or the steamship plows the ocean. Is it not true of all art and of all artisanship that thoroughness and truthfulness are what we need; the refusal to slight work and the refusal to attempt any results except by legitimate, and honest, and appropriate means? And is it not true also that thoroughness and truthfulness in any work of art or artisanship must come not from economy but from principle, not from the sense that they alone can really produce the effect, but from the profound conviction that, whatever be the effect which they produce, they alone are right.

and worthy for a man to use? This is the faculty of genius. And all religious action ought to have, must have, some of the quality of genius in it. Every work of art, and every work of artisanship which has, as all artisanship ought to have, something of the spirit of art about it, must be kept pure, noble, unmercenary and ideal by its constant relation to and consciousness of first principles, which are indeed nothing but the ideas of God.

This is hardly more than suggestion. Think again of the more serious struggle, the struggle with ignorance and error and with wrong ideas and faiths. There are two different views which may inspire the combatant with error. He may think of error as mischievous, or he may abhor and dread error for itself, apart from its consequences, as an intrusion and a misery in a world whose vital atmosphere is truth. Is it not clear what a different thing his fight will be, according as he takes one or the other of these views? If he takes the first view he will be liable to limit his fight with error by his perception of its mischievousness. The error which he does not happen to think mischievous he will tolerate or ignore. There is no thoroughness in that. And he will also be too apt to fight a mischievous error with what seems to be a less mischievous error, and to do evil that good may come. How much of that the world has seen! "I know this fight of mine is not conducted on the highest ground, but still this thing I am trying to set up, bad as it is, is not nearly so bad as what it seeks to destroy. Let me defeat this lie with a lesser lie, this sham with a less harmful sham." There is no bathing of the sword in heaven there. To strike for absolute truth, to tolerate no falsehood, however useful for the time it seems, that is not possible unless the man counts his fight God's fight and despises any method which it is not worthy of God and of the Son of God to use.

The same is true of the fight with sin. Think of sin as a mistake, or as an inconvenience, and you stand in great danger, first, of compromising with it, and second, of using low and even sinful methods of opposing it. But think of sin as a frightful wrong in itself, a blot and curse in the universe of God, and you grow at once absolutely intolerant of it, and at the same time watchfully anxious about the nature of the weapons which you shall use to fight it with. How often has even the Christian Church fought sin with sin! How often has the selfishness which looked to an eternal luxury and privilege in heaven, been arrayed against the selfishness which was hungry for meat, or thirsty for drink, here upon the earth! How often has insincere profession been offered as the medicine for doubt! How many men have been transformed from cold indifference to hot partisanship, and thereby seemed to have been made religious! How many revivals have been sensational and superficial and demoralizing! The fury of persecution called in to kill out heresy—what is that but the sword bathed in hell, the sword drunk with the evil passions of the worst humanity! And everywhere it would be possible to show that such horrible misuse of weapons came from a misconception of the nature of the enemy. Only, my dear friends, when we see sin as God sees it, only then can we be sure of using no weapons that are not divine for its removal. Only when pity for it joins with horror at it in our hearts, as they join in the heart of God, each keeping the other strong and pure, only then can we go out to meet it with a perfect determination, bound never to lay down our arms so long as there is any sin left in the world; and at the same time, with an absolute conviction that no impatience to rid the world of sin must tempt us for a moment to use any means for its destruction which are not pure and just; an absolute conviction that it is better that sin should be left master of the field, than that it should be fought with sin.

Oh, how the history of brave men whose lives have been long fights with wickedness, have borne terrible testimony of what a hard thing it is to get that conviction and to keep it. O how full of faith the man must be who sees a giant evil stalking through the land, ruining human lives by the million, and knows how by some act or policy which is not true and sound and pure he might arrest that evil, and save precious lives, and yet withholds his hand and says, "I cannot." There is no struggle for a man like that, no agony so deep, no test of bravery so searching. The world stands by and plies its well-worn maxims, "Of two evils choose the least," "A half loaf is better than no bread." "Nay, but my sword must be bathed in heaven," the soul replies, and I will not stir until each blow may have in it the strength of a conscience void of offence.

Thank God, if the waiting and inaction has indeed been of this noble sort, the time is sure to come when the long delay is more than justified. The time comes when, without a hesitation or misgiving, the soldier of God sees that he may strike, and may call every good power to witness that he does right in striking. Then it is evident that his plunging of his sword in the eternal righteousness has not merely made it powerless for evil but has made it fiery for good. Then men who called him coward because he would not strike at the wrong time, stand by in amazement as they see him harvesting the field with every great sweep of his unhesitating arm. For now he is a true Sir Galahad.

> "His strength is as the strength of ten
> Because his heart is pure."

O my dear friends, never let yourselves do evil that good may come. If you do, you hinder the coming of the real, the perfect good in its due time. Never try to set a wrong right by another wrong. You are only putting off the day when the true right shall be established. Never plot villany against a villain; never comfort affliction with a falsehood; never try to silence error with an argument which you do not believe; never fight God's battle with any weapon of the devil. Far rather would He have you stand aside useless, and let Him fight His own battle. It is not necessary for Him that you should help Him. But it is necessary for yourself that you should be true. Nothing but a clear faith that the battles which we are fighting are God's battles, can make us strong enough for all this.

We look up to the summit of our humanity, where Jesus stands, and there we see the fire of this faith burning in perfect light. Behold him in the Gospels. Men came to him and said, "Do this! Do that!" "Speak to my brother that he divide the inheritance." "Restore the kingdom to Israel," and how he waved them aside. "Who made me a judge or divider over you?" "Put up thy sword into its sheath." "My hour is not yet come."

One of the marvellous things about Jesus is the union of fire and patience. He saw his Father's House turned into a place of merchandise, and instantly the whip of small cords was in his hands and he was cleansing the sacred place with his impassioned indignation. And yet he walked day after day through the streets of Jerusalem and saw the sin and let the sinners sin on with only the remonstrance of his pure presence and his pitying gaze. Base and blind is the man who lets himself misread that patience. Base and blind is he who excuses his easy tolerance of wickedness, his comfortable carelessness about the sin of the world, by quoting to himself the fact that Jesus did not call down the lightning out of heaven to destroy the wicked city of the Jews. But blind also is he who does not learn the true lesson of that divine patience, the truth which the Lord himself put into His parable of the tares, the truth that only in God's own time and God's own way can the battles of the Lord be fought. The general holds his army till the right moment for launching them upon the foe. It is heroism to stand still and wait under fire as truly as it is heroism by-and-by to rush upon the guns of the enemy. It is disobedience and weakness to be self-willed and fight wrongly, as truly as it is to run away and refuse to fight at all. There is no self-will in Jesus. He is one with His Father and lives by his Father's will. Every act that he did came forth, therefore, out of the eternal nature. His sword was always bathed in heaven. The devil said to Him, "Worship me and you shall have this world you want so much, and save it to your heart's content." "Not so," said Jesus. "It is not just to save the world, but to save it righteously. To save it unrighteously is not truly to save it at all. Get thee behind me, Satan!" O for a courage like this, growing out of a faith like his!

I have spoken of the battles against sin as if they were altogether battles with the world's sins, with sin outside ourselves. Let me, before I close my sermon, speak to you in a few words about that harder battle which goes on in a man's own soul, his battle with his own sins, and see how the truth of which I have been preaching applies especially to it; how there most of all the sword must be bathed in heaven. To know first of all and deepest of all, that that battle which goes on within us is God's battle, is of supreme importance. What are our sins? What is your selfishness, your untruthfulness, your cruelty? Is it something which hurts and hinders you? Indeed it is. But beyond that it is something which usurps a kingdom which belongs to God. It is His enemy. And every movement of your conscience, ever sense of usurpation and of incongruity, is not merely the revolt of your own outraged soul. It is also the claim of the true King upon his Kingdom. It is the sound of the monarch's trumpet summoning the rebellious castle to surrender. Believe this, and what a dignity enters into the moral struggle of our life. It is no mere restless fermentation, the disturbed nature out of harmony with itself. It is God, with the great moral gravitation of universal righteousness, dragging this stray and wayward atom back into Himself. O deep divine mysterious process, that goes on wherever in silent chamber or in crowded street the humbled penitent lies prostrate in the dust, or the resolute struggler stands wrestling with his temptation!

But if the battle be God's battle, then it must be fought only with God's weapons. That must follow in our struggles with our sins as well as in our struggles with the world. You want to get rid of your selfishness. You must not kill it with the sword of another selfishness, which thenceforth shall rule in its place. Have we not all known men who in their youth were profligate and reckless? They flung the gold of health, and purity, and good esteem into the mire of licentiousness. By-and-by they saw how foolish and how fatal all that was. They were killing themselves with this which they call life. Then they reformed. They took care of their health. They nursed their reputation. They grew even to be very patterns of propriety. The town has no such censors of wickedness to-day as they are. They are as uncharitable as they once were unscrupulous. And they are just as selfish to-day, as they were twenty years ago when they were living in the furious indulgence of their appetites. They have killed one selfishness with the sword of another selfishness. It is the old story of the Book of Kings. Sennacharib king of Assyria is slain by his sons, as he is worshipping in the house of Nisroch his God. And Esarhaddon his son reigns in his stead. And so the Assyrian despotism goes on still!

Or think of the way in which the man who finds himself indifferent about truth, and wants to conquer his indifference, betakes himself to partisan intolerance, and grows narrow and bitter on principle. Think of how the skeptic, by-and-by, weary of skepticism, shuts his eyes upon the light and calls his wilful blindness faith. The instances are numberless. The killing of sin by sin, of selfishness by selfishness, of death by death!

But he who dares to count the battle of his soul God's battle, must rise to loftier and purer methods. For him selfishness can only be cast out by self-forgetfulness and consecration; and false liberality and license can only be overcome by larger and truer liberty; and skepticism, which is the glamor of the twilight, must never dream of going back into the darkness, but must press forward to the noonday.

Here only is there any real enthusiasm and hope. Sometimes I know it must have seemed to some of you as if the prospect of life were very doleful, because it offered nothing but the wearisome monotonous alternation and exchange of sin for sin. When the sins of recklessness could be no longer indulged in, then should come the sins of prudence; when the vices of youth were over, then welcome the other vices of old age. O my dear friend, there is something better than that. It is possible to bring down to the earth the perfect standards of the heavens, to stop thinking about safety and comfort and salvation altogether, and to be splendidly inspired with the consciousness that we are soldiers under God; to think of our own sins not as the things which are going to condemn us to eternal torture, but as the enemies of Him, the hindrances that stand in the way of His victorious designs; to see their badness not in their consequences, but in their nature, not in their quantity but in their quality; and so to bring to bear upon the very least of them the intense hatred and intolerance which the very nature of sin must always excite in him who has attained a true passion for holiness.

Can you imagine Jesus discovering in the robes of his spotless holiness, one single spot of sin? Behold him as he gazes on it! Is there any question in him as to whether it is great or small? The positive horror of its being there swallows up all questions of its size. Is there any question as to what its consequence will be? The present horror is enough. The future is not thought of. Only, all the Godhood that is in Jesus is instantly summoned to destroy this spot of sin. All the ocean of the divine power and holiness is implored to pour in and wash this speck of wickedness away.

So it is possible for us to deal with every sin, little or great, that we discover in our hearts. To count it God's enemy and to fight it with all His purity and strength; that is what it means for us that our sword should be bathed in heaven! Courage can only come with thoroughness. But with absolute thoroughness, courage must come. Resolve to-day that every strength of God which it is your right to invoke, because you are His child, and which prayer and consecration can bring into you from Him, shall be devoted to the overcoming of your sin, and then your sin shall certainly be overcome. May He whose enemy that sin is, as well as yours, grant that victory to you, and win it for Himself!

SERMON XVI.

The Knowledge of God.

"As the Father knoweth me, even so know I the Father."
ST. JOHN X. 15.
"Then shall I know even as also I am known."
1 CORINTHIANS XIII. 12.

THE first of these two texts is from the words of Jesus. He is telling the people of his relation to them on one side, and to his Father on the other. He says he is like a shepherd in the charge of sheep. Between him and the owner of the sheep, who has put him in charge of them, there is the most perfect confidence, a mutual knowledge which is absolute. The second text is from one of the epistles of St. Paul. He is anticipating the completion of life. He is looking forward and saying what man will be when he comes to his completeness. And what he prophecies is just exactly what Christ declares as already present in himself. Paul says, "some day I shall know God as God knows me." Jesus says, "As God knows me, even so do I now know God."

Do not these two verses, taken together, give a very striking picture of the general method of the

Christian faith? Do they not in their combination make that same impression which is made by the whole New Testament? Behold here in almost identical words are the eager hope and the calm assurance of accomplishment. Here is man reaching out for a great spiritual attainment, for the knowledge of God; and here is The Man saying, "I have attained it, I do know God." That is the very spirit and soul of the New Testament, the hope of man already fulfilled in Jesus Christ, the possibility of man made already manifest in Jesus Christ. Among the differences which have been in the world since Christ's religion came, is not this one of the greatest, that the best men in all their hopes and struggles have hoped and struggled in the presence of a visible success? In all times, under every faith, the men of hope and struggle have carried in their hearts a deep assurance that the thing for which they strove was possible. Under every discouragement, untouched by any skepticism or contempt of scornful friend or foe, there has lain at the bottom of the soul a conviction too deep for reason to give an account of, that this which seemed so impossible could be done. The soul could break through its selfishness, could despise danger and pain, could enter into communion with God. There could be no struggle at all buoyant and enthusiastic without such certain convictions lying at the bottom of the soul. But now what happened—one of the things which happened—at the incarnation was that this assurance, which had lain at the bottom of the human heart, came forth and was a living, manifest Being. It put on human flesh. It spoke with human lips. It worked with human hands. Christ was what man had felt in his soul that he might be. Christ did what man's heart had always told him that it was in his humanity to do. The new man which the old manhood had always felt struggling within itself came forth, and men knew themselves, their true selves, for the first time manifest in Him. This was what made man's hope thenceforth another thing. The stars at which men had guessed, knowing with what they called certainty that they were there, lo! in the Incarnation they burned out visibly. Thenceforth it was with a new and different assurance that the believer said, "I shall some day know as I am known," when Christ had once said, "As the Father knoweth me, I do now know the Father."

I know that there may seem to some of you to be something strange in talk like this. Have you been in the habit of thinking of Christ as of one so far away, so different from us, that what he is and does seems to throw no light on what we may be and do? But such a thought as that denies the very power of the Incarnation. Here stand our human lives, all dark and lustreless. Here stands one human life in which has been lighted the fire of an evident divinity. Shall we look on and see the fine lines and the fair colors of human nature brought out by the fire which burns within, and not make any glowing inference with regard to our own humanity, with regard to its unfulfilled possibilities and the attainments for which it may confidently hope? Surely not so! If

He can conquer temptation, then to be conquered by temptation, however it may seem inevitable to-day, cannot be the hopeless doom of man. If he cannot merely be known of God, but know God, then we too may be above the fear of any base agnosticism and look forward to the day in which we too shall know as we are known.

Let us believe indeed that in the experience of Christ there is such revelation of the possibility, such confirmation of the hopes of our humanity! So only does his life become that beacon on the mountain-top, that bugle cry at the army's head, which he evidently counted it to be, which it has so often been through all the Christian centuries!

One special illustration of all this is in these two texts, which I have chosen for this morning. The knowledge of God, a knowledge of Him such as He has of us, this Christ declares that he possesses. This, because of Christ's possession of it, we dare to believe that we shall some day possess. Let us try to understand this belief more deeply, that we may make it more thoroughly our own. Let us study first Christ's assurance about himself, and then St. Paul's hope for all believers.

"As the Father knoweth me, even so know I the Father." The words are full of that idea of mutualness which gives so much of warmth and richness to all life. Any relation which is all one-sided is unsatisfactory and dull. It is not vividly interesting. We love to think of any two objects, any two beings which have to do with one another as ministering each to each, each sending to the other something in answer to that which it receives. That fills the relationship with motion, and with motion come light and heat. The sun and the earth, the insect and the plant, the nation and the citizen, the teacher and the pupil, the parent and the child, the sound that strikes the rock and the rock which gives back reverberation to the sound, the air which, filled with light, gives to the light its substance and its swiftness, in every relationship there is this principle of reciprocity. Nothing alone is thoroughly alive; all complete life subsists in the reaction of mutuality. To give is never perfect life; it needs the complement, the fulfilment of taking. To take is never perfect life; it needs the complement, the fulfilment of giving.

Jesus declares that this is true of knowledge, of the knowledge of himself and God. To be known and to know—these two together make the fulness of the relation of lives to one another.

"The Father knoweth me." Those words must have summed up for Jesus a large part of the meaning and power of his life. They must have brought back to him the time when, as a child, he had felt about for the deepest connection of his newly conscious life, and behind every dearest connection with his fellow-men had become aware that the Creator of the world, the Being who was behind all other beings, knew him. He had read the assurance of that knowledge in all the sacred history of his people. Then he had found the confirmation and witness of it in his own soul. And, once completely grasped and understood, it had become the inspiration and the strength of everything he was and did.

I am not speaking now of that which was unique and singular in Jesus. I am not thinking of the peculiar and separate relation in which he stood to his Father. I am thinking only of that which he shared with all mankind. Simply as man, he felt the knowledge of God reaching out and laying hold of him. He felt his being bosomed on the divine intelligence. "Thine eye did see my substance yet being imperfect, and in thy book were all my members written." So David had sung, and as we listen to his song we feel how in that knowledge which God has of him, he is finding, as it were, his naturalization into the universe. He is becoming able to count himself no stray and foreign particle. What God knows has its place, its right, within the universe of God. It feels that knowledge of God seizing it and holding it as the new planet flung into the system feels gravitation seizing it and holding it in its great, warm, tender, mighty hand. All this was real to David. How much more real it must have been to Jesus!

It would be easy, if we had time, to point out what this sense of being known of the Father brought to Jesus. It brought independence. Out of the questionings and cavillings, and hootings, and revilings of the crowd he retired into the heart of it, and was strong. I see him enveloped in it, as in a cloud of safety, invisible but real, while he stood in the tempest of reproach and objection in the temple. "My Father knoweth me." I see him wrap it around him like a cloak as he faces Pilate upon Gabbatha. It brought him unity. That comprehensive certainty of being known involved the cradle, and the cross, and all that lay between, and made one single total life out of it all. It gave him charity. God's knowledge of him interpreted to him God's knowledge of his brethren, and let him freely leave them to the same great knowledge. We enumerate what it gave to him We tell these blessings of it one by one. But, after all, we know that it was more to him than our enumeration can describe. It was the element in which he lived. It was the air he breathed. It was his life.

And now what shall we say about the other side? Was there no response to this knowledge? Was it only that the Father knew the Son? Did not the Son also know the Father? There is such a one-sided knowledge, a knowledge in which one is only known, and the other only knows. The wise man knows this globe on which we live. He knows the rock and river; he knows the animal and plant; but animal and plant, river and rock do not know him. His live intelligence beats on the surface of an absolutely passive, unconscious, unresponsive world. It gets no answer back. But it is altogether different with this consciousness of Jesus. "The Father knoweth me, and I know the Father," he declares. The very knowing that he was known by God, of which I have just now been speaking, was in itself a knowledge of God by him. That independence and unity and charity which came into his life with the certainty that he was held in the intelligence of God, they were themselves an answer to the recognized fact of the divine intelligence. But even more directly there was a perception of what God was. There was a recognition by the sympathy of a kindred nature of the essential character of the nature into which it found itself pressed. What shall we say? Was it not like the answer which the plant makes to the sunshine that is poured upon it? The sunshine knows the plant in radiance, and the plant knows the sunshine in grateful bloom.

Jesus was no agnostic. No dreary conviction that there might be a God, but that if there were, he were hopelessly hidden from mankind, unknowable forever—no such dreary negative conviction was possible for him. He knew the Father by the direct perception of a kindred life. Not perfectly! He himself is careful to tell us of the limitation of his knowledge. The prison of his incarnation, of his abiding in mortality enfolded him. But he knew God. He sent back adoration, trust, exuberant love in answer to the recognized care which was always pouring itself upon him. Now and then, in the calm, cool night between the hot and weary days, when he went apart upon the silent mountain-top and prayed, he went to the God whom he knew, that he might know him more clearly. But the knowledge was a continual fact. He knew the Father, as nature knows nature, by direct perception.

Surely it must forever stand as a most impressive and significant fact, a fact that no man who is try-

288 The Knowledge of God.

ing to estimate the worth and strength of spiritual things can leave out of his account, that the noblest and most perfect spiritual being whom this world has ever seen, the being whom the world with most amazing unanimity owns for its spiritual pattern and leader, was sure of God. I cannot get rid of the immense, the literally unmeasurable meaning and value of that fact. It comes to me when God is clearest to me, bringing me new and yet more glorious assurance. It comes to me when doubt is with me, and I know my doubt is a mistake, and I sit even in the midst of doubt, joyously waiting for certainty; as the watcher for sunrise sits joyously expecting the time when the radiance which is already shining on the summits of the hills shall pour down into his valley where it still is dark. It comes to me in sorrow and in joy, in hope and fear, in ignorance and wisdom, in work and rest, the great fact, radiant with significance, that Jesus was sure of and believed in and knew God.

Nor must we let our thoughts rest solely on this large knowledge of nature by nature, which is the broadest statement of the truth. The knowledge which the Father had of the Son, and the answering knowledge which the Son had of the Father, referred also to the details of action as well as to the elemental facts of existence. "The Father knoweth me;" surely when Jesus says that, it means more than just that God was aware of his existence. That word "know" on the lips of Jesus is always a deep and pregnant word. To know any man is not merely to be sure of his existence, but to have some conception of what his existence signifies, and what it is for. For God to know Jesus was for God to have in his soul some purpose and will about the life of Jesus. The Jesus whom God knew was not a mere name, not even a mere nature. It was Jesus the Saviour of mankind, Jesus the Teacher, the Revealer of Divinity, the Pattern of Righteousness, the Victim of the Cross!

Is not this truly a great step forward? It was much for Christ that he was never for a moment unaware of God's existence. It was much that every instant he felt God's being under his being, as the ship feels the ocean under its great sides; but when we add to this the definite and clear conviction that God had a purpose with regard to every deed which filled those gracious days, how much is added! Now it is not merely a flood of light poured over the whole life, but it is this same light taken up and broken into countless points of brilliance; the whole experience tremulous and palpitating at every promontory with the consciousness of immediate communication of divinity. The miracle, the sermon, the word of sympathy, the pang of suffering— it was not merely because the Son saw that it was good and right; it was because the Father wanted it, and willed it, that it came. Here is transfiguration. Here is glory. What sense of drudgery, what monotonousness or weariness could there be in a life like that? It was no longer simply a great glassy ocean flooded with the sun. Every wave of the ocean had caught its own little sun, and the whole was full of infinitely varied yet identical life and light.

And now to this detailed knowledge of God, which means purpose and will, to this also comes its own response. "The Father knoweth me." That means, "God has a will for every act of mine." What then can "I know the Father," mean, except, "In every act of mine, I do the Father's will." Obedience becomes the organ and utterance, nay becomes the substance and reality of knowledge on the side of him who is aware that in this more special sense God knows him. I think of Jesus on that day when he called Lazarus back from the dead to life. He travels all the way from Galilee to Bethany. At last he stands beside the tomb. His soul is full of sympathy. He sees the tears and feels the misery of his poor friends. The dreadfulness of death oppresses him. Then he becomes aware of a will of God. God knows all that is going on there, the whole sad sorrow, the bereavement, the horror. And God cannot know anything in pure passivity. He always wants something to be done about the thing he knows. Every knowledge of God involves and issues in a will. God's will then shines on Jesus: and then behold! He lifts his head. His face shines like the sun! The gloom is gone! He stretches out his hand! He opens his lips with the cry of life! "Lazarus, come forth!" "And he that was dead came forth, bound hand and foot with graveclothes!"

God's will and Christ's obedience! Here then

there is the perfect mutualness, the absolute understanding and harmony of the Father and the Son. If it were not the morning of the miracle at Bethany, but the awful morning of the cross, it would be still the same. "Father, into thy hands I commend my spirit." There, in those words of completed obedience, the mutual knowledge of Father and Son is perfect, and being blends with being; the vail and barrier of the human flesh no longer hangs between.

And so as it concerns this first division of our subject, have we not reached a picture of existence which may well enchain us with its richness and beauty. Father and Son have come close to one another. In mutual knowledge, in harmony of will and obedience they are absolutely one. Of no act that the strong gentle hands do, can we say anything but this, that Father and Son together do it, making one power, working one result. Who is it that calms the sudden tempest on the lake? It is the Father and the Son. It is God in Christ. It is Christ filled with God! Who is it that speaks the parable of the prodigal son, instinct with divine authority and wisdom, tremulous with human tenderness and sympathy? Is it not the divine Father and the human Son, making one power, that utter together those wonderful words which have moved almost like a great personal presence down through the restless or the sluggish generations of mankind? "My Father worketh hitherto, and I work." It is not two confederates taking hold of hands. It is one system of power, in which two elements perfectly blend; which is a fragment and not a whole if either of the two be lost; which beats with one life-blood, knows but one standard, and issues at last embodied and expressed in one perfect unit of result. That simplicity and richness, wedded to each other, we try to take into our understandings when we hear Jesus say, "As the Father knoweth me even so know I the Father."

And then comes St. Paul. Years have passed away. The life and work of Christ have become the pattern and inspiration of the world. A higher and more spiritual standard of life has been set up. St. Paul is always stating it. He states it in that passage of his Epistle to the Corinthians which is the second of our texts. Let me give what little time remains to a few thoughts upon that passage.

"Then shall I know even as also I am known," says Paul. I have already bidden you observe how exactly Paul's hope is identical with Christ's consciousness. A knowledge of God answering to God's knowledge of him, that is what St. Paul expects. And the correspondence between Paul and Jesus is complete. It includes both of the two kinds of knowledge which, in speaking of Jesus, I have been trying to define.

First, it includes the larger knowledge of nature by nature. "God knows me," says St. Paul. "He knows me as the Maker knows His work. He knows me as the Father knows the child." That was the fundamental conviction of the great apostle. He went about his daily work enfolded by that conviction. "In Him we live and move and have our being," he cried to the Athenians. But that conviction for him inevitably involved another. If the Father knew the child, then it must be in the child's power to know the Father. Ignorance he could understand. Hindrance, darkness, perversion and mistake, he saw them everywhere. But the power to know God he knew was in man. Some time certainly it must come forth and be powerful. God might be unknown to many men, Athenians and others, but God was not unknowable by man, not unknowable by any man that lived.

St. Paul, like Christ, was no agnostic. In these days, when a whole school of philosophy takes upon itself not merely to disparage the poor flickering knowledge of God which man has yet attained, but to draw a sharp line, to build a high wall, beyond which the knowledge of man can never go, it is good to resort to the assured confidence of this great soul. To dwell upon how much is unknown may be often very good for us. To declare anything of God to be intrinsically and eternally unknowable by man, is unreasonable. May we not even say that it is insolent, insulting both to God and man. Here we may say, as St. Paul essentially says, as we seemed to hear Jesus say when we were listening to his words, that to know that God knows us is itself a knowledge of God, and promises what depth of future knowledge no man can begin to say.

Let us keep this distinction always in our minds,

and so be always full of hope. The unknown is not by any necessity the unknowable. Now there is mercy holding me, of which I hardly know more than that it is there, and that it is merciful. There is wisdom guiding me of whose existence I am certainly aware, but whose ways I cannot comprehend. But it shall not be always so. Now I am known perfectly, but I know in part, in the very least and weakest and dimmest way. But the time shall come when I shall know as I am known. Let me be sure of that, and with what hope I live. Nay, it is more than hope. For to be sure that such a knowledge shall be mine some day, is in a true sense to know now. Such a hope for the future is a possession in the present.

The other mutualness of knowledge we saw was that which lay between a special will or purpose of God and the corresponding activity of man. That was complete in Jesus. To the completeness of that too we may look forward in ourselves. "He spake and it was done," says David. That is a declaration of the oneness of God with His creation. His will is instantly echoed in its being and its action. The answer is so instantaneous and sure that the oneness between His will and His world is perfect; so perfect that often men's eyes have not been able to distinguish one from the other, and have said the world was God. Is not that a magnificent picture of the oneness which we would have between God's will and our action? No force of nature ever fails in its response. The seasons in their coming and their going, the sun in its rising and its setting,

The Knowledge of God. 295

the tempests and lightnings, fire and hail, snow and vapors, wind and storm fulfilling his word, all of these are absolute; they never vary; the glory of science is in finding out how invariable they are. They are of lower order. They are of easier submission. Their obedience then is just a type and picture, just an image and a prophecy, of what shall come to pass when in our higher world, our world of free thought and free action, we too shall become as obedient to God as are wind, fire, lightning and sunshine in their lower world.

Oh how one longs for it sometimes! With perfect freedom, not turned into machines, still keeping all the glory of our liberty, to answer perfectly to every will of God with absolute obedience. To do the right because it is His will, and to do His will because it is right always. We know that there alone is peace and power. Such a standard cuts right across our ordinary standards. The feeblest life, perfectly harmonized thus with God's, outshines the mightiest life in which that harmony fails.

Is it not evident that the great hope which St. Paul holds up before us all, and which our hearts recognize and claim, must include this or it is not sufficient. Simply to know God, though the knowledge were complete, simply to know God if it were possible without obedience, would be a barren privilege. O how we separate our knowing and our obeying powers, our mental and our moral natures, as if they could be separated, as if either of them could live without the other! No, the promise that we shall know includes the promise that we shall obey! So it attains its fullest richness.

When we say that, eternity springs into life and lives. No longer a bare doctrine, no longer a great arid fact, that we shall live forever, but a great, actual reality! Hark, through the atmosphere of that belief can you not hear the music of the activity which fills the streets of the New Jerusalem? I hear the feet hurrying over the glassy pavements, the voices calling to each other in the joy of service, the ringing of the hammers on the anvils where in the fire of the love of God eht perfect obedience of His redeemed is forging his perfect will into the instruments of perfect deeds.

Have I wasted your Sunday morning with abstract truths, and far-away visions of the future? It would be waste indeed if abstract truth must not always lie at the heart of concrete action, and if the visions of the future, thoroughly believed, were not the realities of the present. What Christ was we shall be some day, and because we shall be it some day, we may begin to be it now. What is the meaning and result of all that I have said to you this morning? O my friends, it is this! You need not live alone, for you may, if you will, know and obey God. You and God, you and God, one system of power knit together in mutual knowledge, and in common standards! That is what Christ claimed you for. Give yourself to Him, and you shall come to that. Behold Him! Hear Him! Come by Him to the Father, and then live! O Christ, draw us, thy Father's children, to our Father now!

SERMON XVII.

An Evil Spirit from the Lord.

"The spirit of the Lord departed from Saul, and an evil spirit from the Lord troubled him."—1 SAMUEL xvi. 14.

WE probably should be surprised if we understood how very little people really know about the Bible and what is in it. We deceive ourselves regarding our own knowledge. The sacred Book has lain so long upon our tables, and we are so familiar with its outside look, that we get a vague idea that we have read it. But if we really brought ourselves to the point we should be amazed at our own inability to tell even the simplest of its stories rightly. And we imagine sometimes that all the rest of the world know more about the Book than we do; but every now and then something gives us a glimpse of what they do know, and we are startled at the imperfectness and carelessness of their knowledge of the richest and most familiar and most important Book in all the world. There are many of you who are eager for each new book, who are anxious if each Saturday night does not find you read up to the line of the week's new literature, who probably never read the graphic, brilliant, stirring story of Saul, the first King of Israel, in all your lives. We circulate the Bible by the million. Some parts of it we read as a religious duty. But there are whole books of it teeming with interest which few of us ever touch. One sometimes feels that some day or other a great increase of the spiritual power of the Bible will come with what will be almost a re-discovery of its literary attractiveness. When people break through the strange feeling which has gathered around it that it is dull and unreal, and find that it is the most interesting book in all the world, then they will be open for its deeper power to lay hold upon their consciences and hearts.

Saul's life, as it is told to us in the first Book of Samuel, is the perfection of a tragedy. If it were not the story of a real man who lived in the Jewish tribe of Benjamin, it might be the most sublime allegory that ever was written of human life in the tragical aspect of it, which is always suggesting itself, and sometimes presses itself upon us so urgently that we can see no other. There is one chapter, the tenth chapter of the first Book of Samuel, which is as fresh as a spring morning. A farmer's boy, lighthearted, innocent and strong, striding away over the hills to find a flock of asses that had wandered from his father's fields. He talks with his servant; he questions the group of girls whom he meets at a town gate. At last he meets a venerable prophet, who tells him what fills his young frank eyes with wonder, and makes his heart leap with the mysterious birth of noble ambitions—that he is to be the first King of the new Kingdom of Israel. It is all as fresh and bright as innocence and hope can make it. Then there is another chapter, the twenty-eighth of the same Book, which is like the bleakest, bitterest day when the year is dying in December. The same Saul grown old and wretched, with his country all in confusion, with his conscience tortured by memories, the subject of insane fits of melancholy and frenzy, encamped now with his army on a cold hillside, with the Philistines camped opposite to him, and knowing that he must fight them in the morning, and that they are too strong for him. This Saul at midnight creeps stealthily across the mountain to find a witch, who brings up before him an apparition of Samuel the prophet, the same who had first told him that he should be king; who tells him now out of his ghostly lips that God has become his enemy, and will rend his kingdom out of his hands. All is as dark and bitter as guilt and despair can make it. Jealousy, superstition, frenzy, pride, have closed down together on this ruined man. And what is the misery of this half-savage life, we say, but just, in strong bold colors the picture of what our smoothed and civilized lives are? It is the same thing, only more vivid. The same tragedy of the changing life is everywhere. Everywhere are bright enthusiastic boyhoods turning into the guilty and desperate old age of weary Sauls.

The verse which I have taken for our text this

morning contains one statement about this tragical history of King Saul, which well deserves our study. It is one of those epitomes of a life which open the deepest questions. It is said that "the spirit of the Lord departed from him, and an evil spirit from the Lord troubled him." We catch at once the character of the representation. It is entirely realistic. There is a vivid picture in it all. God is seen by him who writes it, standing surrounded by spirits who are in His control, to be sent wherever He shall please. Some of them are good and are his spirits pre-eminently; others of them are evil, the spirits that vex and torture and distress the men to whom they come. God sends these spirits as he pleases. He speaks to a spirit of blessing and the spirit flies to make some saint better and happier. He turns to a spirit of evil, and he hurries to do his dreadful work of punishment on some poor sinner. God's spirit of good has been with Saul, but at one point, one crisis in his life that spirit departed from him, and an evil spirit from the Lord troubled him.

That picture of the court of God with its company of various spirits has grown dim. No such clear and objective picture stands before us. But the truth still remains, which that picture tried to express, the truth that the evil spirit, like the good spirit, came out of God's presence; that when the life of Saul had altered, and the blessing of his early innocence had left him, it was not as if he had been cast out into a region over which God has no control, not as if God had nothing to do with him any longer. As the old blessing had come out of his relationship to God, so the new curse came out of that same relationship. As it was God who made his first life noble and happy, so it was God who made his last life desperate and wretched. He could not get outside of God. Whatever spirit, good or evil, came to him, came to him from the Lord.

This is a strange, perhaps at first it sounds as if it were a dreadful, truth. But we shall understand it better if we look and see what were the circumstances of the change when the evil spirit supplanted the good in the King's life. There were two acts in Saul's life, occurring near together, which seemed to mark the point of change. One was the unwarranted performance of a religious rite. The people were in a sad strait. They had been crowded and driven by the Philistines. Saul was waiting, as he had been bidden, for Samuel to come and offer the sacrifice which was to call down God's blessing on the host as they met their terrible enemy. When Samuel did not come, Saul grew impatient; and by-and-by, neglecting every command, casting every scruple to the winds, he offered the burnt-offering himself. Not long after came the second action. Saul had gone against the Amalekites. Samuel, speaking for the Lord, had bidden him to conquer them and to destroy them. The King did conquer them, but for the ostentatious glory of his own triumph and for a splendid sacrifice to God, he spared the life of their King Agag and the choicest of their sheep and oxen. These were the two. It does not seem that the madness and misery were sent in direct punishment for these two actions, but these actions mark the time when the King's life begins to change. The clouds begin to gather. God seems to be against him. The winds that used to help him on, blow now in his face, and all grows harder and darker till the bitter end. They seem only trifling actions, but they both mean the same thing. They mean rebellion. Self-will is the essence of them both. They mean that he who had been frankly obedient, only asking to know the will of God that he might do it, now chooses to do his own will. That is the point where the change comes. From the time when he begins to disobey God, God works against him, and the prophet of God, who in the first scene was blessing him and telling him of his great mission, in the last scene appears, rising like a ghost to rebuke him and tell him of his doom; as the hopes and chances of a man's early youth rise ghostlike before him, when he has grown old, to reproach him with the failure of his life.

Now I think we shall understand this story best if we consider how wide the law of life is that it opens to us. The law is that a beneficent power, if we obey it, blesses and helps us; but the same power, if we disobey it, curses and ruins us. That law runs everywhere. See how most manifestly it is true in nature. There was a time when the ignorance of man divided all natural forces into two hostile camps. One army was fighting against man. The other army was fighting for his good. The sunshine was his friend, the cruel lightning was his enemy. But what have we learnt since, as science has brought us more into the soul of nature? Is it not this, that there is no force which is deliberately set to do man harm; that the most hostile force, if we can understand and obey it, treat it after its laws and nature, becomes our friend and ally? The cruel lightning carries our tenderest messages like a pitying slave. Everywhere, man says that he rules nature and she does his work. The truth is that she does none of his work except as he obeys her, docilely studies her ways, and suits himself to them. You obey fire, and she will forge your iron and cook your dinner. You disobey fire, and she will sweep your city in a night off the face of the earth. This is the meaning of applied science: man humbly learning nature and by obedience turning her from his enemy into his friend.

The same is true of government and law. Here are you sitting to-day peacefully in your house, without a fear, and yonder in the jail is some poor wretch for whom there is no escape until the dreadful day when he shall be led out to his dreadful death upon the scaffold. The same government, the same law makes your safety and his danger. The same beneficent power protects your life and takes his life away. The change came with his disobedience. There is something picturesque and awful in the instant change which a sudden crime makes in the whole relation which a man holds to the state he lives in. He has grown up protected by his nation's law. It cared for him even before his birth, and there has never been a moment in his boyhood, youth or manhood, when its shield has not been over him and its sword drawn to strike down any one who dared to do him harm. Some day he does a sudden crime, he disobeys the law, he takes a brother's life, and instantly, as his dagger pierces and the life-blood flows, everything alters. The law which has protected him becomes his enemy. Her sword is pointed at his heart. Her shield is spread before him, only lest any one should snatch him from her certain punishment. Instead of trusting in her quiet smile he quails under her pitiless eye. She is transformed the moment that he disobeys.

The same is true about a man's relation to the art he practices. Find out and thoroughly obey its fundamental principles and all the genius of your art is with you. Its history and tradition are the solid backing of your life. Every man who ever worked in it, or who is working in it to-day, is your ally. But disobey its principles, be wilful, try to excel or shine, not by conformity to its nature but by some fantastic violation of it, and all your art contends against you and balks you at every step.

One illustration more. All this is true about our friends. We obey our nobler friends and their friendship helps us. We disobey them, and their friendship harms us. Obedience seems a hard word to use of friendship, and yet there must be obedience, there must be docile conformity, a shaping of your life upon that higher life, a reaching up, a stretching out of what you are, to try to match what he is. If there is that, then how his nature ministers to yours; how first as standard, then as impulse, and continually as elevation and as joy he gives himself to you. These are the commonplaces of every ennobling friendship. But if there is no obedience; if, bound to his higher life by obligation or by that mere liking which may have no relation to your character, you insist on living your own life, what then is the result? How he rebukes you every day. How every deed he does exasperates you. How, by-and-by you hate the goodness which you will not imitate and which builds up a wall between you and your friend, whom you would like to have a man just like yourself. Was not Judas cursed by the same friendship with Jesus that perfected John? And if we try to picture to ourself the life of a man living in constant association with the noblest people, yet absolutely wilful and refusing to conform to any of the higher laws of life which they are always setting before him, we shall surely see him in our imagination growing more and more reckless and defiant. Yes, men are ruined by their best and dearest friends—not simply by wanton indulgence and foolish fondness, but by the noble example that is never followed and the noble invitation never answered.

These are the illustrations of our Law. They show the absolute necessity of obedience everywhere. Obedience is the only key that can unlock the treasures of nature or of man. Obedience has an absolute power. To the obedient man nothing can refuse its richness. Nature flies open and takes man into her inmost heart. Government opens her arms and surrounds him with her most secure protection. The best men make their goodness as much his as theirs. But if obedience is not there, nothing can take its place; no mere excitement of the taste, no rapturous affection can cover over and change the fact of wilfulness. This was so strongly stated by Samuel in his rebuke to Saul. Saul said that he had disobeyed God because he honored Him and wanted to do Him supreme reverence. He had saved the sheep and oxen when Jehovah had bade him destroy, in order to sacrifice to Jehovah. "And Samuel said, Hath the Lord as great delight in burnt-offerings and sacrifices as in obeying the voice of the Lord? Behold, to obey is better than sacrifice, and to hearken than the fat of rams." They are great words. They are words full of the strength of life. If you would be strong you must learn to obey. Self-will is weakness; but to find the nature and will of everything that is higher than you are, and bend yourself to it with complete docility, that makes the richest treasure it possesses, yours. O learn to obey, learn to obey! Obedience is the only mastery and strength.

And now let us return to the description which is given of the disastrous change in the life of Saul. "The Spirit of the Lord departed from him, and an evil spirit from the Lord troubled him." This phrase, "an evil spirit from the Lord," is used again and again to account for the disturbed and wretched life which the unhappy monarch now began to live. What does it mean but just this truth, which we have been studying, brought up and found to be also true in its application to God. The truth is that every beneficent power which helps us so long as we obey it, turns by its own nature and harms and hinders us so soon as we are disobedient. Is this then true of God? If God is the most beneficent of all powers, the central goodness of the universe, it cannot but be true of Him. "I form the light and create darkness," says Jehovah in Isaiah. "I make peace and create evil." "They rebelled and vexed his Holy Spirit, therefore He was turned to be their enemy, and He fought against them." So it is said about God and his people. It is an idea which runs through all the Bible. In many forms it is continually reappearing. It must be so, for God in the Bible is uni versal. He fills all things. No creature of his can creep away out of his sight, and live in a realm with which He has nothing to do. And God in the Bible is positive. No life can lie here close to his life, and not be affected in some way by that power of righteousness. He must be something to us; what he shall be to us depends on what we are to him. Saul is obedient, and God is brightness, courage, hope, happiness. Saul disobeys, and his soul becomes melancholy, gloomy, irritable, suspicious, envious, distracted. Did the God who made the light have anything to do with the making of this darkness afterwards? How shall he think of Saul in his desperate old age? Is that mountain over which he climbs in the dark to find the witch of Endor in her cave, somewhere quite outside the world where God

An Evil Spirit from the Lord.

is everything—outside the world in which lay the sunny valleys of Benjamin, along which the young Saul had passed seeking his father's asses? No, it is the same world; a world capable of holding such diverse scenes because it is all under the same God. Where it opens itself to Him it is He that makes its sunshine. Where it hides itself from Him it is no less He that makes its shadow. Without the sun there could be no more the depth of the shadow than the brightness of the light; and if there had been no God, the bitterness of Saul's old age would have been as impossible as the beautiful happiness of his boyhood.

It bewilders us to think how far-reaching this truth is. So long as God is in the universe, every soul that is in the universe must feel His power. No space can be so wide, no time so long as to exhaust His influence. He that obeys, must feel the ever-present God in joy. He that disobeys must feel Him in pain everywhere and forever. These are the terrible necessities of obedience and disobedience. We may state it; the Bible often does state it judicially. We may speak of God's vengeance. It may seem to be the angry revenge of one who has been insulted and ignored. We may picture to ourselves His wrath. With realistic fancy we may imagine to ourselves the flames of His anger consuming the rebellious souls, which yet are so like him who punishes them that they can never die. Such pictures have their power, as the crudest, coarsest representatives of the essential truth that to the disobedient God must come in suffering, as He comes to the obedient in joy. The essential truth of heaven and hell is ineradicable in the universe. But greater and truer than any picture of angry vengeance, more solemn, more sublime, more impressive to the fear of a reasonable and thoughtful man, there is the mighty image of God standing in the centre of all things. And all things have to touch Him. And as all things touch Him, according to their characters, he becomes to them blessing or curse. He is the happiness of obedience, and the misery of disobedience throughout his world. He looks with sympathetic joy or with profoundest pity on the souls He judges, but the judgments both come from Him. The right hand and the left hand, are both His. Burning there like the sun of all the world, He must be a comforting and guiding light, or a consuming fire—one or the other—to every soul.

Is this all theory? At the best is it all a revelation of something of which otherwise we could have had no knowledge? Or is there anything in our experience that testifies to such a double power belonging necessarily to the very existence of a God? If in our lives there has been any difference between those days in which we tried and those in which we did not try to do God's will; any such difference as made us feel on the first set of days thankful and glad, and on the other class of days wretched and almost indignant that there was a God in heaven; then we do know this truth of Saul's life in our own life. You do wrong. You have chosen to do wrong. You are sitting here with your bad choice enshrined in your heart. You did it yesterday. You mean to do it again to-morrow. You are deliberately and wilfully disobedient. Tell me, is it the same to you that in the heavens, and pervading all the earth, there is a power of righteousness, a great pure, dear Being, whose child you are, who loves you, who has a right to your obedience, whom you are disobeying—is it all the same to you as if there were no God, as if that choice of yours were a mere whim of your own fancy, made in the face of no eternal righteousness and against the protest of no pleading love? Would it be then as dogged, as obstinate, as bitter, as poisonous a thing in all your life as it is now? Ah, a man has to hug his sin very tight that the almost despotic love of God may not wrest it from him. He has to hide its venom very deep in his blood, that the great physician may not find it out and kill it. And just so far as you are worse to-day for living under the grace of a God who has been trying all these years to make you better, just so far as the truth that you have heard has made you more callous, and the duties you have had put before you have made you more faithless, just so far as you have not merely lost the freshness of your youth but have grown hard and bitter from living in a world that teemed forever with the invitations to truth and charity, just so far that has come to you which came to King Saul. Not merely "the spirit of the Lord has departed from you," but "an evil spirit from the Lord has troubled you."

Here is the fatal power of disobedience, of self-will. It makes God our enemy and turns His power against us. Not that the worst sin you or I can do will make him cease to love us. Ah, that cannot be! And that is the tragicalness of it all; the certainty that he loves us still, even while he "is turned to be our enemy." Do you see Jesus sitting on the Mount of Olives, looking down upon Jerusalem? Does he love that fair and rebellious city? We do not begin to know how He loved her. We must be the God he was, and the man he was or we cannot begin to know. Can he save her? If he could, he surely would not be sitting here! But, such is the mystery of moral nature and of responsibility, it is himself he cannot save her from. And what is the essence of her curse? Why is this city on the Syrian Hills doomed to a fall of which no other city in the world is capable? Because of his feet that have trod her pavement, and his words that have sounded in her ears. "O Jerusalem, Jerusalem!" "If I had not come and spoken unto them they had not had sin." Here is the fatal power of disobedience. Without quenching the unquenchable love, it turns the divine nature against us, in the same overwhelmingness, by the same necessity with which, if we were only obedient, that nature would help us and bring us to perfection.

In this truth of ours lies certainly one key to a question which theologians have very much debated. Wherein lay the power of the life and death of Jesus? What was the atonement he accomplished? Did the change which he wrought come in God or man? But we have seen how man's disobedience inevitably made a change in God—not to destroy His love, but to set His loving nature into hostility to the soul that would not do his will. And if the life and death of Jesus breaks down in penitence, as we know it does, the self-will of man, and make him once more gratefully, loyally obedient, what then? The change in God must follow. Not the restoral of a love that was withheld, but the free utterance for help and culture of a love that has been never held back, but which has, by the man's false position, been compelled to work against him. The wind is blowing all the time. The man is walking dead against it, and it buffets him and is his enemy. You turn the man round and set him walking with the wind. The wind blows on just as before. But now it is the man's friend. The wind has not changed, and yet, with the man's change, how completely the wind has changed for him.

How clear this makes the great question of every man's life. Is God with you or against you, O my friend? Is the power which comes out from Him to you a power of help or harm? It must be one or the other. Over a broad open plain there blows a strong steady wind. It never stops, it never changes. All over the plain there are men and women on their journeys. Hear them cry out. "This wind, this dreadful wind!" cries one, all out of breath and gasping. "How bitter it is, how cruel, how it hates me!" "This wind, this blessed wind!" cries another, within hail of him. "How kind it is, how helpful, how it loves me!" Are there two winds, or has the one fickle wind its favorites? No, the one constant wind is blowing steadily and is no respecter of persons; but one man has set his face against it and the other man is walking with it. That is the reason why it seems to hate the one and love the other.

Through this great open world moves God like a strong wind or spirit, finding out all the public and the secret places of the life of man. In the breath of that spirit we are all journeying; no one can escape for a moment. But while your brother at your side is full of the sense of God's love, to you God seems the hindrance of your life; His righteousness defeats your plans, His purity rebukes your lust, His nature and being smite you in the face like a blast that blows bitter and cold from a far off judgment day. Does God hate you and love your brother? No, he loves you both: but you with your disobedience are setting yourself against His love. You must turn round. You must be converted. And then, when your will is by obedience confederate with the will of God, every breath of His presence shall be your joy and salvation.

If there were not some such law as this discernible, how terrible life would be! If man went on, and whether he were good or bad, whether he obeyed or disobeyed, there came no change in God's attitude to him, only one long, weak, undiscriminating indulgence, where would be any limit to the depth of wickedness into which man might fall? What a moral chaos everywhere! You tremble when you think of all that happening in your own family. We cannot picture to ourselves how dreadful it would be in the great family of God.

My friends, my mission is—and more and more do I delight in it—to preach to you the love of God. I have preached that love to you to-day. But I have spoken to you, not as if you were sick children who must hear nothing but the tenderest words, but as if you were reasonable, responsible men and women, who want to face the facts of life, and who know that the truth is best. I have tried to show you out of the story of the old Hebrew King, that however God has chosen a soul, and given it great tasks, and surrounded it with privileges, and apparently made it necessary to His designs, He will not, cannot keep that soul, if it is disobedient. He must let it go its way and take another for His work. There is no privilege which we may not turn into a curse. God does love you, and never will cease to love you, no matter where you go, no matter what you are, no matter through what depths of vice your soul may plunge in any world whose possibilities we cannot guess; but His love shall be to you a spirit of help or a spirit of harm, according to your obedience or disobedience to Him.

This is the truth to preach to men and women who are in the midst of the reality and the solemnity of life. It is strong, manly doctrine. The Bible rings with it. All powerful and vital Christianity is full of it. It is not hard and cruel. It is not weak and sentimental. I beg you to take this truth. Let it fill your life. Let it make you serious, brave, thoughtful, hopeful and fearful both. Let it make you men of God, living in His service, rejoicing in His love, and feeling already in your obedient souls the power of His everlasting life.

SERMON XVIII.

Going up to Jerusalem.

"Then Jesus took unto him the twelve, and said unto them, Behold, we go up to Jerusalem, and all things that are written concerning the Son of man shall be accomplished."—LUKE xviii. 30.

EVERY true life has its Jerusalem, to which it is always going up. A life cannot be really considered as having begun to live until that far-off city in which its destiny awaits it, where its work is to be done, where its problem is to be solved, begins to draw the life towards itself, and the life begins to know and own the summons. Very strange is this quality of our human nature which decrees that unless we feel a future before us we do not live completely in the present where we stand to-day. We have grown so used to it that we do not realize how strange it is. It seems to us to be necessary. But the lower natures, the beasts, do not seem to have anything like it. And we can easily picture to ourselves a human nature which might have been created so that it never should think about the future, but should get all its inspiration out of present things. But that is not our human nature. It always must look forward. The thing which it hopes to become is already a power and decides the thing it is.

And so every true life has its Jerusalem to which it is always going up. At first far off and dimly seen, laying but light hold upon our purpose and our will, then gradually taking us more and more into its power, compelling our study, directing the current of our thoughts, arranging our friendships for us, deciding for us what powers we shall bring out into use, deciding for us what we shall be: so every live man's Jerusalem, his sacred city, calls to him from the hill-top where it stands. One man's Jerusalem is his profession. Another man's Jerusalem is his fortune. Another man's Jerusalem is his cause. Another man's Jerusalem is his faith. Another man's Jerusalem is his character. Another man's Jerusalem is his image of purified society and a worthy human life. You stop the student at his books, the philanthropist at his committee, the saint at his prayers. You say to each of them, "What does it all mean? What are you doing? What is it all for?" And the answer is everywhere the same: "Behold we go up to Jerusalem." We draw back the vail of history, and everywhere it is the same picture that we see. Companies, great and small, climbing mountains to where sacred cities stand awaiting them with open gates upon the top. The man who is going up to no Jerusalem is but the ghost and relic of a man. He has in him no genuine and healthy human life.

There never was an exhibition of all this so fine and perfect as that which we see in Jesus. His manhood shines out nowhere so clear and strong as here. Think how his life gets its glory and beauty from the way in which it is always, from the very first, tending on to the thing which it was at last to reach. That tendency began at his birth, and it never ceased until he was hanging on the cross outside the city gate. Then he had come to Jerusalem and it was finished. The angels sang about Jerusalem when the shepherds heard them. The boy's thoughts were full of Jerusalem as he worked in the carpenter's shop. Egypt, where they carried the babe to get him out of danger was on the way to Jerusalem, where he was finally to be killed. The visit to the temple when he was twelve years old, was a nearer glimpse of the Jerusalem to which he did not then really come, though his feet trod its streets, but which he then accepted as the only sufficent issue of his life. He was baptized in consecration to the life-long journey to Jerusalem. "For this cause was I born. For this cause came I into the world." "My time is not yet come." Those words, and words like those, dropped here and there, along his path, are like foot-prints in the road he walked, all pointing to Jerusalem. At last he came there, and in the tragedy of Good Friday he laid down his life. He had reached Jerusalem at last. The most intense, persistent purpose that the world had ever seen, had reached its completion. He had come to the Jerusalem of his intention, and mankind was saved.

With Christ as the great image and pattern of it all before us, let us speak this morning of the Jerusalem of every life, the steady tendency of every life to come to some appointed result of which it is growingly conscious as it moves upon its way towards it. Let us speak first of the existence of such a result, and then of the struggle by which it is reached.

First, then, may we not say that the appointed result of any man's life will consist of his character multiplied by his circumstances. Find the product of that multiplication, and you can surely tell what the man will attain. It is because both of these terms are vague; because, look as deep into him as you will, you cannot read his character perfectly; and because, study his circumstances as carefully as you may, you cannot tell just what is going to happen; for these two causes, the final issue of his life is not entirely clear; the Jerusalem to which he is travelling, is vague and cloudlike. And yet it is good, indeed it is necessary, for us to know that both of these elements do enter into the decision of a man's life, and that neither of them must be left out. You leave out a man's character, and think that his circumstances only must control his destiny, and at once you are a fatalist. On the other hand you leave out his circumstances, and think only of his character, and you have set a premium on wilfulness. At once men go about complaining that the circumstances, which they did not take into account, are hindering them from being what they have found it, they think, in their characters to be!

But see! here is a man who has heard the doctrine which I have preached thus far in this sermon. He wants to apply that doctrine to himself. "Where is my Jerusalem?" he says. "What is there to which my life is moving? What is there which I must hope ultimately to attain?" That man, I say, must multiply his character by his circumstances and see what the product is. He finds himself by character a scholar, and by circumstances a citizen of America in the nineteenth century after Christ. Those two things he must put together. As the result, a certain image of scholarship, humane, practical, broad, hopeful, distinctly modern, distinctly different from mediæval scholarship, burns before him on the hill. On that his eye must be fastened. To that his feet must struggle.

Or he might have found himself a man with a soldier's heart in the third century, or with a saint's heart in the first century, or with a discoverer's disposition in the fifteenth century. The time and the man together decree the possible career.

Or, if you talk of it within a narrower range; here in town there is a man poor and full of enterprise; there is a rich man all alive with sympathy; there is a quiet, meditative soul, pushed on by the accidents of its existence into perpetual contact with fellowmen; there is a brilliant flashing genius doomed to solitude. In either case it is the condition and the man, it is the circumstances and the character multiplied into each other which make the life. The circumstances are the brick and mortar; the character is like the architect's design; out of the two Jerusalem is built.

He then who would know his Jerusalem must know both of these elements. He must know himself and he must know his conditions. See how at once the full activity of man is called for. You cannot simply look at what other men are doing and see in their activity the disposition of your time and fling yourself out into their forms of action, regardless of the fitnesses and the limitations which are in your own nature. On the other hand you cannot just study yourself and then demand that the age and the place in which you find yourself shall take you and find use for you, however you may be out of harmony with its disposition and its needs. From both of those causes there have come great failures. Who are the men who have succeeded in the best way? Who are the men who have done good work while they lived, and have left their lives like monuments for the inspiration of mankind? They are the men who have at once known themselves in reference to their circumstances, and known their circumstances in reference to themselves; true men, sure of their own individuality, sure of their own distinctness and difference from every other human life, sure that there was never another man just like them since the world began, that therefore they had their own duties, their own rights, their own work to do, and way to do it; but men also who questioned the circumstances in which they found themselves and asked what was the best thing which any man in just those circumstances might set himself to do? These are the men before whom there rises by-and-by a dream, which later gathers itself into a hope, and at last solidifies into an achievement. It is something which only they can do, because of their distinctness and uniqueness. It is something which even they could not do in any other circumstances than just these in which they do it now. Columbus discovers America because he is Columbus, and because the study of geography and the enterprise of man have reached to just this point. Luther kindles the Reformation because he is Luther, and because the dry wood of the papacy has come to just the right inflammability. You and I, who are not Luthers nor Columbuses, but simply, by the grace of God, earnest, true-hearted men, conceive some purpose for our lives and keep it clear before us, praying we may not die before we do it; and at last doing it before we die, because we are we, and because the world in which we live is just the world it is. It is every young man's place to realize, to make real to himself, both himself and his circumstances, what he is and where he is. Are the young men here doing that? If they are not, their lives are stagnant or drifting, and who knows which of these two is worse? But if they are, then there is certainly shaping itself in the misty future a purpose of their life which slowly will grow clear to them, which they will pursue with ever deeper joy and ardor, which they will humbly rejoice in when they come to die, and which men will thank God for, long after they are dead!

"But how shall I realize myself and my circumstances?" some one says. I wish that I could make you see it as clearly as it seems to me. The answer is that you must realize them both in God. Jerusalem, as we go up to it, shines through its atmosphere to us. We see it through and because of the vital air which is poured around both it and us. Now God is the atmosphere in which we "live and move and have our being." He made our characters, and He made our circumstances, and it is His hand that moulds the two together and bids arise into existence out of them a definite, appropriate purpose for our life, a thing for us to be and do.

Here are you, let us say, who have seriously decided that you will be a lawyer in this city and this time. If you have come to that decision seriously and intelligently, and not by mere whim, you have reached it by a knowledge of your character and your circumstances, as I tried to describe. You have recognized certain powers in yourself, and certain needs in the community. Tell me, will it not make both of those recognitions clearer if behind them both you put the thought, the certainty, of God? If you are able to think of One who made you for your time, and made your time for you; if you are able to see, with the eye of faith, as we say, the eye which sees the unseen—if you are able to see the divine wisdom and foresight standing with your nature in its hands, and saying, "This nature will need such and such chances," and so making for it this Boston and this profession of the law, and also see that same wisdom and foresight standing with this Boston and this legal profession in its sight, and saying, "They will need such and such a man," and so making you. "Ah," you say, in your mock humility, "I cannot really think that I am of as much consequence as that." "Ah," you say, in your crude independence, "I will not let any power choose and appoint my life for me. I will do it for myself." Let the two outbursts modify and rectify each other. Let your humility make you rejoice that God has appointed for you the Jerusalem up to which the whole journey of your life must climb. Let your instinct of independence, your instinct of personal life, give you assurance that God cannot have chosen your Jerusalem for you so absolutely that it will not rest with you to find the way to it through every bewilderment, and to keep it continually in your sight.

All this is illustrated in the life of him to whom the picture of our text belongs. The life of Jesus Christ is full of this atmosphere of God. He calls Himself, "Him whom the Father hath sanctified and sent into the world." What does that mean but just what I have been saying? God made the world and He sent Jesus. The world needed Jesus the Saviour, and Jesus the Saviour bore in His mysterious nature the power to save the world. The two met and there was Jerusalem, the sacred city, the city where the sacrifices had smoked in prophecy for years; the city where Herod and Pilate tarried for their victim; the city where the judgment-seat, the condemnation, the cross, the resurrection morning were waiting. As Jesus goes up to that Jerusalem, He goes because He is He, and Jerusalem is Jerusalem, and because both are themselves in God; because the Father hath sanctified him and sent him into the world. When he came there and the cross seized and held him, character and circumstances had perfectly met in their complete result. The Saviourhood and the world's need of being saved had come together, and here was salvation.

Would it not be a vast thing for us if we could be far more aware than we are now of some such great Christlike sweep of our lives towards a purpose? The truth which Jesus first manifested in his living, and then taught in his doctrine, the truth that man is the child of God, is pregnant with that consciousness. Whenever any man has learned it he grows strong and eager. He no longer loiters and plays. A friend comes to you and says, "Do this with me!" And you quietly reply to him, "I cannot;" and he answers you, "Why not?" And you say, "I am going up to Jerusalem." There is an end of it. You have not to sit on a stone at the road side, undetermined, until every speculative question has been settled, until you have decided just whether the thing is wrong, and just how wrong it is, and just how bad it is for this other man to do it, and just how near a thing to it you may allow yourself to do. Simply the thing is not on the way to your Jerusalem, and so you press on past it and leave it far behind. Ah, how men spend their time in debating just how wrong things are, which, whether they be more or less wrong, these men know that it is not for them to do. It is as if a traveller in a great highway refused to pass by the opening of any side lane until he knew just how deep was the bog or the wilderness into which the lane would lead him if he followed it, which he has no idea of doing. The power of an apprehended purpose saves us from all that. The hope of our Jerusalem draws us on, and will not let us stop.

And, to come to the second part of what I want to say, this power of our purpose, this attraction of Jerusalem, is not destroyed, nay, is not weakened, nay, is intensified and strengthened, when the vail is lifted, and it is distinctly shown to us that our purpose can be attained only by struggle and self-sacrifice and pain. This surely is one of the most interesting things in all our study of mankind. I see a man who has caught sight of how his character and his circumstances unite to designate for him a certain work and destiny. He is inspired by the vision. He has set out with all his soul to realize it. I can see lions in the way which he cannot see. I dread to tell him of the deserts he must cross, the fires through which he must force his way before He can go into that open gate, and be what he has made up his mind to be. At last I feel myself compelled to tell him, and I do tell him with a trembling heart. I look to see him falter and sink down, or else turn and run. Instead of that I see his eye kindle; his whole face glows; his frame stiffens with intense resolution, and I see him a thousand times more eager than before to do this thing which he has recognized as his. Listen to Jesus as he says the words following our text: "Behold we go up to Jerusalem, and all things which are written concerning the Son of man shall be accomplished. For he shall be delivered unto the Gentiles, and shall be mocked and spitefully entreated and spitted on, and they shall scourge him and put him to death." What a catalogue of miseries! How clear and how certain they evidently are, as we hear through the ages that calm voice rehearsing them, while the Lord and the disciples walk along the road. But tell me, as we hear that voice through the ages, is there any faltering in it because of these miseries which it foretells? Are you not sure that the steadfast feet go pressing on all the more steadfastly as they keep time to the tragical catalogue which the calm lips are telling? O this is a wonderful power in man, this power which shines out supremely in the Man of men, this power to be inspired by danger, and to desire a good and great thing all the more because of the deserts and the fire and the death which must be gone through for its attainment!

We hear it said sometimes that it was wonderful that Jesus, having undertaken the world's salvation, did not draw back at the sight of the cross. Would it not have been wonderful if, being Jesus, he had drawn back and refused to go up to Jerusalem because of what was waiting for him there? Can we imagine that? Would we not have said at once, "No, ᴜᴇ is not the Christ I thought he was—or else the cross with all its terrors never could have frightened Him."

I think the same is true of all devoted souls—of all souls who have really seen their Jerusalem and set their faces towards it. I do not expect them—they ought not to expect themselves—to be turned back by the difficulties and terrors which stand in the way. The wonders of life are not in deeds, but in characters. Given the character, the deed does not surprise me. Let me look into the martyr's soul and see the perfect consecration which is burning there, and then there is no wonder in my spirit when I see him walking next day to the stake as to a festival. The wonder would be if I saw him turn and run away. Let me thoroughly understand how the humble missionary loves his Master and thinks that Master's service the one precious thing on earth, and then I can perfectly comprehend why he turns his ship's prow all the more steadfastly shoreward when the savages come howling down to the beach to seek his blood. The wonder is that they should be the men they are. When they once are the men they are, the things that they do are not wonderful.

No deed is wonderful except in relation to the strength which does it. It would be wonderful that a robin should swim, but it is not wonderful that a fish should swim. It would be wonderful if you or I should write a Hamlet. It was not wonderful that Shakespeare should do it. The wonder is that he should be Shakespeare; but, he being Shakespeare, Hamlet is no miracle. It would be unspeakably wonderful if any man should stand upon the mountain top and bid the morning rise out of the sea. But God does it day by day, and we are not astonished. Granted God, and what deed of God is marvellous? God is so marvellous that He exhausts all marvel in Himself. God is the one only wonder of the universe. With Him in the universe, the most stupendous prodigies are natural.

What does this mean for us? What is its bearing on our lives? Something very direct and definite, I think. If you are going up to Jerusalem, and as you go you become aware that you can only reach your Jerusalem, your purpose, through suffering, perhaps through death. What then? Where shall you look for your release, and the solution of your fear? Shall you expect it in the change of circumstances, in the muzzling o the lions so that they shall not bite you, in the palsying of death so that it shall not kill you? No! you must seek it in the strengthening of your own life, so that it shall be nothing strange for you, being the man you are, to scorn the lions and to laugh at death.

Men watch you. They say, Is it possible that he will not be frightened, but will go on to his appointed end through everything? You, knowing your own heart, are sure that you will not be frightened, sure that you will indeed go on. Some friend who really knows you, quietly says, "Yes, he will conquer," and evidently thinks it nothing strange.

It is no gift of prophecy in him. It is simply that he does know you, and knowing your strength, the trial that awaits it does not seem too great.

O, do not pray for easy lives. Pray to be stronger men! Do not pray for tasks equal to your powers. Pray for powers equal to your tasks! Then the doing of your work shall be no miracle. But you shall be a miracle. Every day you shall wonder at yourself, at the richness of life which has come in you by the grace of God.

There is nothing which comes to seem more foolish to us, I think, as years go by, than the limitations which have been quietly set to the moral possibilities of man. They are placidly and perpetually assumed. "You must not expect too much of him," so it is said. "You must remember that he is only a man, after all." "Only a man!" That sounds to me as if one said, "You may launch your boat and sail a little way, but you must not expect to go very far. It is only the Atlantic Ocean." Why man's moral range and reach is practically infinite, at least no man has yet begun to comprehend where its limits lies. Man's powers of conquering temptation, of despising danger, of being true to principle, have never been even indicated, save in Christ. "Only a man!" that means only a Son of God; and who can begin to say what a Son of God, claiming his Father, may become and be and do?

Therefore the fact that with our purpose clear before us, with something which we believe that it is our place to accomplish in the world, there still are fears and pains and difficulties in the way, that fact may not have any power except a power of inspiration. You tell the mother that her child is in danger, and that she cannot save it except by vast self-sacrifice, and the question never arises for an instant whether the sacrifice shall be undertaken and the child saved. The whole power of the tidings is just to summon a deeper flood of that self-sacrifice which is the very essence of her motherhood, and which laughs at danger with a quiet scorn.

So may it be with you! I look across this congregation and I know that to many of these young eyes some Jerusalem has shown itself, some purpose far away upon its hill. You have multiplied your character into your circumstances and seen what you ought to do with your life. I bid you know it is not easy to attain your hope. I bid you clearly know that if the life which you have chosen to be your life is really worthy of you, it involves self-sacrifice and pain. If your Jerusalem really is your sacred city, there is certainly a cross in it. What then? Shall you flinch and draw back? Shall you ask for yourself another life? O no, not another life, but another self. Ask to be born again. Ask God to fill you with Himself, and then calmly look up and go on. Go up to Jerusalem expecting all things that are written concerning you to be fulfilled. Disappointment, mortification, misconception, enmity, pain, death, these may come to you, but if they come to you in doing your duty it is all right. "It cannot be that a prophet perish out of Jerusalem," said Jesus. "It is dreadful to suffer except in doing duty. To suffer there is glorious." That is our translation of his words into our own life.

May God let us all first see our Jerusalem and then attain it. What is that prayer but the great prayer of our Collect in the Prayer Book—that by his holy inspiration we may think those things that are good, and by his merciful guiding may perform the same, through our Lord Jesus Christ. Amen.

SERMON XIX.

The Safety and Helpfulness of Faith.

"They shall take up serpents, and if they drink any deadly thing it shall not harm them. They shall lay hands on the sick and they shall recover."—MARK xvi. 18.

THESE are the last words that Jesus spoke on earth. The next verse says, "So then after the Lord had spoken unto them, he was received up into heaven, and sat on the right hand of God." The cloud which hid their Master from the disciples' sight left these words of promise still ringing in their ears. "These signs shall follow them that believe," he said. And those who knew that they believed in him must have turned and gone back from the scene of the ascension, with eyes full of the expectation of miracle. By-and-by they began to see the fulfilment of the promises. When Peter and John went through the Beautiful Gate into the Temple, and looking upon the lame man bade him, "In the name of Jesus Christ of Nazareth, rise up and walk," and "he leaping up stood and walked," the disciples who stood by must have looked into one another's faces and said, "Yes, this is what the

Master promised." When Paul at Melita shook off the viper into the fire and felt no hurt, the words of the Lord must have come back to them, and they must have said, "Behold still the signs that He foretold should follow them that believe." And no doubt they were right. Christ's farewell words did find such fulfilment for a time. But by-and-by there came a change. Those miracles became more and more rare. Men still believed, but their belief gave them less and less power over material nature. Perhaps then the disciples grew bewildered and perplexed. Can it be that the power of Christ's promise is exhausted? Had his gift a limit so that it has lost its virtue? But as they asked that question, gradually they must have become aware of a more profound fulfilment of the promise. No longer over outer and material things, but now over the inner and spiritual life, the power of faith began to show itself. No longer over the danger of the serpents which the hands could handle, or of the sicknesses which flushed the cheek with fever or crippled the tortured limbs, did their belief prove itself mighty. The serpents of the soul, the sicknesses of the heart and mind, they learned to see that these were more dangerous enemies, and that their faith came to its supreme test when it grappled with and tried to conquer these. This conviction grew with the deepening spiritual life of Christianity, until at last the words changed their tone, and now it is a promise of spiritual victory over spiritual difficulties, when the disciple hears his Lord declare, "You shall take up serpents, and if you touch any deadly thing it shall not harm you. You shall lay hands on the sick and they shall recover."

It is in this fullest sense of course that I want to study the great eternal promise of Christ with you this morning. It is as bright to-day as it was on that fresh morning when our Lord passed into the cloud which still hides him from our sight. Nay, it is brighter. The sun that goes behind a cloud always diffuses its light over the heavens not instantly at its first disappearance, but not till some few moments after the cloud has hidden it, and when the cloud itself helps to diffuse the light of the sun which it has hidden. So when Christ became unseen, the world only gradually learned the richness and completeness of his unseen presence. And so we are studying not something whose glory is outworn, but something whose light is growing brighter in the world continually, when we study the promise of the ascending Christ.

The promise then is this: that the believer shall drink poison and it shall not harm him, and that life shall go out of him to cure the sick. And first of all we must notice what is the cause of privileges such as these. Then we shall better understand the full nature of the privileges. These signs are to follow "them that believe." It is to men who believe, through their belief, that privileges such as these are to be given. The essence and ground of the promised power is faith. That old word, Faith! That old thing, Faith! How men have stumbled over its definition and bewildered and ensnarled themselves and those who heard them! God forbid that I should bewilder you to-day. I want to be as clear and simple as I can; and though I would be far from disparaging any of the subtler and more elaborate descriptions of what faith is, I am sure that we may give ourselves a definition which is true beyond all doubt, and which is full enough to answer all the need of definition which we shall meet to-day. Faith then, personal faith, is this, the power by which one being's vitality, through love and obedience, becomes the vitality of another being. Simple enough that is, I am sure, for any man who will think. I believe in you, my friend; and your vitality, your character, your energy, the more I love and obey you, passes over into me. The saint believes in his pattern saint, the soldier believes in his brave captain, the scholar believes in his learned teacher. In every case the vitality of the object of faith comes through love and obedience to the believer. Faith is not love nor obedience, but it works by both. A man may love me and yet not have faith in me. A man may obey me, and yet not have faith in me. Faith is a distinct relation between soul and soul; but it is recognizable by this result, that the life of one soul becomes the life of the other soul through obedience and love. Now faith in Christ, what is it? Just in the same simple way, it is that power by which the vitality of Christ, through our love and obedience to Him, becomes our vitality. The triumph of the believing soul is this, that he does not live by himself; that into him is ever flow-

The Safety and Helpfulness of Faith. 337

ing, by a law which is both natural and supernatural, a law that is supernatural only because it is the consummation and transfiguration of the most natural of all laws—there is always flowing into him the vitality of the Christ whom he loves and obeys. His whole nature beats with the inflow of that divine life. He lives, but Christ lives in him.

And then add one thing more. That this vitality of Christ which comes into a man by faith, is not a strange and foreign thing. Christ is the Son of Man, the perfect man, the divine man. Add this, and then we know that his vitality filling us is the perfection of human life filling humanity. "They that believe" are not men turned into something else than men, by the mixture of a new and strange divine ingredient. They are men in whom human life is perfect in proportion to the completeness of their faith through the Son of Man. They are men raised to the highest power. The man in whom Christ dwells by faith is the man in whom the divine ideal of human life is perfect, or is steadily becoming perfect, by the entrance into him of the perfect life of the man Christ Jesus, through obedience and love.

And now turn back to our promise. These signs shall follow them that believe, them that have the complete human life by me—Christ says. "If they drink any deadly thing it shall not harm them—and they shall lay hands on the sick and they shall recover." Is that a prize? Is it wages which is offered for a certain meritorious act which is called faith?

Not so, surely! It is a consequence. It is a necessity. Safety and helpfulness. These come out of the full life of Christ in the soul of man as the inevitable fruits. Safety, so that what hurts other men shall not hurt him. Helpfulness, so that his brethren about him shall live by his life. These are the utterances of the vitality of him who is thoroughly alive. See what we have reached already. It is by life, by full, vigorous, emphatic existence that men are safe in this world, and that they save other men from death. I glory in such a statement as that. It makes my Bible shine. Men everywhere are trying to be safe by stifling life; by living just as low as possible. Men everywhere are trying not to do one another harm, trying to spare each other's souls by tender petting, by guarding them against any vigorous contact with life and thought. The Bible comes glowing with protest. "Not so," it says. "Only by the fulness of life does safety come. Only by the power of contact with life are sick and helpless souls made whole. None but the live man saves himself or quickens the dead to life; saves himself or saves his neighbor." It is a noble assertion. The whole Bible, from its first page to its last, is full of the assertion of the fundamental necessity of vitality; that the first thing which a man needs in order to live well, is to live.

Let us take now these two parts of the promise of Christ in turn. He tells his disciples that if they believe in him, they shall drink deadly things and not be harmed, and they shall be able to heal the sick. Safety and helpfulness, these are the two privileges of full life; these two together make a successful and complete career. And first let us consider the safety which Christ offers. Notice it is a safety not by the avoidance of deadly things, but by the neutralizing of them through a higher and stronger power. There is no such idle promise as that if a man believes in Christ a wall shall be built around his soul, so that the things out of which souls make sin cannot come to him. The Master knew the world too well for that. His own experience on the hill of his temptation was still fresh in his memory. He knew that life meant exposure, that sin must surely beat at every one of these hearts. Nay, that the things out of which sin is made, temptation, moral trial, must enter into every heart; and so he said not, "I will lead you through secluded ways where none but sweet and healthy waters flow :" but, " Where I lead you there will be the streams of poison. Only if you have the vitality which comes by faith in me, your life shall be stronger than the poison's death ; if you drink any deadly thing it shall not harm you."

One thing we see immediately in such a promise, one condition which belongs to its fulfilment. It is that only in the higher action and mission lay the safety from the lower influence; and therefore that the lower influence was to be powerless over the disciples only as they met it incidentally in the direct pursuance of their higher task. Jesus had made this same promise once before. When he sent the seventy disciples out to preach, he said to them almost exactly these same words, which now he said as he looked into his disciples' eyes for the last time on Olivet. They too were to find the deadly things they touched robbed of their venom. The poison was to be harmless as they drank it. But then Christ spoke it of their special mission. It was while they went on this particular preaching journey that the pestilential powers of nature were to lose their mischief. But now, on Olivet, he is giving his disciples a life-long career. He is sending them forth consecrated to a service which is to last until they die. So now the special promise becomes general, and covers all their life ; now they are constantly to be armed against the poison; but still the essence of safety is to be in their perpetual mission, their unbroken consecration. It was not that they might sit down at ease and drink what pleasant poison they would, and yet be unharmed. It was only while they were living, believing, working, only as they lived and believed and worked, that they were safe.

And the meaning of that, when we translate it into the terms of our life, is clear enough. Only those temptations which we encounter on the way of duty, in the path of consecration, only those has our Lord promised us that we shall conquer. He sends us out to live and work for him. The chances of sin which we meet while that divine design of life, the life and work for Him, is clear before us, shall not hurt us. When we forget that design, our arm withers, our immunity is gone. This is what we really mean, what we often put blindly enough, when

The Safety and Helpfulness of Faith. 341

we ask whether such a man is a religious man or not. We mean, or we ought to mean, whether religion or the service of God is present with him as a continual purpose; not whether he is ever tempted; not whether he ever sins; we know the answers to those questions well enough; but whether behind all the temptation, under all the sin, his soul is still set toward God with genuine and strong devotion. If it is, we know that he must come out safe. This is the real question after which men are often fumbling when they seem to make some mere outside thing like an amulet worn about the neck, or a church-membership written in a book, a pledge and token that what would be sin to other men is not sin to some privileged, protected soul.

It is only when we are about some higher task, only when they meet us as accidents in the service of Christ, that we have a right deliberately to encounter temptation and the chance to sin, and may claim the Lord's promise of immunity. Think in how many places that law applies. Have I a right to read this skeptical book, this book in which some able, witty man has gathered all his skill against my Christian faith? It is a book of poison. Have I a right to drink it? Who can say absolutely yes or no? Who does not feel that it depends upon what sort of life the reader brings to meet the poison? If in your soul there is a passionate desire for truth, if you do really love and serve Christ, and want to know him better that you may love and serve him more, if this book comes as a help to that, part of a study by which you shall get nearer to the heart of the truth and him, then if you drink that deadly thing it shall not harm you. Nay, you may rise up from the reading with a faith more deep. Whatever change your faith may undergo, it shall win a profounder life. But if there is no such earnestness, no such life as this, if it is mere curiosity, mere desire to be fine and liberal, mere defiance, a mere wantonness, then the poison has it all its own way; there is no vigorous life to meet it; and its death spreads through the nature till it finds the heart.

This is the only true discrimination. The old policy which makes indexes of forbidden books can never do anything for faith. Whatever a man can read in honesty and humility and consecration, and the pure desire of truth, let him read it; and if there be any deadly thing in what he reads it shall not harm him. I say this solemnly, deliberately, thoughtfully, knowing that many young people are hearing, and I hope are noting what I say. I say it without hesitation ; only I beg you to remember how profound are the conditions which alone give one the right to read the skeptics and yet hope to keep his faith. It is a solemn thing for a man first to be sure that he has indeed honesty, humility, consecration, and the pure desire of truth. The very solemnity and responsibility with which he searches himself that he may be sure of that, will be his safest safeguard.

There are dabblers in unbelief on every side of us, who are being poisoned through and through by the

The Safety and Helpfulness of Faith. 343

scepticism which they drink in. There are other men who know vastly more than they about what unbelief has said, who are more full of real faith for all their study. Everything depends upon the state in which their spiritual constitutions met the struggle and upon what it was that took them into the midst of doubt. And so it is eveywhere with all exposures of the spiritual life. "What took you there?" "What right had you to be there?" These are the critical questions on which everything depends. If you are passing through temptation with your eye fixed on a pure, true life beyond it, temptation being only a necessary stage upon your way, so long as you keep that purpose, that resolution, that ideal, you shall be safe. If you are in temptation for temptation's sake, with no purpose beyond it, you are lost.

Two men walk through the vilest streets here in our city. One of them has nothing in him but selfishness and low love of self-indulgence. The other is glowing with human charity, seeking perhaps some child of his who has wandered into that dreadful hell, or longing, it may be, to pluck out of the burning some man's or woman's life, whose fiery iniquity makes those streets the streets of hell. Why is it that one man fills himself full of the iniquity through which he walks, steeps himself in its vileness, and the other comes out with garments all the whiter for the fire? Is it not what Jesus said, "This sign shall follow them that believe. If they drink any deadly thing it shall not harm them"?

Two men go into politics. One of them wants office;

the other wants honesty in government, faithfulness to national obligation, the preservation of the public purity and credit. What shall be their personal fate, the fate of their personal characters there, in the political turmoil? One of them has no faith. It is faith that sends the other where perhaps his feet half refuse to go. According to their faith so is it unto them. And when, while one man sinks from depth to depth of unscrupulous selfishness and shameless corruption, the other seems to breathe the foulest air without a weakness or a taint, I seem to see as clear a fulfilment as the world can show, of that which Jesus said, "This sign shall follow them that believe. If they drink any deadly thing it shall not harm them."

The religious man who lives and works in one church, one denomination, is saved from the poison of narrowness and sectarianism by the larger faith with which he believes and rejoices in the work of Christ his Master, and the salvation of men his brethren, wherever he can see it going on. The woman in social life bears a charmed life through all its deadening frivolity, because the life of Christ is in her, and she ever counts herself and all of those whom her life touches in the lightest contact, the children of God, sacred, and capable of pure and beautiful life. Everywhere the amulet is faith, some great idea, some large, long hope. Everywhere, where death rages most wantonly, "the just shall live by faith."

What would you say to the young man who you

knew was asked to go into some dangerous trade? Not a trade where boilers sometimes exploded or where poisonous gases crept into the lungs, but a trade where honesty was constantly beseiged, or where temperance was hourly solicited, or where a man was always dragged down towards hard and cynical thoughts of his fellow-men. What would you say to him? If the danger was a certainty, if no man could possibly live in that trade and not be cursed with its curse, then there would be only one thing to say. He must not go at all. No man has any right to be doing that hateful business anywhere upon the earth, no matter how it may seem as if the world would suffer if all men gave it up. That case is plain. What shall it profit a man if he gain the whole world and lose his soul? But if that is not so. If men do live in this dangerous trade and keep their souls pure, what then shall you say to your young friend who thinks of entering into it? "Be sure, be sure that you have faith. Be sure that you are one of them that believe. Be sure that you are going there for something more than money. Be sure that you reverence the life you carry there. Be sure that you go there as the child of God. If you go so, then go, and Christ's word shall be fulfilled to you. In fear of him, in reverence for yourself, in charity for your brethren shall be your safety. And protected by that faith, "if you drink any deadly thing it shall not harm you."

There is a deep solemnity about the sight when a group of young men, a generation of young men, come up to life together. To whom among them will it be life indeed? to whom will it be death? It is as if we saw a line of men march into a region where a fever raged. How we should search their faces to see which among them carried the vitality which could keep them safe. The pestilence is not whimsical or indiscriminate. It knows its victims when it sees them coming. And so the world of wickedness, the world of corruption, impurity and spiritual death—it too must know its victims. It too must laugh with anticipated triumph as it sees coming up to it a frivolous and faithless soul, must cringe and know its powerlessness when some man filled with faith, comes humbly, strong with the strength of Him in whom he trusts. For him the world in vain may mix its poisons. This is the criticalness that one feels as he sees any group of men beginning life; any class of young men leaving college; any generation meeting the novel needs and dangers of a new age of the world.

So much I say distinctively of the first part of Christ's promise to the faithful man. He promises him safety. But that is not all. Hear once again the other part. "If he drink any deadly thing it shall not harm him," and " He shall lay hands on the sick and they shall recover." Safety and helpfulness. He shall be safe and he shall save others too. These two things go together, not merely in this special promise of the Saviour, but in all life. Safety and helpfulness. So is the whole world bound into a whole, so does the good that comes to any man tend to diffuse itself and touch the lives of all, that these two things are true. First, that no man can be really safe, really secure that the world shall not harm and poison him, unless there is going out from him a living and life-giving influence to other men. And second, that no man is really helping other men unless there is true life in his own soul. Both of these seem to me to be great and ever-present truths. Men try to act as if they were not true, and thence comes much bad, useless living. Men think that they can be safe without being helpful, and thence come all the selfish notions of salvation. Merely to crawl through life with face and mouth so bandaged up with caution that the foul air of life cannot affect us; merely to strike out from the wreck of a fallen world and swim ashore, shaking off all the drowning men who clutch at us in the wild water, and leaving the screaming wretches to their fate, the man who seeks salvation so, finds at last to his disappointment and dismay that he is not saved. It is not the hands that catch us and hold on to us, it is the hands of helpless men which we shake off in our selfishness that drag us down.

And then the other truth. No man can really save another unless he saves himself. It is the good man by his good deeds that gives life to the world. The vitality which bad men by their bad deeds seem to give, is not vitality, but death. You remember how they taunted Jesus on the cross. "He saved others, Himself he cannot save," they said. But they were wrong. It could not be as they said. We know that he was saving himself while he saved the world. He was fulfilling his work. He was glorifying his Father. He was entering into life as death crept over him. And always it is the living, not the dead, who give life. It is the man not who has sinned deeply but who has known by intense sympathy what sin is, how strong, how terrible, and yet escaped it for himself. He is the man who helps the sinners most. He is the anointed one who carries on and carries round the Christ's salvation. In their deepest need the wickedest men look to the purest men they know; the deadest to the livest; first to those who they think have most escaped sin, then to those who they think have been most cleansed of sin by repentance and forgiveness.

These two things belong essentially together—Safety and Helpfulness—and both of these Jesus promises to the men who believe in Him. Turn then for a few hurried moments to the second helpfulness or the life-giving, the life-strengthening power. "They shall lay hands on the sick and they shall recover." If I read those words spiritually, if I make them the promise and prophecy of that wonderful power which in all times, in all religions, spiritual life has had to extend itself, like fire, from any one point which it has already occupied, to everything within its reach which is inflammable, which is capable of the same burning life, it seems to me that the way in which the promise is fulfilled is by the clothing of the believing life with two qualities which are expressed by these two words—testimony and transmission. Here is a man in whom I know that the promise of Christ is certainly fulfilled. He is a believer, and through his open faith the life of Christ flows into him constantly, and is his life. Full of that life, he gives it everywhere he goes. The sick in soul touch his soul and are well again. The discouraged find new bravery, the yielding souls are clad anew with firmness. The frivolous grow serious, the mean are stung or tempted into generosity, and sinners hate their sin and crave a better life, wherever this man goes. Oh! there are such men in the world. There always have been. The world finds them out, and souls half-conscious of disease creep to their doors. Friends bring their friends into the presence of these healing lives as of old the men of Jerusalem "brought forth the sick into the streets, and laid them on beds and couches, that at least the shadow of Peter passing by might overshadow some of them."

The power of these life-giving lives seem to me, I say, to be described in these two words—testimony and transmission. It is first in the testimony which they bear by the very fact of their own abundant life. They show the presence, they assert the possibility of vitality. And very often this is what souls whose spiritual life is weak and low need to have done for them. Men half alive grow to doubt of the fuller life in anybody. Men try to realize the descriptions of religion which they hear, and, falling short of them, they grow ready to believe that religion is a thing of excited imaginations, and to give up all thought of making it real in themselves. It is

350 The Safety and Helpfulness of Faith.

not only the badness in the world, it is the dreadful incredulity of good, it is the despair and lack of struggle, which tells how low ebbs out the tide of spiritual life. Then comes the man in whom spiritual life is a real, deep, strong, positive thing. The first work which that man does is to bear the simple testimony of his life that life is possible. Already, just in acknowledgment of that, the sick faces begin to revive and the sick eyes look up to him. The brave and godly boy among a group of boys just learning to be proud of godlessness and contemptuous of piety—the man of golden principles among the skeptics of the street—the one true penitent rejoicing in a new and certain hope out of the ranks of flagrant sin—these instantly, the moment that they begin to live, begin to bear their testimony of life, and so make life about them. The hand just trembling with the mute and awed but certain consciousness of its own new life, though it be but a child's hand, feeling for support, there is a wondrous power in it, if it falls upon some poor decrepit faithless soul, to work there the fulfilment of the Saviour's promise that they which believe shall lay hands on the sick and they shall recover.

And besides testimony I also said transmission. The highest statement of the culture of a human nature and of the best attainment that is set before it, is that, as it grows better, it grows more transparent and more simple, more capable therefore of simply and truly transmitting the life and will of God which is behind it. The thought of a man, as he im-

The Safety and Helpfulness of Faith. 351

proves and strengthens, getting the control of his own powers and becoming more and more a source of power over other men, this thought, which has no doubt its own degree of truth, is limited and vulgar beside the breadth and fineness of the other idea, that as a man is trained and cultured, as the various events of life create their changes in him, as tempests beat him and sunshine bathe him, as he wrestles with temptation and yields to grace, as he goes on through the spring-time, the summer and the autumn of his life, the one highest purpose and result of it all is to beat and fuse his life into transparency, so that it can transmit the life of God. For all good is from God, and he uses our lives, all of them, to reach other men's lives with. Only the difference is this: upon a life of sin, all hard and black, God shines as the sun shines on the black, hard marble, and by reflection thence strikes on the things around, leaving the centre of the marble itself always dark. But on a life of obedience and faith, God shines as the sun shines on a block of chrystal, sending its radiance through the willing and transparent mass and warming and lighting it all into its inmost depths.

I wish that there were time to develope and describe the privilege and power of belief to become the transmitter of that which it believes in. The figure which I have just used tells the story, and I must leave it with you as I abruptly close. Only remember that no words can tell, no figure can begin to represent the fulness of the privilege of life which belongs to those who genuinely believe in Jesus

Christ. Nothing but his own life can tell us fully what the life is that he means to give to us. Safety and helpfulness. As safe as he was, as able to touch the blackest sin and yet be white, to taste of death and thereby be more thoroughly alive. So safe shall His complete disciples be. As helpful as he was; as full of the testimony of life and its possibility to half-dead souls. As purely transparent in obedience, in self-forgetfulness, in essential sonship kept clear and unclouded by filial love. So helpful shall they be who believe in Him. As live as he was, nay, as live as he is forever, shall we be when our human life becomes the utterance of his, as his divine Life is the utterance of God's.

SERMON XX.

The Great Expectation.

AN OLD-YEAR SERMON.

"Let your moderation be known unto all men. The Lord is at hand."—PHILLIPPIANS iv. 4.

IT is not easy to decide just what the apostles expected with reference to the second coming of the Lord. Sometimes it seemed as if they looked almost immediately to see the opening sky and the descending chariot. At other times, with a more general faith, they seemed to anticipate what has come to pass, the slow and spiritual occupation of the standards and purposes of human life by the spirit of Jesus, to be quickened at some future day and brought to some great consummation which it is impossible to describe beforehand, but which, when it comes, will centre about him and crown him as the Master of the world. Sometimes one of these thoughts, sometimes the other seems to represent St. Paul's anticipation. But, whatever was the form which their expectation more or less definitely assumed, the great fact about him and the other disciples was that they always were expecting. Their look was always forward; and they found abundant clearness and abundant inspiration in their expectancy when they described the thing which they expected as a "coming of the Lord." "Maranatha." "The Lord will come." It was one of their customs to greet one another with that salutation.

We cannot probably imagine how completely this habit of expectation had possession of their lives. It must have given color and meaning to everything they did. Every step they took in life brought them a little nearer to that great end and purpose. They set out on a voyage, and as they turned their eyes away from the fading shore and looked across the broad waters, they seemed to be sailing out to meet the coming Lord. Two of them parted from each other, not knowing when they were to meet again, and they said to themselves. Whenever it is it will be in some nearer presence of the Lord. One of them moved to a new dwelling, and, as he entered into the door of what was to be his future home, its rooms became sacred to him because in them he was to witness the approach of Christ; in them Christ was to be nearer to him than ever in the house which he had left behind. "Now is our salvation nearer than when we first believed." Those words which once came from the apostle's lips, expressed the feeling and the power which was always in all the apostles' hearts.

And it has been this expectation of a coming of the Lord which, ever since the time of the apostles, has always been the inspiration of the Christian

The Great Expectation. 355

world. The noblest souls always have believed that humanity was capable of containing, and was sure sooner or later to receive, a larger and deeper infusion of divinity. The promise of Christianity is as yet but half fulfilled. All that has been done yet in all the Christian centuries is only the sketch and prelude of what is yet to be done. This has been the faith of every Christian reformer. This is what has made it easy for souls which loved the dear associations of the past as much as any others, to cut loose from them and sail out on unknown seas. It has not been mere wilfulness. It has been really the profoundest faith. It has dared to think of human history not as a great flat plain on which men wandered pleasantly but aimlessly, always coming back at last to the dead camp-fires where they had slept before, but as a flight of shining stairs up which men were to struggle toilsomely but eagerly toward a day of the Lord, a kingdom of heaven which was waiting for them at the top.

And as the noblest souls have thought of the world's history, so the most earnest men and women have always thought of their own lives. The power of any life lies in its expectancy. "What do you hope for? What do you expect?" The answer to these questions is the measure of the degree in which a man is living. He who can answer these questions by the declaration, "The Lord is at hand: I am expecting a higher, deeper, more pervading mastery of Christ"—we know that he is thoroughly alive.

And, as I have already intimated, one of the

great signs of how strong life is in such a man will be the way in which he leaves his past. What a difference there is in men about that! Some men are always driven out of their past and leave it only because they cannot stay there. Other men go forth from their past because they have grown weary and disgusted with it, and are willing to flee from it for pure love of change. Other men leave their past full of honor for it, full of gratitude for the equipment which it has given them for their future life, but full also of the attraction of the future in which the equipment which their past has given them is to be used. Here on a ship's deck which goes sailing out of port some day there are three men together. All of them are leaving the home-land. Behind all three alike, standing on the same deck, the same land fades away and is lost out of sight. But is it the same thing to all of them? Has leaving home for all of them the same meaning? One is an exile, who, having committed flagrant crime, is permitted to live only on condition that he shall leave his country and never come back to it again. One is an idler, who, having exhausted the surface of the land where he belongs, is sailing now to feed his restlessness in mere change, in the mere sight of things he never saw before. The third is a discoverer, who has gathered all the knowledge and character which he could gain at home, and is now set to use them in reading the secret of some hidden country and making the world larger for mankind. How different they are! with what different eyes they see the familiar shore sink down into the sea! But they are not more different than are three men who leave any one period of life behind them and go out into a new one, one of them simply with the feeling that he cannot help himself, another with the vague sense that the past has grown tame and the future will offer something new, and the third with the eager hope that the Lord is at hand, that in the larger circumstances and with the maturer powers he will come nearer to and know more of Christ.

You know of course why I have thus begun to speak to you to-day. It is the last Sunday of 1884. The year which came to us twelve months ago, all fresh and young, is old and weary. Before next Sunday a new year will come to crowd him from his place. On such a Sunday it is not a mere habit, it is a natural and healthy instinct, which makes us stand between the new year and the old, between the living and the dead, and listen to them as they speak to one another. Can we not almost hear the words they say, and is not their deepest burden something like this which I have tried to express? The old year says to the new year, "Take this man and show him greater things than I have been able to show him. You must be for him a richer, fuller day of the Lord than I could be." The new year says to the old, "I will take him and do for him the best that I can do. But all that I can do for him will be possible only in virtue of the preparation which you have made, only because of what you have done for him already."

We want to think then about men going forward to greater things, leaving the past, in hope and expectation of a greater future. As I announce that subject, I can almost hear some cynical bystander say, "You may spare yourself the trouble of that sermon. For one half of your hearers it will be needless. For the other half it will be useless. The young people know without your telling them, know better than you can tell them, that the future is very great and glorious and splendid; and you will not convince the people who are no longer young that the future will be in any great way different from the past. Perhaps there are a few just trembling between youth and age, not having wholly lost the vision of the one nor gained the insight of the other, whom you may persuade to cling to their illusions a little longer; but is that really worth your while? By-and-by the eyes must open and the vision disappear, and then the monotony of life must be accepted, and the man give up all expectation of anything except running the same round of routine till he dies."

I want at least to bear a protest against the mockery of such words as those, and to assert that that cry, "The Lord is at hand," may and ought to be in the ears of every man as he goes from the old year to the new.

There are really two divisions of our subject. We may think first of the way in which a man becomes more conscious of the God who is already close to him, and second of the way in which God actually comes closer to him, year by year. They are what the philosophers would call the subjective and the objective thoughts of God's nearness. And we start with that which must be true, the assertion that the more varied and manifold a man's experiences have become, the more he has the chance to know of God, the more chance God has to show Himself to him. Every new experience is a new opportunity of knowing God. Every experience is like a jewel set into the texture of our life, on which God shines and makes interpretation and revelation of himself. You hang a great rich dark cloth up into the sunlight, and the sun shines on it and shows the broad general color that is there. Then one by one you sew great precious stones upon the cloth, and each one, as you set it there, catches the sunlight and pours it forth in a flood of peculiar glory. A diamond here, an emerald there, an opal there, the sun seems to rejoice as he finds each moment a new interpreter of his splendor, until at last the whole jewelled cloth is burning and blazing with the gorgeous revelation.

Now a much-living life, a life of manifold experiences, is like a robe which bursts forth of itself to jewels. They are sewn on from the outside. They burn out of its substance as the stars burn out of the heart of the night. And God shines with new revelation upon every one. And the man who feels himself going out of a dying year with these jewels of experience which have burned forth from his life during its months, and knowing that God in the New Year will shine upon them and reveal Himself by them, may well go full of expectation, saying, "The Lord is at hand."

Life may be always expecting new sight of God, because life is always acquiring new experiences on which, through which, God may declare His nearness and His love. We may, if we will, turn the jewelled cloth away from the sun, but if we let him shine upon it, he must make himself known. To most of you—shall I not say to all of you?—have come in this past year, some new experiences, some things which you have never known before. Some of you have known for the first time what it is to be poor. Perhaps some of you have known for the first time what it is to be rich. Some of you have had your first sickness. Some of you have felt for the first time the keenest suffering in the death of your best beloved. Some of you have begun the new joy of family life. Some of you have become fathers or mothers. Some of you with yet deeper changes, which bore no outside witness of themselves, have laid hold upon new and inspiring ideas. Some of you have given yourselves up to a profession; some of you have made a new friend; some of you have entered into the communion of the Church and put on Jesus Christ. These are the jewels on the cloth of gold of your life. As you go forth, knowing that God must have something new of himself to show to you through these experiences as they become more and more set and fastened in your life as its habits and possessions, can you help being full of expectation?

Can you help saying to yourself: "The Lord is at hand"?

Is there not something of the same kind when in the midst of some great experience you look forward to meeting again, with the power of that new experience in you, your most noble and many-sided friend? "It may be," you say to yourself, "that this experience will be the key which I have needed to unlock that closed chamber of his nature, before which I have so often stood and wondered." You see him coming to you, and new light streams forth from him. You have gained a new power of reflecting him. Henceforth your whole life with him is going to be a richer, deeper thing. Make this mutual; let each of two friends, with multiplying experience, gain new power to reflect the other's light; and have you not the whole philosophy of deepening friendship, of the way in which those who are true friends become more and more to each other every year, the longer that they live?

A soul goes forth from this world and enters into heaven. Surely a part of that intensified and deepened sight of God which is to be its privilege and glory there, will lie in the abundance of experience which it has accumulated here, and which will belong to it forever. Every treasured experience will be to it like an eye with which to gaze on God. We shall know him better forever and forever, because of that success or this disappointment, because this friend played us false, or because the market turned just as our fortune was on the point of being made. Could anything make the events which happen to us here on earth seem more interesting and significant than such a truth as that?

Thus much we say of the way in which the Lord is constantly coming by the ever increasing capacity, the ever multiplying experience of man, to discover and display more and more fully how near He is already. But this subjective interpretation is not all. There is the other, the objective side. We must pass to that. In these days man is so conscious of himself, so large a portion of his time and thought is given to the consideration of himself, he is so aware of the fact of his own activity, that sometimes it seems as if God were wholly passive, standing off there and waiting for man to come to Him; and meanwhile only making revelation of Himself to man as man turns to Him this or that side of his reflecting nature. Other times have been full of the truth of the activity of God. The Old Testament is all alive with that idea, and constantly in history there have recurred ages full of the spirit of the Old Testament, which think of God as He was thought of in those vigorous and stirring books. That God is seeking after man, changing His methods of treatment according to man's behavior, actually coming nearer to or going farther off from man, not simply making Himself known as near or far, but actually changing from near to far, from far to near, that is the Old Testament truth; and the New Testament, with the Incarnation for its light and glory, evidently has not lost or thrown away that truth.

No religion can live and be thoroughly strong unless it keeps that truth of the activity of God. Some religions, like Calvinism, have kept it so strongly that they have lost or made little of the other truth, of the activity of man. In our time, as I said, man is so aware of himself, and of what he has to do, that there is sometimes danger lest he forget—sometimes he certainly has forgotten—the activity of God.

Let us remember that great truth, and then, does not man's expectation of the future lift itself up and become wonderfully enlarged? Not merely, I shall grow so that I shall be able to understand vastly more of what God is and of what He is doing. God also will be ever doing new things. He is forever active. He has purposes concerning me which He has not yet unfolded. Therefore each year grows sacred with wondering expectation. Therefore I and the world may go forth from each old year into the new which follows it, certain that in that new year God will have for us some new treatment which will open for us some novel life.

The world, as it looks back upon the past years, knows that God's active care for it has proved itself abundantly in all his various treatments. One year He lifted the curtain from a hidden continent, and gave his children a whole new world in which to carry out His purposes. Another year He revealed to them a strange, simple, little invention which made the treasured knowledge of the few to be the free heritage of all. Another year He touched the solid frame of a great spiritual despotism, and it trembled and quaked, and thousands of its slaves came forth free men. Another year, in our own time, in our own land, He sent the message of liberty to a nation of bondmen, and the fetters fell off from their limbs. We call these events of history. They have a right to be called the comings of the Lord. They all are echoes and illustrations of that great coming of the Lord from which they who have known of it agree by instinctive consent to date their history, the birth of the child of Bethlehem, the Man of Nazareth and Calvary, into the world.

When we once think thus of the events of history as the activities of God, as the comings of the Lord to man, then there comes a great vitality into the story of mankind. It is all alive. And then we stand before the yet unopened history of a new year, and say, " What will God do ? " Something of what he will do we can guess, as a child can guess something of the future actions of the wisest man by intuitions of his character; but what we guess is very little and very vague. Still there is enough left on which to feed our wonder. What will God do this year? How will he come near to man? It may be, O that it might be! that he will break up this awful sluggishness of Christendom, this terrible torpidity of the Christian Church, and give us a great, true revival of religion. It may be that he will speak some great imperious command to the brutal and terrible spirit of war, and will open the gate upon a bright period of peace throughout the world. It may be that he will draw back the curtain and throw some

The Great Expectation. 365

of his light upon the question, of how the poor and the rich may live together in more cordial brotherhood. It may be that he will lead up from the depths of their common faith a power of unity into the sects of a divided Christendom. Perhaps he will smite this selfishness of fashionable life, and make it earnest. Perhaps by some terrible catastrophe he will teach the nation that corruption is ruin, and that nothing but integrity can make any nation strong. Perhaps this! perhaps that! We make our guesses, and no man can truly say. Only we know that with a world that needs so much, and with a God who knows its needs and who loves it and pities it so tenderly, there must be in the long year some approach of His life to its life, some coming of the Lord!

And if we know this of the world, shall we not also know it of ourselves? For us too God is certainly active. We look forward into the opening months and we say, Yes, no doubt something will happen, some change will come. It may be one thing or another. It may be fuller life; it may be death. It may be what we wish or what we dread. When we are young men we try to anticipate what is coming. As we grow to be older men we are very apt to give that up in hopelessness and merely wonder what will come. If we have no religion (or do not use the religion which we have, as many religious men do not), we think of what will happen as the falling of accidents or as the maturing of self-ripening processes. If we think of it at all religiously, we talk about God sending messages to us. If our religion is a real life thing, we feel God actually coming to us Himself, in all the unknown things which are to happen to us before another New Year's day. Ah, after all, that is everything. To know that there is no accident. To know that indeed there is no such thing as a mere message of God. To know that He is always coming to us. To know that there is nothing happening to us which is not His coming. To know all that, is to find the most trivial life made solemn, the most cruel life made kind, the most sad and gloomy life made rich and beautiful.

These are the two ways then in which the Lord comes, is always coming, to His servants. He opens their eyes to see how near He is already, and He does actually draw nearer to their lives. And now I must say a little about the other words of St. Paul in this text of ours, in which he describes what ought to be the result of this expectation of the coming of the Lord upon a man's life. "Let your moderation be known unto all men. The Lord is at hand." Moderation! Is not the word almost strange at first? Does it not almost chill us? Moderation! we cry. Nay, but in him whose soul is full of glorious expectation will not enthusiasm be the great condition? Will not his soul expand and claim its larger heritage? Will not those other words of Paul describe him to himself: "All things are yours!" Who shall talk to him of moderation? What a hard, cold word it is!

But this word moderation—forbearance, the new version renders it—is one of St. Paul's great words-

The Great Expectation. 367

Men are known by their favorite words. And as Paul uses this word it has more meaning in it than we can put into any one single word by which we can translate it. Indeed it is one of those words descriptive of character, which have no hope of being understood except as they find a conception of the character which they try to describe already present in the mind of him to whom the description is given, and are able to point to it and to say: "That is what I mean." It is self-restraint, it is self-possession.

There is—all man's self-knowledge has borne witness to it—there is somewhere in the human mind an image of human character in which all wayward impulses are restrained, not by outside compulsion, but by the firm grasp of a power which holds everything into obedience from within by the central purpose of the life. This character dreads fury and excitement as signs of feebleness. It hates exaggeration of statement, because exaggeration of statement means weakness of belief. It shrinks from self-display just in proportion as it accepts the responsibilities of selfhood. It is patient because it is powerful. It is tolerant because it is sure. It is hopeful for every man because it has found solid ground in the midst of the great turmoil for itself to stand on, and believes that all other men have the same right to solid ground to stand on as itself. It is this character, I think, which St. Paul calls by his great word moderation. It is self-possession. It is the self found and possessed in God. It is the sweet reasonableness which was in Jesus, of whom it was written that he should not strive nor cry, neither should his voice be heard in the streets; that he should not break the bruised reed, and the smoking flax he should not quench until he sent forth judgment unto victory. In these words I think we have the true description of what St. Paul means by moderation.

In the midst of eager and sometimes frantic struggles after virtue and after power, is there not something very great and refreshing in this setting up of moderation as the perfection of life? Be yourself in God, it seems to say, and virtue and power will take care of themselves.

And St. Paul says that this great self-possession in God must come to any man who really expects the coming of the Lord. O, my dear friends, if you knew that in the most evident of all ways, which is by death, the Lord were coming to you to-morrow, and if you could be perfectly free from all base feeling, from fear and flurry, from defiance and from dread, from exaggerations and depressions belonging to that awful moment, if so you could calmly lie and listen while the great, quiet footsteps came nearer and nearer to your door, what would be the condition which it would make in you? Would it be anything like this which I have tried to describe? Would it be any elevation, refinement, solemnity, and broadening of life? Would it be the calming of frivolity, the release of charity, the kindling of hope? Would it not be all of these?

Not yet for us does that great solemn footfall sound

The Great Expectation.

outside the door. But none the less is the Lord at hand. I have preached to you in vain to-day unless I have made you feel that He is always at hand. All expectation may be expectation of Him. All expectation then ought, if Paul is right, to be the birthplace of this lofty character of moderation. And is it not? Tell me, what would you like to do for any friend of yours, or for your son, who was foolishly exuberant, overrunning into frivolities and quarrels and silly theories of life, into petulant discontent and all the base ambitions of the hour? What would you like to do to save him? Would you not be sure that if you only could set a noble expectation before him, and give it dominion over his whole soul, he would certainly be saved?

That is St. Paul's doctrine! There is salvation for us all. Oh friends, the old year is fast slipping back behind us. We cannot stay in it if we would. We must go forth and leave our past. Let us go forth nobly. Let us go as those whom greater thoughts, and greater deeds await beyond. Let us go humbly, solemnly, bravely, as those must go who go to meet the Lord. With firm, quiet, serious steps, full of faith, full of hope, let us go to meet Him who will certainly judge us when we meet him, but who loves us while he judges us, and who, if we are only obedient, will make us by the discipline of all the years, fit for the everlasting world, where life shall count itself by years no longer.

JUN 1 1991

Printed in the USA
CPSIA information can be obtained
at www.ICGtesting.com
LVHW050345261023
762112LV00003B/72